*FIVE BILLION
VODKA BOTTLES
TO THE MOON*

INTRODUCTION BY

Herbert Friedman

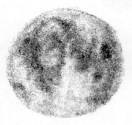

Five Billion Vodka Bottles to the Moon

Tales of a Soviet Scientist

Iosif Shklovsky

*TRANSLATED
AND ADAPTED BY*
Mary Fleming Zirin
AND
Harold Zirin

W. W. NORTON & COMPANY
NEW YORK LONDON

Copyright © 1991 by Eugen Shklovsky, Alla Shklovskaya, Mrs. Iosif Shklovsky
Translation and adaptation copyright © 1991 by W. W. Norton & Company, Inc.
All rights reserved.
Printed in the United States of America.

The text of this book is composed in 11/13.5 Century Old Style,
with the display set in Onyx Typositor.
Composition and manufacturing by the Haddon Craftsmen, Inc.
Book design by Margaret M. Wagner

First Edition

Library of Congress Cataloging-in-Publication Data
Shklovskiĭ, I. S.
Five billion vodka bottles to the moon : tales of a Soviet scientist / Iosif
Shklovsky ; translated and adapted by Mary Fleming Zirin and Harold Zirin ;
Introduction by Herbert Friedman.
p. cm.
Translation from the Russian.
Includes index.
1. Shklovskiĭ, I. S. 2. Astronomy—Soviet Union—History. 3.
Astronomers—Soviet Union—Biography. I. Title. II. Title: 5 billion vodka
bottles to the moon.
QB36.S56A3 1991
520'.92—dc20
[B]   90–19905

ISBN 0–393–02990–5

W.W. Norton & Company, Inc., 500 Fifth Avenue, New York, N.Y. 10110
W.W. Norton & Company, Ltd., 10 Coptic Street, London WC1A 1PU

1 2 3 4 5 6 7 8 9 0

Contents

Photographs appear on pp. 123–31.

Introduction

HERBERT FRIEDMAN

I MET Iosif Shklovsky in Moscow in August 1958 on the occasion of the Tenth General Assembly of the International Astronomical Union. It was a lavish affair, the first gesture of open hospitality by the Soviet Union to the world community of scientists. Although the event had been scheduled years earlier, the successful launches of Sputniks I and II no doubt spurred an effusion of national euphoria that made for a glittering occasion.

Shklovsky was already widely known for his brilliant research publications, but he had rarely met face to face with Western scientists. Circulating from group to group with a broad smile, he was obviously thrilled to recognize individuals whom he had known only by the proxies of their published papers. To his surprise many of us appeared much younger than he expected. Americans achieved status and travel privileges much earlier than their Soviet peers.

While freely expressing his admiration for the American way of life, he was uninhibited in pointing to our political embarrassments. "Why were American marines sent to Lebanon and why did we persist in high altitude nuclear tests?" He was concerned about the treatment of minorities in the United States as well as in Russia but understood that the daily drivel in the Soviet press about lynchings in the American South was a gross distortion of the truth.

Engaging him in personal chit chat, I discovered that he and I were born the same year about a week apart. His father was a rabbi in the Ukrainian town of Glukhov, where Shklovsky was born. I came from a very Orthodox Jewish home in Brooklyn, New York, and my childhood had been steeped in biblical studies. In 1958 he and I no longer practiced our religion in ritual fashion, but our cultural Jewish ethos was deeply ingrained. Throughout his book Shklovsky makes incidental references to his Jewishness and to the trials and tribulations that afflict his race in the Soviet Union.

As Shklovsky explains in his introduction, he was headed for a career as a portrait artist but was seduced by astronomy.* I had spent my undergraduate years as an art major and came late to physics. Both Shklovsky and I were intrigued with the early gleanings of x-ray astronomy. His theoretical insights and my early rocket probing of the x-ray spectrum were synergistic, and we quickly cemented a warm friendship that took advantage of every opportunity to meet up to the summer of 1984, the year before his death.

Shklovsky was a free spirit, always outspoken in criticizing the disgraceful violations of human rights, anti-Semitic prejudices, and stupidities of a totalitarian regime, while he risked the

---

*"... In my childhood, I was far removed from any technology, feeling only a depressed repulsion toward it. By calling [I am] an artist. From the age of three I began drawing with any means at hand—chalk, pieces of broken brick. (I had no other graphic tools; times were difficult and our poverty was total.) I drew almost everywhere and all the time from then on. Until the time I graduated from the physics department of Moscow University in 1938 I was still wavering in my choice of vocation. When I made my choice, however, I gave up art completely."—*History of the Development of Radio Astronomy in the USSR Cosmonautics,* Astronomy Series, no. 11 (Moscow, 1982): 3

prospect of repressive measures that were inevitably taken against him. His sharp tongue was quick to challenge unsupportable scientific claims as well as bureaucratic incompetence. Even his admired colleagues felt the bite of his sarcasm when he believed they had demeaned themselves in any way. All his life he remained emotionally Russian through and through and never had a serious thought of defecting, although he was constantly wooed with offers of professorships at universities here and abroad. What he wanted most was freedom of intercourse with his scientific peers in foreign countries and the privilege of traveling wherever he pleased.

For most of his life travel to the West was denied him. He began foreign travel with an exhilarating experience as a student participant in a solar eclipse expedition to Brazil in 1947. He reminisced later on: "I took it for granted that the forthcoming expedition to the Tropic of Capricorn, to a faraway Brazil as beautiful as anything in a fairytale, was just the *beginning* and that many more fine and soul-stirring things yet unknown lay ahead. After a poverty-stricken youth and the harsh suffering of the war years, the world had at last opened up for me." How wrong he was! He had to wait nineteen years before he could revisit the Western hemisphere.

The euphoria of the South American voyage for young Shklovsky, who had never previously been outside his native country and entertained in an affluent society, is recalled in the humorous vignette *"Amado Mio,"* Chapter 7, where he describes his first encounter with a French menu and the etiquette of a formal dinner table. During the thaw of the Khrushchev era Shklovsky regained the privilege of travel even though, as he recounts in Chapter 18, "Paris Is Worth a Dinner," he could never quite fathom the bureaucratic manipulations that let him slip through the iron curtain several times within a few years. In the last decade of his life the tide of restrictions seemed to turn against him once again.

In 1933, Shklovsky entered the physics and mathematics department of Vladivostok University, but he soon yearned for escape from the shivering cold. Two years later he matriculated in the physics department of Moscow University. By 1938 he knew that his destiny lay in astrophysics rather than art and was accepted as a graduate student in the Shternberg Astronomical Institute, a department of the University of Moscow with which he retained a lifelong affiliation. The first formal course in radio astronomy anywhere in the world was given by Shklovsky at the Shternberg Institute in 1953. He soon expanded the course to include "all wave" astronomy made possible by observations from rockets above the atmosphere.

Shklovsky's bitter denouncements of the horrors of Stalinist terrorism crop up repeatedly throughout the book. In 1936, the People's Commissariat of Internal Affairs (NKVD), the forerunner of the KGB, instigated a rash of purges and mass terror, aimed particularly at intellectuals. Only now are the full horrors being revealed. As a beginning student Shklovsky barely escaped the period of the bloody purges of astronomers at the Leningrad Institute of Astronomy and the Pulkovo Observatory. Typical of those years from 1936 to 1938 is Shklovsky's tale of how a Pulkovo graduate student who could not pass his qualifying examination for the Ph.D. vindictively accused Boris V. Numerov, founder and director of the Leningrad Institute of Astronomy, of suspicious association with German scientists. Numerov was one of the leading astronomers in the Soviet Union and widely respected in the Western world. When he was arrested he was so certain that he would be cleared of the ridiculous accusation that he reassured his wife and three children he would very shortly be released. He never saw his family again. Instead, he was so severely tortured that he broke down and signed a falsified confession that he was the ringleader of a counterrevolutionary group of astronomers, a "fascist-Trotskyite-Zinovievite terrorist organization" operating as an arm of German intelligence and dedicated to the establishment of a fascist dictatorship in the USSR Numerov's forced confession was immediately followed by a widespread roundup of Leningrad astronomers one night in November 1936. Many of the most brilliant minds in Soviet astronomy were caught up in the dragnet. After five years' imprisonment, Numerov was shot to death before the German army overran his prison camp. Other leaders of Soviet astronomy fared no better than Numerov. All told, between two and three dozen astronomers were arrested between March 1936 and July 1937, and few survived.*

With the advance of German armies into the Soviet Union during World War II, Shklovsky and a cadre of graduate students were conscripted for technical military service and relocated in Central Asia. The journey of the motley corps of science students in a traveling freight-car university on the Moscow-Ashkhabad railway is recounted in the first chapter. After the war he was appointed to a professorship at Moscow University and served until 1953. He then headed the department of radio astronomy at the Shternberg Astronomical Institute. From 1972 until his death he was chief of the astronomy program at IKI, the Institute of Space Research in Moscow.

Shklovsky's stories in this collection have comparatively little to do with science itself, but he surveys the Soviet scene from the unique perception of a deeply concerned scientist. He died just before glasnost, and when he wrote most of the stories he had little hope that they could be published in the Soviet Union, let alone in the United States. He explains that he was impelled to write the truth fearlessly because he had nothing more to lose; it was obvious that he had been permanently blackballed from election to full membership in the Soviet Academy of Sciences. With his sharp wit he recounts the tragicomic situations of his hero colleagues and exposes the true colors of the villains, scientific hacks as well as vindictive party bureaucrats,

---

*See Robert McCutcheon, "Stalin's Purge of Soviet Astronomers," *Sky and Telescope* (October 1989): 352–357.

whom the Soviet system provided in abundance. He could wound even his friends when they failed his test of honor, but there was never any lingering hatefulness. He was generous and warm with younger scientists and students and helped substantially to promote their careers. The ranks of leading Soviet scientists today contain many of his former students.

For the reader to appreciate Shklovsky's credibility as a raconteur it helps to have a sense of his truly remarkable scientific achievements. In the following brief account I try to trace lightly the record of his research without getting into complicated detail. In the immediate aftermath of World War II, astrophysics was poised to examine the cosmic scene with a rush of brilliant new insights, and Shklovsky was one of the remarkable generation that led the way. With keen intuition he sensed every important new development early on and came up with startling new explanations.

Shklovsky's candidate (1944) and doctoral (1949) dissertations were concerned with the physics of the solar corona. Astronomy had been focused on relatively commonplace low energy processes, characterized by temperatures of a few thousand degrees, but Shklovsky was intrigued with high energy phenomena that implied million-degree plasmas. At the time, the far-reaching outer atmosphere of the sun was a source of great puzzlement. From a variety of indirect evidence it was inferred that the solar coronal temperature was over 1,000,000° C., even though the temperature of the solar disk was no more than 6000° C. It seemed to defy the second law of thermodynamics that heat could not flow from the cool photosphere to a hot corona. In 1944 he proposed that hydromagnetic waves could be a source of coronal heating through the viscous dissipation of wave motion. A year later he correctly predicted the strong emission of x-rays and extreme ultraviolet light in the superheated coronal plasma of highly stripped atoms. By 1949 his ideas were largely confirmed by the earliest observations of solar x-rays by my colleagues and me in the United States with captured German V-2 rockets.

Radio astronomy was developing rapidly after the end of World War II, and Shklovsky was one of the first to realize its great potential. Radio waves are emitted not only by broadcasting stations but by every object in the universe as well. The sun was the first major target of study because its radio emissions are so easy to detect. Shklovsky recalled how he entered a conference hall at the Academy of Sciences Physics Institute in Moscow searching for a friend in the audience and

> unwittingly began listening to the speaker—a middle-aged man wearing colonel's epaulets. . . . At that point he was speaking about the fact that during the recently ended war officers of the radar service of the British Royal Air Force had discovered that the sun was emitting radiation at meter wavelengths. The news literally stunned me. The speaker had long since gone on to another purely radio-technology subject, while I, sitting in the back of the large auditorium, concentrated on what that unique astronomical phenomenon could mean. At that time I had already spent three years working on problems of the solar corona . . . I was internally attuned to what I had just heard. One way or another I had already comprehended the phenomenon of solar radio emission (and it was only by accident that I had come into the hall less than half an hour earlier). But in life there are moments of illumination like that (alas, very rare ones). I have experienced them in my scientific life only two or three times afterward.*

In 1947, for the eclipse expedition to Brazil, he brought along a radio telescope, the first ever to be used in studying an eclipse.

In the late 1940s Shklovsky moved from solar physics to a wider spectrum of problems in galactic radio astronomy. He was particularly intrigued with the prediction of a young Dutch astrophysicist, Hendrik van de Hulst, who theorized during the war years that neutral hydrogen would radiate a characteristic wavelength of 21 centimeters. Extending van de Hulst's calculations, he concluded that the Galaxy would be so bright in this neutral

*History of the Development of Radio Astronomy in the USSR, pp. 7–8.

hydrogen glow that it should be readily detectable with radio telescopes of that time. In 1951 this prediction was confirmed by H. I. Ewen, a graduate student in physics at Harvard University. Subsequently, radio astronomers measured the intensity of the 21-centimeter radiation in all directions and were able to map out the spiral arm structure of the Milky Way.

Continuing to move ahead, Shklovsky calculated that microwave radio emissions from the Galaxy should contain characteristic spectroscopic signatures of several species of molecules in the interstellar medium, most notably OH, CH, and SiH. At the time it was commonly believed that interstellar gas was almost entirely atomic hydrogen. He derived theoretical radio wavelengths for four spectral lines of OH near 18 centimeters that served as a guide for the search that led to its discovery ten years later. His prediction for CH was confirmed seventeen years later. Thus did he open the way into astronomical microwave spectroscopy, which today accounts for a catalogue of nearly 100 interstellar molecules, some composed of as many as a dozen atoms. Shklovsky's predictions of the power of molecular microwave spectroscopy for studying the Galaxy were well ahead of the observational capabilities of the time, and it took many years for the radio astronomy community to catch up with him.

In the early 1950s only a few celestial radio sources had been identified. One of the most intriguing was the Crab Nebula, a tangled web of luminous filamentary debris from a supernova explosion that had been noted by Oriental observers in A.D. 1054, when it flashed to the brilliance of Venus for a fortnight. Much of the light of the nebula had an amorphous, continuous spectral character unlike that of other nebulous sources. It was fundamentally different from the thermal radiation that astronomers identified with most celestial bodies. Shklovsky grasped the idea that this strange light was synchrotron radiation of the type produced when energetic charged particles move at nearly the speed of light in a magnetic field. Generically, synchrotron light in astronomy is the same as the radiation that sweeps outward from the particle beams circulating in the racetrack accelerators that physicists employ to create ultra-high energy particles. With this bold insight he advanced the correct explanation in 1953 for galactic supernovae and the active radio galaxies, non-thermal sources that generate the highest energy radiation in the universe.* Furthermore, he predicted that cosmic synchrotron sources discovered in the radio spectrum would produce continuous radiation extending through the visible spectrum to x-rays and gamma rays. As a supernova remnant radiated synchrotron light, Shklovsky proposed that it would deplete its supply of high energy electrons and steadily fade away. That prediction was confirmed with convincing precision for the bright radio source Cassiopeia-A, the youngest known nebulous remnant of a supernova.

Around 1957 Shklovsky began to take a leading role in the creation of new space science initiatives in the Soviet Union, realizing how important it was to observe astrophysical phenomena in all regions of the spectrum from radio waves and infrared to x-rays and gamma rays. One of his early successes was an "artificial comet" experiment associated with the second Soviet moon rocket. Sodium vapor was released from the rocket and fluoresced strongly under the influence of solar radiation so that it could easily be seen from earth and serve as a tracking aid. Later the technique was applied to studies of the Earth's upper atmosphere and the interplanetary medium. In 1960 Shklovsky was honored with the Lenin Prize for his "artificial comet."

The name "planetary nebula" is a misnomer since they have nothing to do with planets. Nineteenth-century astronomers ob-

---

*Swedish physicists Alfvén and Herlofson had proposed synchrotron radiation as the source of radio emission in discrete sources in 1950, and Shklovsky's Soviet colleague, Vitaly Ginzburg, did likewise in the following year. But it was Shklovsky who made the most important application of the synchrotron concept to the Crab Nebula and other supernova remnants.

served these fuzzy, colorful luminous disks and were struck by the resemblance to the rings of Saturn. Shklovsky correctly described a planetary nebula as a great bubble of gas that blew off the top of an unstable, bloated red giant while its stellar core collapsed to a white dwarf. The tiny bright remnant star can be seen through the bubble, while its ultraviolet light bathes the nebula and excites its colorful fluorescence. He further postulated that the compact core could be a pre-supernova star.

Among Shklovsky's seminal predictions, soon confirmed, was the binary pair model for x-ray stars. If one of the coupled stars is a neutron star, it can draw a tidal flow of gas from the normal companion. The accreted gas delivers an enormous amount of kinetic energy to the magnetic poles of the compact star and creates the very high temperature plasma that radiates x-rays. As little mass as a sugar cube dropped onto a neutron star can release the energy of a Hiroshima bomb. These examples illustrate the virtuosity of Shklovsky's scientific genius.

From the time of the Moscow Assembly of the International Astronomical Union (IAU) in 1958, Shklovsky's star was in the ascendancy as the world of astronomy recognized his achievements. He was besieged with invitations to lecture and participate in scientific meetings abroad. But he was outraged at growing signs of anti-Semitism in admissions of Jewish students to universities and in discrimination with respect to promotions in academic and research institutions. His outspokenness about politics and human rights deprived him of the privilege to travel abroad. He was not allowed to attend the IAU triennial assemblies in the United States in 1961 and in West Germany in 1964. It was a bitter pill to swallow for a man who had such a burning desire to meet with his peers abroad.

There followed a brief thaw in the iron-curtain mentality under Khrushchev, and Shklovsky was permitted to appear at the "Texas" conference on relativistic astrophysics in New York in 1966, to his unbounded delight. Abruptly in 1973, the door to the West was shut again, and Shklovsky together with many of the best Soviet astronomers was not permitted to attend the IAU symposium in Australia. When some forty members of the Soviet Academy of Sciences signed a public declaration condemning Andrei Sakharov, Shklovsky wrote a courageous letter in his defense. His punishment was a ban on his attendance at the IAU meeting of 1976 in Grenoble, France, even though he had been invited to deliver one of the most prestigious discourses of the occasion. When foreign friends asked about his failure to appear at scientific meetings, Soviet attendees would give the standard stock of answers: "He is too busy"; "There is not enough money for any individual to travel more than a very limited number of times"; or most frequently, "His health is too poor." After the last excuse from a prominent Soviet representative at one meeting, I learned that Shklovsky was on a wilderness vacation, canoeing and cross-country skiing. When one American astronomer met him during this bleak period with the greeting "I hear you have been ill," Shklovsky rejoined: "Yes, I have diabetes. Too much Sakharov!" (The Russian word for sugar is *sakhar.*)

While Shklovsky's renown grew abroad, his recognition at home was mixed. In the Soviet Academy of Sciences there are two ranks, full member and corresponding member, the latter usually a stepping stone to full membership. Elected a corresponding member in 1966, Shklovsky never advanced, undoubtedly because of a combination of his Jewishness and his maverick behavior in support of human rights issues. But he had the satisfaction of election in 1973 to the U.S. National Academy of Sciences as a Foreign Associate, an honor shared with a mere handful of other Soviet physicists and astronomers.

Every American astronomer who had the pleasure of knowing Shklovsky personally has a stock of anecdotes to recount. He had a mannerism of grabbing you by the arm with one hand while gesturing excitedly with the other and recounting fantastic ideas in which it was hard to tell the science fiction from the real thing.

With tongue in cheek Shklovsky could suggest bizarre ideas about extraterrestrial life. It is well known, for example, that Phobos, the inner of the two Martian moons, slowly spirals inward at a rate that suggests a very low density. Shklovsky, addressing popular science audiences, argued that Phobos was in fact hollow and that it must have been constructed by a now extinct Martian civilization capable of carrying out such a large public works project. Of course, more conventional physical explanations can now be offered.

In recent years there has been much scientific speculation about natural catastrophes, such as the impact of a large asteroid or comet, that may have led to the demise of the dinosaurs. Shklovsky loved to concoct catastrophe theories. Early on, he and his good friend, Valerian Krasovsky, had suggested that a nearby supernova could have profound influence on genetic mutations by irradiating the earth with a flood of cosmic rays that would produce radioactivity in the earth's atmosphere. A very large dose of radiation, a thousand times the present natural level, would only double the mutation rate of short-lived species, but an increase in exposure of only three to ten times normal could have a profound effect on long-lived species. Shklovsky speculated that a supernova might have stimulated the origin of life on earth. He also suggested that such a radiation anomaly might account for the luxuriant vegetation of the Carboniferous period.

Shklovsky's interest in extraterrestrial life went far beyond whimsy. He had a counterpart in the United States, astronomer Carl Sagan, who was seriously studying the possibility of interstellar radio communication. In 1962, Sagan sent him a preprint of a paper on his ideas, and Shklovsky responded almost immediately. He had written a book, *Universe, Life and Intelligence,* expressing confidence that the power of the new astronomies would lead to the detection of extraterrestrial intelligence. The ideas he expounded were similar to Sagan's. It was very natural for them to collaborate, but they were continents apart and co-authorship was difficult. Sagan translated Shklovsky's chapters and added his own material to produce a manuscript that was published in 1966 in the United States as *Intelligent Life in the Universe*. They met face to face only several years later, by which time the book had generated worldwide scientific interest in the subject. Shklovsky was especially proud that his original work was published in Braille.

Shklovsky's enthusiasm for the radio search for extraterrestrial intelligence began to wane in recent years. He argued that here on Earth our high-tech civilization was compressed within the twentieth century after three billion years of the evolution of life. If intelligent life was abundant in the galaxy, he reasoned statistically that many civilizations would have advanced far beyond our space travel capabilities millions of years ago and would have sent robot messengers to roam the galaxy far and wide, including our solar neighborhood. Why was there no evidence of robot visitors from any planets of the billions upon billions of stars in the Milky Way Galaxy?

At a meeting of the International Astronomical Union in Montreal in 1980, Shklovsky had been invited many months in advance to chair a symposium on extraterrestrial life, but his visa was not forthcoming and he had virtually abandoned hope of attending. At the last possible moment he was informed that he could leave. He arrived barely in time to assume the chairmanship. At the end of the session, one of the participants asked: "Dr. Shklovsky, what is your own best personal assessment of the existence of extraterrestrial intelligence?" He replied, "Yesterday I thought there was no possibility whatsoever that I could be here for this meeting, yet here I am." In recent years he felt that the possibility that we were the only intelligent life, at least in the local system of galaxies, was a much richer concept philosophically, ethically, and morally than the presumption of a Universe teeming with life.

Shklovsky relished his few happy experiences in the United States. The first began at the Second "Texas" Symposium on

Relativistic Astrophysics January 1967 at the New Yorker Hotel in Manhattan. He was very warmly received by all the American participants, showered with offers of hospitality, and set forth on a Grand Tour of the United States in a style of opulence to which he was totally unaccustomed. His reminiscences were marked with expressions of wonder and admiration for the free and easy democratic mode of life of the American scientific community.

Those of us who were involved have vivid recollections of that first visit. While in New York, Shklovsky asked if I could tour him through Manhattan on foot. His express wishes included a nostalgia meal in a kosher restaurant (no longer to be found in Moscow), a walk across the Brooklyn Bridge, an excursion to the Statue of Liberty, and a museum that had paintings by El Greco (none to be seen in the Soviet Union). He and I covered the city on foot from the East Side garment district, where we found the ethnic flavors he savored, to the Metropolitan Museum, where he gazed with admiration at the El Grecos. At the kosher restaurant he tasted a wide selection of dishes from matzo ball chicken soup to stuffed derma and compared each serving with gourmet precision to youthful memories of his mother's cooking. His mother won the competition by a wide margin. As we strolled north on Fifth Avenue he devoured the exciting New York scene, commenting that everybody looked Russian.

That night, after the symposium banquet, my wife and I set forth with Iosif to continue his sightseeing agenda. It was bitter cold and windy, certainly no weather for a walk across the Brooklyn Bridge. With some disappointment on his part we adopted a compromise plan—to hire a taxi and request the driver to cross the bridge at the slowest possible speed. The bridge seems to hold a special mystique for Russians, who admire a romantic description by the poet Vladimir Mayakovsky. Had Iosif been alone I am sure that he not only would have crossed on foot but also would have examined the views from below as described in the poem.

Our next target was the Statue of Liberty, which could be viewed close up from the Staten Island ferry. While my wife and I drank hot coffee inside the lounge area, Iosif stood exposed on the deck, bracing himself against the stiff wind. He was ecstatic over the marvelous view of the New York skyline and the symbolic beauty of Miss Liberty as we passed close by. At that late hour on a weekday, the ferry was deserted except for us, but when we disembarked we found a waiting taxi. I instructed the driver to take us back to the hotel by way of Greenwich village, which would be jumping with life at any hour of the night. Enroute Shklovsky and I were talking about astronomy when, to my astonishment, the driver turned his head and addressed Shklovsky in Russian. He too was an emigré astronomer, an amateur, and owned his own telescope. He claimed to recognize Shklovsky's name and for the rest of the ride monopolized a Russian conversation with our guest. I wondered what Shklovsky thought—could this be entirely circumstantial or was he being monitored? If there wasn't friendship and trust he could easily have suspected a plant—just like home!

Immediately after the symposium was over, Shklovsky set out on a whirlwind trip to San Francisco, Palomar, Disneyland, and Los Angeles and worked his way back to the National Radio Astronomy Observatory in Charlottesville. From there the plan called for him to take the plane to Washington and visit with me for a day at the Naval Research Laboratory. That night he would fly to New York and return to the New Yorker Hotel, rejoin his comrades, who had followed another itinerary, and they would all head home on Aeroflot.

The morning of his scheduled departure from Charlottesville he awoke to look out upon a familiar Russian scene. The ground was covered with deep drifts of snow. All airline transportation was grounded. He was put on the train, which made the trip to Washington at a slow crawl. My wife and I met him at Union Station after hours of waiting, too late for a visit to my laboratory. Our impromptu plan was to remain in town for dinner at the Cosmos Club and for Iosif to stay overnight at our home in

Arlington. With luck the snowfall would end and we could find a way to get him to New York the following day in time to rejoin his Russian group for their return to Moscow.

Around the corner from the Cosmos Club is the Phillips Museum with its incomparably fine collection, including especially Renoir's famous "The Boating Party." We felt that he ought to see it. With my wife's special persuasion we gained entrance for a brief visit, even though it was past the official closing hour. He was especially impressed with the collection's Kokoschka paintings. At the Cosmos Club, I took him for a quick tour of the upper floor. When we returned to the lobby two men were in conversation with my wife. They were Frederick Seitz, president of the National Academy of Sciences, and Donald Hornig, science adviser to President Lyndon Johnson. After introductions, which Shklovsky did not grasp at all, I invited Seitz and Hornig to join us for dinner, which they graciously accepted.

Shklovsky had come to Washington dressed as he would for a Russian winter—heavy boots, crewneck sweater, no jacket or tie. Indeed, he looked very scruffy for dining at the club, but the room was almost empty because of the forbidding weather and formalities could be suspended under the circumstances. During the course of the evening other diners drifted in and paused at our table to exchange greetings. Two were from Los Alamos and associated with atomic-bomb and thermonuclear-fusion work. Shklovsky held forth in high style with comic stories that drew everybody's laughter. After the dinner broke up and our guests had departed, Shklovsky asked my wife again to identify his dinner companions. When he finally understood that he had dined so informally with two of the highest-ranking members of the scientific establishment, he was stricken with embarrassment and contrition for some of his coarse jokes and what he thought must have appeared as gross indifference to the importance of the people he had met. I had to explain to him that I had not arranged for Seitz and Hornig to be there and that the informality that accompanied our chance meeting was typically

American. He replied that under no circumstances could he ever visualize himself socializing in that manner with Academician Keldysh, president of the Soviet Academy of Sciences, or a member of the Politburo.

Iosif stayed at my home that night, and the next day we got him on the train to New York. He had received enough honoraria in his travels to make him temporarily rich in dollars. There was no point in bringing that money home, where it would be confiscated, so he had bought the largest suitcase he could find in California and filled it so full of electronic computer gear and other treasured gifts that he could hardly manage to carry it aboard the train. He struggled with his luggage from Penn Station to the New Yorker Hotel, unable to get a taxi in the miserable weather, and arrived ten minutes before departure time with an expression of carefree nonchalance on his face to impress his colleagues.

Shklovsky was now one of a happy group of "exit comrades," as he called them, who seemed privileged to travel. Why he had this new status he could not fathom, but while it lasted he would enjoy it. He returned for another tour of the United States in December 1968, starting this time in Charlottesville, headquarters of the National Radio Astronomy Observatory, to present the prestigious Jansky Lecture. Next he revisited us in Washington. After picking him up at the railroad station we drove through Washington, D.C., toward our home in Virginia. En route Shklovsky asked if we would pass anywhere near the Soviet embassy. He wanted to see it but not be seen. We satisfied his curiosity and continued home. It was Christmas vacation time and my two sons were home. Paul was heading for a career in law and Jon was bent on being an artist. Iosif was amazed that the sons of a successful physicist could study to be anything other than scientists. He could understand Jon wishing to be an artist—after all, he aimed toward that career himself before becoming entranced with astronomy. But a lawyer was beyond his comprehension. In the Soviet Union the only offenses that called for legal defence were crimes against the state. Person-to-person crimes were of little concern.

That night, *Apollo 8* was on its way to orbit the moon in the sequence of test flights that preceded the landing mission of Apollo 11. With TV animation tracking the passage of the vehicle behind the moon while the astronauts' voice transmissions were heard live, Shklovsky and the Friedman family watched and listened with tingling suspense as the spacecraft was eclipsed by the moon. All of us felt a surge of relief as the vehicle emerged again and communication was restored. For Shklovsky, the experience was unlike anything that could have happened in the Soviet Union at that time, when no space operation was permitted to be broadcast in real time. He remained intently absorbed as the broadcast ran through most of the night. We talked in a casual way about whether he ever had thoughts of defecting, but he explained that for all his criticism of the Soviet system he loved his country.

Shklovsky moved on to Dallas for the Third "Texas" Symposium. He was dazzled by the opulence of the occasion, from the great stretch of red carpet at the airport to the richly spread reception at the meeting. Ivor Robinson, a brilliant mathematician, was the organizing genius of these symposia. He was also a skillful politician and pressured the Soviet authorities from the time of the first symposium in 1964 to permit travel of their best scientists to these Western meetings. Not successful at first, he achieved his goal in conjunction with the 1967 and 1968 symposia attended by the Soviet Union's two star representatives, Vitaly Ginzburg and Iosif Shklovsky, who were lionized by their happy hosts.

Shklovsky told a fascinating account of the Dallas meeting, including his personal investigation of the site of the Kennedy assassination, from which he concluded that there could have been only one marksman and that he must have been positioned in the book repository. At the meeting, he met the brilliant Israeli physicist and military intelligence expert Yuval Ne'eman.

They became ardent friends because of their mutual scientific interests but perhaps even more because of Shklovsky's passionate concern for the survival of Israel and his deep need to discuss his views with such an expert as Ne'eman. Iosif recounted how he and other Soviet astronomers were stricken with fear that Israel was doomed at the start of the Six Day War. They received the Israeli news broadcasts from Tel Aviv with their large radio-astronomy telescope and danced with joy when they learned that the Syrian air force had been totally destroyed by the end of the first day.

Shklovsky's good luck with travel seemed to turn bad again after 1968, and he could no longer count himself among the "exit comrades." When he did travel it was under tight control. I could sense the difference when I met him again in Leningrad in 1970. The occasion for my visit was a major symposium on Solar-Terrestrial Physics. I was president of the international organization and received VIP treatment as befit my position in Soviet eyes. My wife and I were put up in one of the best rooms of the Europa Hotel next to Neil Armstrong, who was being displayed to the Soviet people after his dramatic trip to the moon. Shklovsky was reluctant to come up to our room for a visit because he was sure that it was bugged. Instead he suggested that we take a walk around Leningrad, where we could talk freely in the open air. He met us in the lobby accompanied by a friend, Sam Kaplan, a nephew of Ezar Kaplan, who was then Israeli finance minister. Sam had applied time and again for an exit visa to Israel without success because he had been a radar expert during World War II and presumably retained knowledge of military value. He talked with keen insights about the dismal state of affairs in the Soviet Union, feeling no restraint because he no longer held any hope of escape. I learned a few years later that he died in a tragic accident. While passing from one car to another in a fast moving train he slipped to the tracks—perhaps a suicide, perhaps foul play.

After walking for a few hours, Iosif brought us to his favorite restaurant. He ordered a special dish for my wife and me. It was so hotly spiced that it was an agony for me to swallow, but it was the sort of food he loved. The four of us then returned to the hotel, where I had an American paperback of Solzhenitsyn's *Gulag Archipelago* that I had brought especially for Iosif. He felt it was too dangerous for him to take, but Sam Kaplan had no hesitation. He came up to our room, put the book in among the papers of his briefcase, and carried it out of the hotel with a happy smile. It was worth a fortune on the black market.

Three years later I was back in the Soviet Union again as a member of a small delegation of the U.S. National Academy of Sciences holding an annual exchange meeting with their Soviet counterparts. In Moscow, I tried to arrange my usual meeting with Shklovsky but found that I could see him only in the Institute for Space Research. There I was taken to a large conference room, where Shklovsky awaited me with a dozen other scientists. I was invited to talk about the progress of x-ray astronomy in the United States, and we had a lively scientific discussion, but I had no opportunity to be alone with Iosif. When I was ready to leave a car was waiting and Shklovsky with one of his colleagues, Vladimir Kurt, accompanied me. Shklovsky seemed very subdued. The driver dropped him at some midpoint and Kurt continued with me to my hotel. We got out of the car and Kurt walked a short distance with me out of earshot of the driver. He explained that Shklovsky was in some trouble and couldn't see me alone.

Our American delegation hosted a reception at our embassy for the officers of the Soviet Academy and several leading Soviet scientists. Shklovsky had been elected a foreign associate of our Academy the year before and I insisted to Philip Handler, our president, that every effort be made to get him an invitation to our reception. It was delivered to him and he came. He was very pleased to meet the members of our delegation, and as we talked he suddenly pointed out to me that Sakharov had entered the room. He, too, had been elected to the U.S. Academy but had never sent his acceptance. Handler had requested that he come to our embassy party to indicate orally his agreement to join our Academy. He entered the room between two burly KGB escorts, who brought him face to face with Handler for a brief exchange and then was turned around and taken away. The following day the Soviets hosted a reception for the Americans that was attended by many of their academicians, but neither Shklovsky nor Sakharov received the courtesy of an invitation.

I did not see Shklovsky again until the 1979 meeting of the IAU in Montreal. As described earlier, he arrived after receiving a visa at the last possible moment. He was in good spirits and was especially happy to learn that Yuval Ne'eman was also there. Unfortunately, the entire Soviet group seemed to be under tight KGB control. They were all housed in the university dormitory under a curfew and were restricted from fraternizing with Western scientists unless accompanied by a second member of their group. Ne'eman was equally desirous of talking to Shklovsky, but how to arrange any privacy? My wife and I had a room in the Queen Elizabeth Hotel, which was the locale for a special evening lecture attended by nearly all the scientists at the meeting. We arranged to sit with Iosif at the lecture and gave the key to our room to Yuval, who made his way there before the final minutes of the lecture. At the end of the evening session we walked with Shklovsky through the hotel and up to our room, where Yuval was patiently waiting. My wife and I offered to leave them in complete privacy but they insisted that we stay.

Their discussion focused solely on Israel and strategies for dealing with her problems. I was fascinated by the extraordinary amount of information that Shklovsky had and by the seriousness of his discussion about tactics and future developments. He was deeply pessimistic about Israel's chances of long-term survival. Yuval had the optimistic confidence that Israelis were sufficiently resourceful to survive all Arab efforts to destroy them. It was well past midnight when I left alone with Iosif while

Yuval remained behind for a while longer to preserve our deception. As we were ready to leave the room, Ne'eman offered Shklovsky a seat next to him on the El Al plane to Israel in the morning but Shklovsky smilingly refused. We drove to the university gate, hoping that Iosif could slip in without being noticed. I don't know how he explained his night on the town to his KGB watchdog.

The last time we met Shklovsky was at a meeting in Graz, Austria, in 1984, where my wife and I and another colleague, Tom Donahue, enjoyed a day in the country with him. It was a warm and sunny Sunday. We stopped for lunch near a lake and strolled past a miniature golf course. The caretaker stepped out of the ticket booth and, in precise British speech, asked if anyone had a match. Shklovsky, an inveterate smoker, immediately produced a box of Soviet matches. "Oh," said the Britisher, "a Russian spy, I see!" Shklovsky laughed and commented, "What is the probability that a Russian scientist accompanied by three American friends in the middle of the Austrian lake country would be approached by a Britisher at a miniature golf course and accused of being a Russian spy?" ("What is the probability?" was one of his favorite expressions.)

After lunch at a lakeside café, recommended by the Britisher, Iosif announced it was his birthday and we toasted him with the local wine. Appearing healthy and relaxed, he remarked that it was the best birthday he had ever had (Sunday, July 1, 1984). It was also his last. Returning to Graz, he expressed a dreary view of the Soviet future—nothing could change in the next fifty years. How sad that he could not have lived a few more years to see the remarkable transformation that is now in progress.

The circumstances of his death were tragic. Before leaving for a trip to a conference he developed an embolism in his leg. Protesting that he felt fine, he was reluctantly forced to enter a hospital for treatment of the arterial blockage. A surgical instead of a medical procedure released the blood clot to his brain and he fell into a coma. A call was made from the Soviet Academy to

Dr. Frank Press, president of the U.S. National Academy of Sciences, for medical help. Unfortunately, it was too late to save him.

One of his colleagues remarked, "Fifty percent of Shklovsky's ideas are brilliant but no one can tell which fifty percent they are." His legacy of students includes two corresponding members of the Soviet Academy of Sciences, ten doctors of science, and about thirty candidates of science. We shall all remember the great humanity, humor, and intellectual brilliance of this most remarkable man.

Herbert Friedman
Emeritus Director
Space Science Program
Naval Research Laboratory

Translators' Foreword

FIVE BILLION VODKA BOTTLES TO THE MOON is a legacy of the Iosif Shklovsky we admired—an exuberant and opinionated man who was fun to know. These tales from life circulated in typescript throughout the Soviet scientific community, and Shklovsky's controversial opinions and attacks on sacred cows managed to offend almost everybody. The book will undoubtedly be published in Russia sometime in the future, when passions have cooled and others have had their say. Since we can't consult Shklovsky—he died in 1985—we can only hope that he would be tolerant of our stripped-down version for an English-speaking audience of nonscientists and appreciate our efforts to retain the essential spirit of his stories. With great trepidation we have eliminated eleven tales that have little to do with Shklovsky's life or science, rearranged the remaining chapters in rough chronological and topical order, eliminated digressions, and tightened up and reordered some passages for better continuity. Our footnotes are distinguished from Shklovsky's by square brackets.

MARY FLEMING ZIRIN AND
HAROLD ZIRIN

FIVE BILLION
VODKA BOTTLES
TO THE MOON

Foreword

IN the years following my sixieth birthday in 1976, I began to realize that for the most part my life was over. This is an old topic and there's no point in belaboring it; after all, in my time I've seen a few things and met a fair number of interesting people. Since I originally set out to be a portrait painter, I've always retained a strong interest in people and their fortunes, and in my circle of students and friends, I've gotten a reputation for the funny and sad stories I have to tell.

It would be a shame for those tales, all drawn from real life, to perish with my dust. In early March 1981, while I was vacationing at the writers' retreat at Maleevka,* I decided to write some of them down. I felt that I ought to be able to write as well as the prose writers and journalists at the retreat—whom I found overall to be mediocre and often just plain dim—were struggling to do. Irritation also goaded me: some of the

*[A so-called House of Creative Work near Moscow run by the Soviet Writers' Union.]

literary fraternity around me had written about the life of science—and, God, what rosy drivel that was! It's hard for someone outside the field to realize the degree to which scientific complexities have been distorted in our literature and megatons of falsehood and nonsense about science dumped on the heads of our poor readers. In my real-life tales, as in our society, science occupies a special place, and I considered it imperative to give an authentic portrait of the relations among scientists.

It took me two days to make up a list of subjects that I found interesting and typical. I started writing after I got back to Moscow—only as inspiration struck me, but always according to the list. I tried to write without compromise, but telling "the truth and nothing but the truth" is never simple and there's nothing worse than half-truth. Under prolonged storage in the memory, however, truth undergoes curious aberrations, and there's nothing you can do about it: the laws of human psychology are more complex and elusive than the rules for chess. Chaff and error are inevitable—I hope I've kept them to a minimum.

By early 1984, writing most of the stories at a single sitting, I had gotten through the list. The tales had almost literally burst from me, and when they were finished I suddenly felt light and empty. I collected them in a folder on which was carefully inked in red the code title "Convoy," referring to the subject matter of the first of them, "The Quantum Theory of Radiation."

The Quantum Theory
of Radiation

WAS it really over forty years ago that Moscow University was evacuated to Ashkhabad to escape the German invasion? I still remember every minute detail of those unforgettable months in the fall of 1941, a terrible and fateful year. I can close my eyes and see our university convoy, which was put together in Murom from a score of freightcars, as it moved southeast, making long stops at every siding. Ashkhabad was still a long way off, and for the time being a way of life phantasmagoric by peacetime standards but normal during war took shape around the convoy's stoves.

The inhabitants (you can't call them passengers) were very young. I had just finished graduate school at the Shternberg Astronomical Institute* and was among the eldest in the car. My authority, however, wasn't due

*[Known popularly as GAISH from its Russian title (Government Astronomical Institute named for Shternberg), the Shternberg Institute is the astronomy department of Moscow University. It was Shklovsky's scientific home until 1968, when he moved to the Institute of Space Research, known from its Russian acronym as IKI.]

only to my age. As a raw boy, before being admitted to Far East University I had worked as a foreman on the building of the Baikal-Amur Mainline (BAM).* In those days I organically absorbed that distinctive variant of the Russian language in which an appreciable fraction of workers still express themselves even in our era of developed socialism. Later, at the university and at home, I still suffered from that ingrained bad habit of profanity. In the convoy, however, expounding my uncomplicated thoughts that way seemed natural and organic.† The boys, who were in their second and third years as physics students at Moscow University, had already seen hard times during the terrible past summer when, cut off by the war from their papas and mamas, they were sent to dig trenches near Vyazma. They could fully appreciate my "eloquence."

The boys of our convoy were pure gold. There were never any quarrels or conflicts among us. Jokes, laughter, and teasing reigned. Of course, the jokes as a rule were coarse, and the teasing at times far from good-natured, but the general atmosphere was exceptionally healthy and—I'm not afraid to say it—optimistic. After all, those boys were born in 1921 or 1922, and most of them had only months to live. Of the men in that age group called up in the war, only 3 percent survived. A couple of months after our arrival in Ashkhabad the kids were sent to military schools in Central Asia and from there as junior lieuten-

---

*Most people don't realize that the alternate northern line of the Trans-Siberian Railroad was already under construction in the 1930s.

†You have to recognize that foul language bears an *organic character* for people who absorb the idiom while they are still losing their baby teeth. I'll never forget hearing Mstislav Keldysh, the theoretician in charge of our space program, suddenly begin to swear foully during an important conference in his office on Miussy Square at the dawn of the space age. He obviously did it deliberately, to chime in with the style of the rough engineers and technicians present. Coming from the highly intellectual theorist, who never even raised his voice, the obscenities sounded monstrous, unnatural, and absurd. I checked afterward with some of the others present: it made them all uncomfortable and they avoided looking at each other. On the other hand, obscenity on the lips of any veteran of the labor camps can seem organic and even music to the ears.

ants to the front, where almost certain death awaited them.

But now the convoy was on its way to Ashkhabad, and the snow-covered steppes of Kazakhstan echoed with our rousing songs. We sang in the evenings around the blazing stove as it greedily gulped down fencing and other "working wood," which the kids tore up "by the roots" at stations and sidings. Our chorus leader was a strapping, handsome fellow named Lyova Markov, who had a superb, deep baritone. Our repertoire included folk songs, revolutionary ditties, and fashionable Soviet ballads of the prewar years: ". . . train follows train, year rolls after year, at the forty-second siding in the steppe," and so on. There was the latest in folklore.* I can still hear jaunty Lyova leading off:

> . . . Tools grow warm in the summer sun,
> Faroff the boss engineer's barking,
> And comrade students one by one
> Trail their spades to the quarry . . .

followed by a concerted refrain from twenty youthful throats:

> Stand 'neath the grade,
> Dig with our spades,
> All of us working together.
> Digging the earth,
> Cutting the turf (or a cruder variant),
> Keep up our honor in labor . . .

And then there was the ditty sung to the tune of the well-known prewar "Into battle for our native land, into battle for Stalin":

> . . . With a vacuum in our bellies and callused hands,
> And driving rain to soak us to the skin—

*[Songs the students had made up during their summer stint digging trenches.]

Our teeth are honed on the granite of science,
And after granite—clay can never win!

The stove was the physical and spiritual center of the freight car. Here we told improbable stories, traded jokes, and organized games. In November 1941 the great battle for Moscow was on, the city's fate hung by a thread. We had no radio, no newspapers, no way to find out what was happening. Now and then we would give way to nostalgia for the capital and wonder whether we would ever see it again. To distract ourselves from those bitter reflections, we grains of sand caught up in the whirlwind of war found preposterous ways to amuse ourselves. My bunkmate to the right was a boy named Zhenya Kuzhelev, a robust, cheerful fellow decked out in half-rotted rags and a fiery red youthful stubble growing right up around his eyes. He was a convivial chap and a joker. Once around the stove he gave a lecture on the lice that infested us all. He informed us that there were three varieties of those parasites in nature and declared his intention, in conformance with the most advanced teachings of Michurin and Lysenko, of breeding a hybrid of the head and clothing louse around the collar of his incredibly filthy shirt. Every evening he gave us new details of the bold experiment, embroidering his account with fantastic minutiae. The group roared with laughter. I wonder whether Zhenya Kuzhelev is still alive.

We also had an American in the freightcar, a real one, born in Houston, Texas, the future center of American space technology. A rather puny kid by the name of Leon Bell, he delighted our ears by organizing a fantastic musical ensemble that he called Jazz-Bell. His stories on the subject of Texas food evoked even stronger emotions. He regaled us with completely incredible details of transoceanic Lucullan feasts. God, how starved we were! Listening to Leon drove us crazy; his American accent strengthened the impression and lent his stories plausibility. Sometimes the usually silent Boris ("Bob") Belitsky, who had also spent time in America, added his bit to Leon's stories. In the fall of 1971 I was overjoyed to meet Bob, the best simultaneous translator from English in our country, at the unforgettable Byurakan Conference on Extraterrestrial Civilizations. We had a lot of reminiscing to do.

And to my left on the bunk lay a twenty-year-old kid of a different sort. Tall, skinny, and seedily dressed, with deepset eyes and bushy hair, he almost never took part in our schoolboy pastimes. He spoke almost inaudibly and was diligent in doing the menial, dirty work so prevalent in convoy life. Everything indicated that the boy had been ripped by the whirlwind of war out of an intellectual family before his skin had time to thicken. One day he asked me a preposterous favor: "Do you have anything I can read on physics?" he politely asked the "senior comrade"—i.e., me. I should say that most of the kids addressed me in a familiar way, and my neighbor's courtesy made me wince. My first impulse was to use my best BAM curses to send this mama's boy and his ridiculous request straight to hell. "What a great time the idiot's picked!" I thought, but at the last moment I had an unkind idea. I remembered that I had a copy of Walter Heitler's monograph, *The Quantum Theory of Radiation,* at the bottom of my knapsack.

I've never understood why I took the book with me when we evacuated Moscow in such haste on October 26, 1941. Evidently this odd act was connected with what then seemed to me the unsuitable field I went into after finishing my physics degree at the university. Even as a laborer on the Trans-Siberian Railroad, I had set my heart on becoming a theoretical physicist, and fate threw me into graduate school in astronomy instead. Dunce that I was, I dreamed of getting back into physics and from time to time tried to read appropriate literature. I clearly remember buying the Russian translation of Heitler's monograph in April 1940 at a bookstall near the entrance to the old university building in central Moscow. The book tempted me because I thought it would enable me to plunge immediately into the depths of arcane theory and come "up to the mark." Alas, I quickly broke my teeth on it: I couldn't get beyond the introduction and the start of the first paragraph (a discussion of first-order processes). I remember how depressed I was—that was it, theoretical physics wasn't for me! How could I have known that the book is a very difficult one and written in a heavy Germanic style besides? But why on earth did I stuff it into my knapsack?

"I pulled a good one on that kid, giving him Heitler," I thought and forgot the incident almost immediately. Every day was packed with vivid, sometimes dramatic happenings. In triumph we raised a Christmas tree over our car. With great foresight—there would be no forests in Central Asia, after all—we had cut it in Murom and brought it along. Nailed to the roof, the tree made a superb landmark and came to our rescue at junctions clogged with convoys as we made our way back to our freightcar with vats of kasha or pails of boiling water, diving under cars and across tracks. It's no wonder that someone eventually stole it from us. For days afterward we mourned its loss. Happenings like that made me forget entirely about the strange youth, whom I now and then glimpsed subconsciously in my peripheral vision: by weak, flickering lantern light, against the background of preposterous songs and merry tales, the kid lay quietly on the bunk reading. We were close to Ashkhabad before I realized that he was still poring over my Heitler. "Thanks," he said, giving me back the book in its black, badly crumpled cover.

"What, you finished it?" I asked doubtfully.

"Yes, why not?" Astonished, I had nothing to say. "It was a hard book, but very thorough and informative. Thanks a lot," the kid added.

I was beside myself. Judge for yourself: here I was, a graduate student, and no matter how hard I tried I couldn't get through the first paragraph of that damned Heitler, but this boy, a third-year student, not only read it but gave it a thorough workout (I recalled his taking notes), and all this, to put it mildly, under the most difficult conditions. My bitter surprise soon vanished with the completely fantastic, merry, and starved life in Ashkhabad that was like nothing else on earth.

There were many novelties during the ten months I spent there. I went twenty kilometers into the desert and caught turtles in Kara-Kum, and a fellow named Deli Gelfand perished in that same desert. Our dormitory was in a school at 19 Engels Street, near the Russian market. Counterfeiting ration coupons in order to get a dozen bowls of soup with a few measly noodles in each was an epic tale in itself: by straining out the noodles we could make two or three bowls of soup of more or less normal consistency. Everybody did the same thing.

During that unforgettable year 1942, in the desolate but splendid Party Education Building, I gave lectures to my one and only fourth-year student, Solomon Pikelner, who later became such an ornament to Soviet astronomy.* Teacher and student, who differed only slightly in age and were incredibly ragged (and Monya went barefoot, besides), sat in the party educator's office and analyzed the fine points of the Schwarzschild-Schuster model for the formation of spectral absorption lines in the solar atmosphere. My heart still contracts with pain at the thought that Pikelner, the finest person I've ever known, has been dead for nearly ten years. It's funny and sad that to the end of his days he invariably deferred to me as his teacher.

Now and then I saw the kid who had struck my imagination. He was just as ragged and starved as the rest of us. I think he earned something on the side working part time in the dining hall, or as we called it, the "soup-station." (We made up other such word combinations: "soup-tropics," i.e., Ashkhabad; "soupo-stat," the person standing ahead of you in the soup line, and so forth.†

The Ashkhabad evacuation ended, and I went on to Sverd-

*[A gentle, unworldly man, Solomon ("Monya") Pikelner (1921–1975) was Shklovsky's close associate and friend. Pikelner's research was mainly on the theoretical explanation of phenomena on the Sun and in the interstellar medium. After the war he worked at the Crimean Astrophysical Observatory and became a professor at Moscow University in 1959. For fifteen years he edited the Soviet *Astronomical Journal.*]

†[The puns play on the prefixes "sub" and "super."]

lovsk, where my own Shternberg Astronomical Institute was located. That was the worst time of all. Cold was added to the pangs of hunger, my nearsighted eyes kept me out of the army, and sometimes I just didn't want to go on living.

In April 1943—an early bird!—I returned from evacuation. It's strange how little I remember about those days of life in a Moscow that seemed totally empty.

At the end of 1944 my graduate adviser, that dear soul Nikolay Pariysky, came back to Moscow also.* We greeted each other joyfully after three eventful years, reminiscing about everyone we could think of until we exhausted the list of mutual friends and acquaintances and the conversation took a turn to other, less vital issues. Among other things, Pariysky said, "Igor Evgenevich [Tamm—an old friend of his] has a really extraordinary graduate student. He's the first of his kind, even Ginzburg can't hold a candle to him!"†

"What's his name?"

"Hold on, just a minute, the thing is it's such a common name, easy to remember—what the hell, I've gone completely sclerotic!"

Well, that was typical of Pariysky, who is legendary among astronomers for his absent-mindedness. I started thinking, "After all, the entire wartime graduating class of the Moscow University physics department was with me in the Ashkhabad convoy. Where was this outstanding graduate student?" And in an instant I had him: it could only be my bunkmate in the freight-

*[Pariysky was an astronomer and geophysicist who worked on solar system problems and later on the rotation of the Earth.]

†[Tamm (1895–1971) was a distinguished physicist in quantum and nuclear theory, professor at Moscow University, and head of the theoretical division of the Academy of Sciences. Vitaly Ginzburg (b. 1916) is a distinguished physicist in radio astronomy and cosmic rays. He and Shklovsky were friends and classmates at Moscow University, but later a quarrel erupted between the two over priority for discoveries and suggestions, which has continued even after Shklovsky's death. For Ginzburg's account of the dispute, see "Notes of an Amateur Astrophysicist," *Annual Review of Astronomy and Astrophysics* 28 (1990): 30–32.]

car who had surprised me by mastering Heitler. "Is it Andrei Sakharov?" I asked Pariysky.

"That's it, such a simple name, and it slipped my mind!"

After Ashkhabad twenty-four years passed before I saw Sakharov again. In 1966, on my fiftieth birthday, I was elected a corresponding member of the USSR Academy of Sciences (on the fifth try). At the next meeting of the Academy that fall, Yakov Zeldovich* asked me, "Would you like to meet Sakharov?"

We squeezed our way through the dense crowd that packed the lobby of the House of Scientists, and Zeldovich presented me to Andrei. "But we're old friends," he said. I recognized him at once—the main change was that his eyes had sunk even deeper into his face. Strangely, his bald spot didn't detract at all from his noble appearance.

In late May 1971, on Sakharov's fiftieth birthday, I presented him with *that very same* miraculously preserved copy of Heitler's *Quantum Theory of Radiation*. He was deeply touched, and I think that both of us had tears in our eyes.

*[Zeldovich (1914–1988) was a much-decorated physicist who had a successful career in weapons research before becoming one of the world's leading cosmologists. He was Shklovsky's colleague at the Institute for Space Research.]

Born Lucky

WHEN I was a child my mother used to tell me that I was "born in a shirt." To be frank, I still don't know the gynecological definition of that phenomenon. I was never interested, just as even after two heart attacks I'm still not interested in the workings of my poor heart. From fourth grade I recall that it has auricles, ventricles, and valves, but what all that adds up to—I swear to God I don't know and don't care. Of course, this is due to the fatalism which is no small element of my character. As to the celebrated shirt, I should probably have taken more of an interest, since in folk belief being born in a shirt means you'll be lucky. Has this omen justified itself in my fate? Musing about the long years I've managed to survive, I've come to the conclusion that, any way you look at it, I've been quite a fortunate person.

Certainly I had great luck as a twenty year old when, still a shy provincial boy, I was accepted in the Moscow University physics department in 1935. We students lived in a score of two-story wooden barracks in Ostankino on the north edge of Moscow. Of course, I realize now that our dormitory was a dwelling hard to match for squalor. The so-called conveniences were trenches in the traditional Russian railway-station style. I still shudder every time I think of those outhouses, especially in winter, when frozen stalagmites of a repulsive composition were a material element of their "interior." There was one tiny shop for the entire quarter, but the assortment of foodstuffs was much richer than in our present grocery on Eliseev Boulevard.* Transportation to the university was a disaster: there were two painfully slow tramlines, the 17 to Pushkin Square, from which you walked downtown, and the 39 to Komsomol Square and a metro connection. I'll never be able to forget the cruel winters in ice-covered tramcars that inched along and made a long stop at Krestovsky crossing. A one-way trip could take well over an hour.

But all of the boys and girls who lived in those barracks were young and carefree. When your entire life is ahead of you, such "everyday difficulties," as they're called, are trifles, especially in summertime, when we sometimes studied in the shade of ancient oaks in the marvelous old park of the nearby Sheremetev palace, strolled its dirt paths, and swam and boated in the Ostankino ponds. The area north of Moscow had yet to be covered in ferroconcrete, construction on the Industrial and Agricultural Exposition was just beginning, and the monstrous Ostankino

---

*I remember the prices with photographic accuracy: a kilo of bologna cost 8 rubles, frankfurters 9.40, small sausages 7.20, ham 17, butter 17.50, red caviar 9, Siberian salmon 9, black caviar 17, and 10 eggs 5.50. A kilo of black bread was 85 kopeks, and you could buy coarse wheat bread for 1.70. The sausages were pure meat, and we didn't have to stand in line. Fantastic! In the fat weeks of the first half of the month, our usual dilemma in buying provisions at the store was whether to take 200 grams of frankfurters or 200 grams of red caviar (didn't we buy that yesterday?). When our stipends ran low at the end of the month, we switched to a semipenal diet: a kilo of wheat bread, a little sugar, and boiling water. On the other hand, the situation with manufactured goods was catastrophic. I went around in secondhand clothes, and in the winter I wore old felt boots, for some reason both for the left foot. On my twentieth birthday I bought my first—poor-quality—new trousers, and I got my first new suit for my marriage. To order it my future wife Shura and I had to stand in line one entire long winter night in a wretched workshop near the Rzhevsky (now Riga) railroad station.

tower hadn't yet been built. We were close to nature (at times brutally so) and at a healthy distance from deans' offices and university committees.

The latter circumstance to no small degree furthered the free spirit which ruled our life in the Ostankino student quarter. Mass psychoses rolled over us like tidal waves: we were swept away by a peculiar Italian hybrid of volleyball and rugby or ball-bearing billiards or card games. There was no limit to our youthful absorption in those diversions. I once spent the entire night playing twenty-one for small stakes with Vasya Malyutin and ended up gambling away my monthly stipend. God, how I hated the serious and methodical Vasya, how furious I was to lose that idiotically primitive game! The odds had to be absolutely equal, but against all the laws of probability theory, without even a flyspeck of advantage, he won and I lost. I realized then that the greatest passion in life is getting your own back. I don't remember how I managed to finish out the month.

In the 1930s luminaries like Lasker, Capablanca, and Euwe played in international chess tournaments in Moscow. With bated breath we students followed the titanic struggle for the world crown between Alyokhin and Euwe. We were ahead of our time and ideologically already in the postwar years of flourishing Russian nationalism as we rooted furiously for our Muscovite Alyokhin, even though he was an emigré. The tournaments created a propitious climate for the outbreak of an epidemic of chess fever.

A monstrous version of "blitz" without a clock held sway: each move had to be made in seconds, and there was a wild din from opponents and rooters alike. Even today I can hear the triumphant roar of a happy winner, "Gotcha!" as his king knocked over yours (there actually were such cases—we had no concept of checkmate). I skipped classes and played up to forty games a day. Thanks to that "style" of playing, I never did learn chess properly, and now, in my sixties, I'm deeply indifferent to it.

Often we played for forfeits, and your humble servant distinguished himself in the invention of refined punishments for the
unfortunate loser. For a while I roomed with the aforementioned Vasya Malyutin, a tall, bony, silent peasant of incredible
physical strength. Vasya didn't approve of our wild citified pastimes and sat for long hours at the wretched table in our room,
chipping away painfully at the granite of the science that came so
hard to him. Since I found mathematical analysis easy, sometimes I helped him. In the evening when we had our tea, I used
to watch him amusing himself by setting a heap of lump sugar on
the table, pulling back his huge middle finger, and slapping it
down on the heap with such terrible force that the lumps were
granulated. Those sugar lumps were not compressed grains (as
they are today) but enormously hard crystals, and nobody else
ever managed to repeat the experiment.

Vasya's trick gave me an idea for a particularly cruel forfeit:
losers in the chess arena would let him give them sugar-granu-
lating flicks on the forehead. The subtlety of the plan lay in my
calculation that Vasya would use less than full force on me, his
roommate and consultant. Odd as it may seem, Vasya readily
agreed to play the role of dormitory executioner and did so with
regal grandeur. On the honor system, whimpering plaintively,
the unhappy victim would seek out Vasya, who asked calmly,
"How many do you get?" I don't think anybody got a concus-
sion, although it's hard to be sure. In October 1941, Lieutenant
Vasily Malyutin was killed near Kalinin.

We physics students occupied the second floor of our wooden
barracks. Historians lived below us. The traditional wars of
words, teasing, and practical jokes were always starting up between us, but they never went beyond the limits of peaceful
coexistence—to tell the truth, those "contemptible historians"
were not bad kids, on their own level. They were the first students to be enrolled in the history department after an interval
of some years when the discipline of history had been effectively
destroyed in our country. For a long time it was replaced in the

school curriculum by a required subject called "social studies." Not surprisingly, the first recruitment of history majors was quite badly prepared.

In those days I was a feisty, skinny, touchily proud kid. After failing in Italian ballgames and chess blitzes, I decided to prove myself in a more original genre. As an adolescent and youth, I read greedily, mostly in history and geography. I had an exceptional memory (it still hasn't begun to let me down, thank God) and so I announced publicly that any average physicist, being a cultured person, has a good knowledge of history, no worse in any case than the pitiful historians downstairs. And besides we know physics, the queen of sciences, while those poor saps don't even know Ohm's law, not to mention the Schrödinger equations or, let's say, the canonical Gibbs distribution. In short, we were the salt of the earth, and those pitiful individuals living downstairs, the manure. The physicists neighed in approval, and the historians rose in savage rebellion. I proposed an unprecedented duel: I would pose ten questions on the history and geography of foreign lands to any representative chosen by the historians in advance, after which he would put ten questions of his choice to me. I pledged to answer all their questions, but my challenger would have to answer *only one of mine.* Any other outcome would count as my loss.

You can imagine the uproar. The first duel took place on the spot, and to the disgrace of the pitiful humanitarians I won. A dispirited mood set in on the first floor. The historians' grades went up sharply as they studied desperately to put me to shame. I didn't waste time either; I abandoned physics and spent my time secretly studying the basic university courses in history. I went through the standard textbooks on the ancient Orient, the Middle Ages, and Roman history. I could recite the names of the Roman emperors in any order, not to mention various Merovingians, Valois, and Piasts; I was especially strong in dates. All the succeeding tournaments (and they took place roughly once a month) ended in the catastrophic rout of the poor servants of Clio.

I'm sure that the insulting terms of the duels instilled fear in the historians and gave me an edge. An episode with a shy girl from the provinces, Tamara Latyshkina, who was studying for an oral exam in the history of the medieval Orient, illustrates their emotions. The poor girl could never manage to remember the name of the first shogun of the Tokugawa dynasty, the famous Hideyoshi, an early precursor of Japanese militarists like the bogy of my youth Savva Ivanovich Araki (the general was of the Orthodox faith!) and the criminal Hideki Tojo who was hanged after the war.* Moved by burning hatred for me mixed with admiration, Tamara made up a mnemonic way to remember that abstruse name: "Khudo Yose" [Tough for Yosa]—that is, me Iosif. To her grief, the professor examining her did indeed ask her about the shogunate and the name of the man who, four hundred years earlier, had said, "I will go beyond the sea and carry off China like a mat." To the professor's astonishment, Tamara blurted out, "Plokho Yose" [Bad for Yosa].†

I also remember ruining the blood pressure of that dear soul Elka Taubin. Elka was a native of Belorussia and a fanatic admirer of Belorussian culture (a purely Jewish phenomenon). On the other hand, I rated it very low and ended every discussion of the topic with the apparently innocent question: "And tell me then, Elka, how does the lyrical line "Hush, sorrow, hush" sound in Belorussian?" Elka would howl and fling himself on me with fists flying. My implication was that the phrase would be "Shut up, you bore, shut up."**

---

*[Sadao Araki (1877–1967) was Japanese war minister from 1931 to 1936. His specialty was Russian affairs, and he served as an intelligence officer in the St. Petersburg embassy before World War I and played a role in the Japanese intervention in Siberia during the Russian civil war. Since Araki was known to be fiercely anti-Russian, the sincerity of any "conversion" to Orthodoxy is open to question. Tojo was prime minister during World War II.]

†Several decades later, when I met an imposing, stout lady, our eminent Indologist Tamara Devyatkina, we had a good laugh over that episode.

**["Hush, sorrow, hush" in Russian is "Molchi, grust', molchi." In standard Belorussian the phrase would be "Mauchy, sum, mauchy," but there is a dialect variant, "Tsyts',

Junior lieutenant Ilya Taubin was killed on his beloved Belorussian soil at the beginning of the war. A quarter of a century later Elka's son, born after his father's death, looked me up in Moscow and asked me timidly whether I had ever sketched Taubin in the dormitory. He and his mother had nothing but a small pocket-size photo of their father and husband. Luckily, by some miracle a fine portrait of Elka in sanguine had been preserved in my archive, and I presented it with affection to his son and widow.*

Ideological education was at a low level in our dormitory rooms. My roommate, Mishka Dyachkov, was particularly flippant. Plump, clumsy, and squinting, he loved the theater and had once worked as an extra at the Maly. He often recited emotional passages in dead seriousness, while the other fellows rolled in laughter. I'll never forget the time that he suddenly jumped up from the table, threw back his head, and, shaking his fist at the Leader's fly-specked portrait on the wall, hissed: "To hell with you, Iosif Stalin!"† Nobody laughed at that; they pretended not to hear. Mishka called the Führer by the familiar "Adolf," and the Students' Best Friend, "Iosif." At times he improvised incredible comic dialogs between them which anticipated events in the fateful years to come.

I vividly recall another scene involving Mishka. In those "merry" days huge brightly colored portraits of all five marshals

---

nuda, tsyts'," which bears a resemblance to the rude Russian phrase "Tsyt, zanuda, tsyt," or (roughly) "Shut up, you bore, shut up."]

*In those years, carried away by the new technique of sanguine and India ink, I often drew from nature with great success, primarily portraits of my comrades in the dormitory. The sittings were about forty minutes, which was about as long as my models could take. At that time I reached a peak in the art of the portrait. I gave almost all of my drawings to the sitters, but I have a few left, and sometimes I still marvel that I could draw so well without ever having had lessons. In 1938 I abruptly abandoned art, and I've never regretted it.

†["Uzho tebe," a citation from Pushkin's narrative poem "The Bronze Horseman." The pitiful protagonist, a clerk who has lost his beloved in the great 1824 flood in St. Petersburg, uses those words to curse the builder of the city, Peter the Great.]

of the Soviet Union—Voroshilov, Budyonny, Blyukher, Egorov, and Tukhachevsky—hung on the roof of the Yaroslavl station. As each marshal in turn was arrested, his portrait was taken down even before the news appeared in the newspapers. With the low level of technology of those years, the complicated procedure went on for several hours in plain sight of the many thousands of people who thronged Komsomol Square with its three railroad stations. One day Mishka burst into our room and wailed, word for word: "Fellows! The score is three to two— and not in our favor!" He had just seen Blyukher's portrait being removed from Yaroslavl station.*

Most of the boys were splendid, honorable fellows. There were only a few squealers among us, but we soon began to feel their weight. Our comrades started disappearing one after the other. We went on frolicking, like Wells's eloi on a sunny day, while the morlocks worked at night, picking up people in their closed black trucks. Kolya Rachkovsky's disappearance made my skin crawl—I felt that "some hour was fast approaching." We called Kolya "Gogol" because he resembled a larger-scale version of that classic author. He loved chess and Ukrainian literature and recited with heartfelt conviction Shevchenko's "The Minstrel." Was that what led to his downfall? It must have been easy to pin a charge of Ukrainian nationalism on him.†

Three of the boys in our room no. 25 were well matched, merry, and sociable; our first precept was to help our friends. But there is no family without its black sheep: our fourth roommate was a loathsome type who did his best to poison our existence. Nikolay Zykov was older than the rest of us and, to put it mildly, not distinguished for looks. He had a low forehead

---

*[Stalin's purge of the officer corps started with the secret trial and immediate execution of Marshal Mikhail Tukhachevsky and seven other senior officers on June 11–12, 1937. Of the five marshals of the Soviet Union, only Klimenty Voroshilov and Semyon Budyonny survived to play active roles in World War II.]

†[Ukrainian poet Taras Shevchenko (1814–1860) was a freed serf and political activist repeatedly arrested and even forbidden to write by the tsarist regime.]

creased with deep wrinkles, small, close-set, shifty eyes, and a vile, sour odor about him. The feature that for some reason sticks most clearly in my mind is the deep cleft in his chin. We weren't such aristocrats and snobs that we couldn't have put up with that, but Zykov's character was intolerable. He was a spiteful bore and moralizer, a party member who was always trumpeting the fact and preaching at us as a "senior comrade." Since Zykov was impenetrably and militantly stupid, his endless sermons didn't improve the moral and political climate of our room. We soon saw through him, ignoring his sermons and either openly mocking or shutting our ears to his idiotic lectures on love and girls (his favorite themes). Sometimes we played not entirely inoffensive jokes on him. Mishka Dyachkov once asked Zykov, with deadly tenderness, "Kolya, do you think that a kiss brings people together?"

Kolya's mug lit up—at last he had gotten a normal response to his tirades. He started answering Mishka's question tediously and at length in the affirmative.

"Well then," concluded Dyachkov calmly, "kiss my ass!"

God, what a scene that kicked up. "You're making fun of a party member!" squealed the aggrieved Kolya, resorting to the argument he found incontrovertible.

"What's the party got to do with it? You're just a plain fool, Kolya, so to speak, in the personal sense."

That was the last straw. Zykov immediately switched to high-level threats. "Uncrushed Trotskyites! I'll unmask you. I'll *expose* you."

We were the dumb ones, taking that disgraceful scene for mere fun. The year 1937 was not far off, and the outraged activist's accusation of Trotskyism was mortally dangerous; accusations like that led to murder with impunity around some dark corner. What idiots we were not to realize it!

Zykov hated me with particular ferocity. Although he worked to exhaustion, science came hard to him. I was foolish enough (pure childishness!) to conceal my dogged long hours of work in the Lenin Library and pretend that I never bothered to study. I used to infuriate Kolya deliberately, driving him into a rage with my pose of idle loafer. He also had a crush on Shura, who was soon to become my wife.

The inevitable happened. I couldn't go on playing the fool and get off scot-free. Abruptly and unexpectedly I began to sense something new and even frightening in the atmosphere of the department. A void formed around me. A vacuum. On the surface everything seemed normal, but that was only appearance. My classmates avoided me like the plague, feigning absentmindedness to keep from greeting me. Even the department watchman started looking at me in a strange way. In those times an atmosphere like that could only mean that somebody had denounced you, the denunciation was serious, and your days were numbered. Even I, free spirit that I was, realized it. I felt inexpressibly vile at heart, and especially whenever I happened to see Zykov, who was less talkative than usual but made no effort to hide his triumph. I almost quit going to the department.

In that overheated atmosphere an outburst could come at any minute, and it finally did, at eleven-thirty one night when all four of us, already undressed, were lying angled across our cots reading.

"Put out the light," growled Zykov. He got up and headed for the switch.

"It's not twelve o'clock yet. We have a right to read."

"I'll show you your rights," he shouted, reaching for the switch.

"You're not really going to do that, are you?" said Vasya mildly, wiggling his huge steel fingers.

"You're making fun of a party member!" Zykov struck up his old tune.

"What's the party got to do with it?" I noted. "You're just a fool."

The scoundrel's face distorted with an anger I'd never seen before. He seemed to be trying to force a grin: "Just wait until our Chekists grab you by the gullet, and you try telling them that. You'll be bleating, 'We never said anything, we never made fun of a Communist.' "

"There's no reason to get so bothered, Kolya! I'm willing to confirm always and everywhere that you're a fool, because it's the honest truth, so to speak, in the court of last resort. If you doubt it, I can write you a certificate to prove it."

Forty-six years have passed since that night, but I remember it all down to the last detail. Zykov stood in the middle of the room in his dirty drawers, shaking from a frenzied anger mixed with joy. "So write it," he wheezed, coming over to my cot and holding out a pencil stub and a page from a notebook. The boys froze on their cots.

"Kolya," I said calmly and even tenderly, "who does things that way? This is an important document, and you give me a pencil. Be so kind as to dip the pen in ink and hand it to me. And give me that book, too, to put under the paper." With trembling hands he handed me the pen and the book. God, how loathsome he was! I wrote briefly and precisely:

CERTIFICATE

I hereby give this to Zykov Nikolay Makarovich in witness of the fact that he really is a fool.

February 1937.   I. Shklovsky

I handed him the certificate and said, "And now you can put out the light; it must be time by now."

I dropped by the department on some urgent business a week later and sensed immediately that the atmosphere had altered sharply. Welcoming faces greeted me; I was asked where I had been, had I been sick. The black storm-clouds which had been piling up on my horizon had vanished.

Years afterward, an old friend from graduate school, the now deceased Yury Lipsky, told me what happened. Zykov had written the department's party committee, which Lipsky headed, and had indeed libelously accused me of Trotskyite agitation. The party committee was obliged to look into it and reach a conclusion.

"Your affair was hopeless," Yura told me. "I was very sorry for you, you fool, but . . ."

Suddenly Zykov, blazing with joyful wrath, burst into the regular meeting of the party committee and handed them a crumpled paper. "You need more evidence of Shklovsky's anti-Soviet activities—just read this."

The committee members read my certificate and burst out laughing.

"You really are an idiot, Zykov. Get the hell out of here," said Lipsky, and the matter was dropped.

The happy ending of that dramatic story can be explained only by my being born in a shirt. During the years at Ostankino I tested the shirt effect several other times as well. It was certainly at work when I received a summons to appear at the Lubyanka early in the summer of 1937. I'll never forget that visit. I recall in particular the elevators and the long empty corridors of that terrible building. I remember pressing up against the wall to make way for a man with his hands behind his back and an escort following three paces behind him. Blood was running down the man's face. For some reason he was strangely calm.

At the Lubyanka they wanted to know details of poor Kolya Rachkovsky's life. I blurbled something about Kolya's peculiar way of playing chess—he took an annoyingly long time thinking out his moves. That was all I knew about the unfortunate fellow. Having failed to get any sense out of me, the investigator wrote me a pass to leave. Never will I forget the delicious sensation, body and soul, when that heavy door closed behind me and I stepped out into a Moscow street flooded with sunshine. I was overwhelmed by a tremendous feeling of love for the people scurrying back and forth as if nothing had happened.

During those two hours my world had turned upside down.

I was incredibly lucky. My entire generation of October Revolution babies had to be born lucky even to survive until the food supply program went into effect after the Civil War. It would be interesting to know how many of us are still alive today.

"All the Same It Moves!"

NIKOLAY KOZYREV was arrested in November 1936, at a dance celebrating the nineteenth anniversary of the Great October Revolution. He was approached by two men as he returned his lady to her seat. Situations like that were quickly understood. "But what about the lady? Who's going to take her home?"

"Don't worry about the lady, escorts will be found!"

Kozyrev was a brilliant twenty-seven-year-old astronomer, the hope of Leningrad's Pulkovo Observatory.* His work on extended stellar atmospheres had been published not long before that in the authoritative *Monthly Notices* of the Royal Astronomical Society of Great Britain.† Kozyrev's arrest was just one small part

---

*[The Chief Astronomical Observatory of the Academy of Sciences, which sits on the Pulkovo heights south of Leningrad, was completed in 1839 under Tsar Nicholas I. From its inception Pulkovo has been one of the great observatories of the world, although its location near the city has reduced its importance in recent years. It was completely destroyed by the Germans and rebuilt after World War II.]

†[Kozyrev showed that the strong ultraviolet excess found in some early stars could be explained by the presence of an extended atmosphere.]

of the catastrophe that battered the famous observatory, the oldest in our country, which in the nineteenth century Simon Newcomb had called the "world capital of astronomy."

Pulkovo Observatory had long been a thorn in the side of the Leningrad authorities—its staff included too many independent intellectuals of the old school. After the murder of Kirov, the observatory's position became, to use an astrophysical term, metastable.*

Disaster struck the institution apparently out of the blue. I have vivid memories of one marvelous fall day in 1960 that I spent as the guest of the phlegmatic, stout Slava Gnevyshev, who had been my comrade on the 1947 Brazil eclipse expedition, at the High Altitude Station of Pulkovo Observatory near Kislovodsk.† As we sat on a sunlight-flooded veranda with a stunning view of Mt. Elbrus, Slava, an old Pulkovite, told me quietly and unhurriedly about the 1937 catastrophe which to all intents and purposes destroyed the observatory.

Apparently it started when a certain graduate student took the qualifying examination in celestial mechanics from his adviser, our country's most eminent astronomer, Professor Numerov.** The graduate student, who suffered from both lack of talent and lousy preparation, didn't take his failure on the exam lightly. Having spotted a pile of foreign scientific correspondence on his adviser's desk, he took out his spite by denouncing Numerov in writing—either to the local party organization or someone higher up. At that time the secretary of the observatory party committee was a shifty, loud-mouthed,

*[The assassination of Leningrad party chief Sergey Kirov on December 1, 1934, was instigated by Stalin, perhaps to get rid of a rising popular rival. The "investigation" of Kirov's death began the purge which reached its peak in the mass arrests of 1937.]

†[Mstislav Gnevyshev established and directed Pulkovo's solar observing station high in the Caucasus Mountains used for studying the Sun's atmosphere or corona, which requires dark mountain skies.]

**Boris Numerov [1891–1941], a corresponding member of the Academy of Sciences, was then director of the Institute of Theoretical Astronomy and a member of the Pulkovo Scientific Council.

disgreeable man named Eigenson. When that scoundrel heard about the denunciation, he decided that the hour had come for him to show "appropriate" vigilance, and he started an investigation that resulted in Numerov's arrest. After being cruelly beaten at his first interrogation, Numerov signed a fabricated paper listing a number of his colleagues who were supposed to be participants in an anti-Soviet conspiracy (twelve in all at Pulkovo and approximately as many at Numerov's institute).

Our famous political police had already shown an interest in Numerov even before the student's denunciation. They had questioned Kozyrev about him but, of course, had gotten nowhere. Despite the paper they made him sign agreeing to secrecy, Kozyrev warned Numerov about the impending disaster. Under torture, the unfortunate astronomer told the investigators about the warning, and that served as a pretext to arrest Kozyrev. Further arrests followed and, to make it short, there was the type of chain reaction so common at the time. In the resulting conflagration (there's no other word for a phenomenon like that), at least eighty percent of the staff of Pulkovo, including the director Boris Gerasimovich, a gifted scientist, were subject to repression, and the majority of them perished.* Among those who died were Eropkin and a number of other important figures in our homeland's astronomy. Kozyrev was also burned in that conflagration.

Of course, 1937 was a disaster for the entire nation, but a great deal depended on the specific situation in each establishment, and here I should describe the astonishing case of my own Shternberg Astronomical Institute. This Moscow establishment is comparable to Leningrad's Pulkovo Observatory in size; you could call it Pulkovo's double. Improbable as it may seem, it is a fact that a certain graduate student at the Shternberg Institute

---

*[Gerasimovich (1889–1937) was an outstanding Soviet astronomer, the author of numerous works on stellar atmospheres and interiors, and director of Pulkovo from 1933 to 1937. Because he had worked at Harvard for three years and was well known in the West, his arrest brought a storm of foreign protests, which were ignored.]

took his celestial mechanics qualifying exam from his adviser, Professor Georgy Duboshin. His performance on the exam was as lamentable as that of his colleague at Pulkovo at approximately the same time, and the Moscow student reacted to his failure in exactly the way as the Leningrader: he denounced his adviser and incriminated him in the same sins—foreign scientific correspondence. The stereotypical behavior of Soviet graduate students in those far-off years is astonishing! The party organizer at the Shternberg Institute was a fellow named Aristov, a typical "activist" of the period, and he resorted to demagoguery, announcing that the institute was discriminating against a representative of the working class—in those times a very dangerous accusation. But forces within the institute, party bureau members Konstantin Kulikov, Yury Lipsky, and Grigory Sitnik, resolutely rebuffed the provocation. The slandering graduate student (I seem to recall that his name was Alyoshin) was expelled and, I think, kicked out of the party as well, and the luckless Aristov and his swordbearer, one Melnikov, soon followed. The conflagration was extinguished. The result was that during those unforgettable prewar years *not a single person* at our institute was subject to repression. It's the only such example I know.

Nikolay Kozyrev was sentenced to ten years and spent the first two of them in solitary in the notorious Vladimir Prison. There an astonishing thing happened to him. He told me about it in the Crimea afterward when we were working together at the Simeiz Observatory. He was the first person I ever met who had returned from that other world. You should have seen the pleasure he took in walking the wonderful Crimean earth, savoring every breath and frightened of being arrested again at any minute and sent back *there.* It was 1949, a year of repeat arrests, and his fear was not an idle one.

Kozyrev told me that he had a remarkable experience in solitary confinement. He spent those unimaginably tough days working out his strange ideas about non-nuclear energy sources of stars and their evolutionary paths. A year after he finished his sentence, Kozyrev defended his doctoral thesis on that fantastic and, to put it mildly, controversial theory.* At one point in his deliberations he needed to know some of the concrete characteristics of various stars—their diameters, luminosity, and so on. During the past terrible two years he had naturally forgotten such details, and ignorance of stellar characteristics might lead the tortuous thread of his logic into any one of numerous dead ends. And, in this desperate situation, through the slot in the cell door the guard suddenly handed him a book from the prison library—the second volume of the Pulkovo astronomy course! It was a miracle: the prison library numbered no more than a hundred books, and a pitiful collection at that. "For some reason," Kozyrev recalled later, "there were several copies of Demyan Bedny's now forgotten jingle, *How the Fourteenth Division Got to Heaven.*"†

Kozyrev realized he couldn't afford to tempt fate and spent all night in his blindingly lit cell working through what was to him priceless information. Although books were usually handed out for a week, the next morning they took that one away again. From that point Kozyrev became a devout Christian. I remember how surprised I was at seeing an icon in his Leningrad office in 1951. Today lots of dapper followers of fashion decorate their persons and apartments with cult objects, but then the adornment was a great novelty.

Solzhenitsyn, by the way, tells this story absolutely accurately in *The Gulag Archipelago.*** Kozyrev got to know Solzhe-

---

*We mustn't forget that Bethe's classic work demonstrating the nuclear nature of the energy sources of the Sun and stars was published only in 1939. Kozyrev had never heard of it. Total isolation from scientific life is a terrible thing for a scientist!

†["Demyan Bedny" (1883–1945) was a hack poet and tireless toady of the early Soviet period.]

**[Details of Kozyrev's ordeal and the incident Shklovsky recounts above are in *The Gulag Archipelago.* Thomas P. Whitney, tr., pt. 1 (New York: Harper & Row, 1974), pp. 480, 481–482, 484.]

nitsyn when the writer, long before his great fame, called him and expressed a wish to talk with him. The two veterans of the camps quickly found a common language. It is curious, therefore, that Solzhenitsyn's multivolume work passes in silence over a considerably more dramatic episode of Kozyrev's prison odyssey, about which he undoubtedly also knew. It's a good example of the way in which an author's position is revealed in the *selection* of materials he presents.

After he got out of prison, Kozyrev was sent to finish his sentence in a camp in the northern Krasnoyarsk region, on the lower reaches of the Enisei.* Properly speaking, it wasn't even a camp, but a small group of people laboring under guard on difficult installation work at a permafrost research station. It was bitterly cold, and this brought out a nontrivial physical trait in Kozyrev: he could install wires in icy winds and temperatures forty degrees below zero *with his bare hands*—and that takes good circulation, indeed. He was amazingly healthy and strong. Many years later in the Crimea I would admire his noble, handsome appearance, fine figure, and light and airy step. Even after suffering so much grief and so many spiritual and physical trials, he seemed to glide effortlessly over the stony paths of Simeiz.

Since it's hard to accomplish much in mittens, Kozyrev's unique ability to work bare-handed in the cold enabled him to fulfill the installation plan many times over. Thanks to his valiant labors, the local bosses treated him kindly; he received supplementary calories and was even put in charge of a production team. This unexpected rise in status cost him dearly. One loathsome type, a petty accountant serving a term for theft, was inflamed with envy of Kozyrev's privileged position and decided to ruin him. He wormed his way into the astronomer's confidence and launched into provocative talk. Kozyrev, starved for an intelligent word and with no idea that anyone could stoop that

---

*[The Enisei is a river in Soviet Asia that runs north into the Kara Sea and the Arctic Ocean. The camp was near Turukhansk, about 200 miles upstream.]

low, took the bait. One day the accountant asked Kozyrev what
he thought of Engels' famous pronouncement that Newton was
an inductive ass.* Of course, Kozyrev reacted appropriately to
the appraisal. The scoundrel sat down and wrote a denunciation,
and the consequences were not long in coming.

On January 16, 1942, Kozyrev was tried in the court at
Dudinka in the Taimyr Autonomous Region.† "So you don't
agree with Engels' pronouncement about Newton?" asked the
chairman of that farcical trial.

"I haven't read Engels, but I know that Newton was the
greatest scientist who ever lived," answered the imprisoned
astronomer.

The farce didn't last long. Wartime circumstances and the fact
that Kozyrev had already been tried under Article 58 and sentenced to ten years (it was before twenty-five–year sentences
were handed out) aggravated his guilt, and they pinned a new
ten-year term on him.** The Supreme Court of the Russian
Republic reviewed the Taimyr decision and rescinded it "due to
the leniency of the sentence." A firing squad became a real
threat to Kozyrev, who had no way of dealing with the ups and
downs of his case from his post at the permafrost station.

There is no doubt that Galileo, on trial before the Holy Inqui-
sition, never muttered the famous phrase ascribed to him, "All
the same it moves!" That is only a pleasant legend. But under
conditions no less grave Nikolay Kozyrev threw a phrase analogous in significance into the mugs of his jailors and executioners.
Such examples are inexpressibly rare, but the fact that they are
sometimes observed among representatives of *Homo sapiens*
justifies the existence of that sinful species.

The terrible days stretched on. A firing squad would have to
make a special trip by sleigh from farther upriver to shoot the

*See that classic author's *Dialectics of Nature*.
†[A camp near the mouth of the Enisei.]
**[Article 58 of the 1926 Criminal Code defined crimes against the state ranging from
treason, terrorism, and espionage to failure to denounce others.]

condemned man. Imagine Kozyrev's situation: a distant point might at any moment appear against the surrounding white wilderness and, as it came nearer, reveal itself as a sleigh hitched with draft animals (reindeer?) carrying his executioners. There was no way to escape. During those unbearable weeks Kozyrev received tremendous moral support from his fellow prisoner Lev Gumilyov, who is today an eminent historian, a specialist in the nomadic peoples of the steppes.*

A few weeks later the USSR Supreme Court reversed the decision of the Russian Supreme Court and let stand that of the regional court.

Why didn't Solzhenitsyn tell that astounding story? I think the reason is his extreme hostility to the intelligentsia or, to use his term, "educated trash" [*obrazovanshchina*]. As a Christian, Kozyrev is comprehensible and acceptable to the writer; as a dedicated scientist, he's an object of deep hostility. It's odd because Solzhenitsyn himself has a half-cocked education in physics and mathematics, but it can't be denied that hatred blinds people.

*[Gumilyov is the son of two great poets, Anna Akhmatova and her first husband Nikolay Gumilyov, who was executed by the Bolsheviks in 1921 for alleged counterrevolutionary activities.]

A Diplomat in Spite of Himself

DURING the forty years that the late Vladimir Turok and I were friends, he told me many engaging tales. He was a splendid storyteller, and it's a shame that he didn't write them down, but he was lazy beyond belief. Lazy and cautious—let's not forget the times!

I can close my eyes and see him sitting in the kitchen, striking a languid Oriental pose, wearing his bathrobe, and drinking strong black tea. Turok has converted me to the Turkish faith (meaning tea), and I am enjoying that potion which burns the gullet. "Pour some more for that bandit!" he orders his faithful life's companion, Koka Aleksandrovna. There is usually a long conversation with Koka's current pet tomcat, a subtle comparative analysis of the animal and the guest—that is, me. The comparison is not in my favor. I've grown used to the pungent odor of cat and bear all these cheerful torments and indignities stoically with the goal of reveling in Turok's stories, which usually begin after the third glass of tea.

He had a lot to tell. The details of Turok's career

aren't clear to me even now. For an extended period in the 1920s he was a TASS correspondent in Vienna, but primarily he was an operative of the Comintern. I remember hearing him tell how he procured a false passport for Georgy Dmitrov. He had known many interesting people who went down in history and then were written out of it again. Now, years afterward, all I can remember are fragments, snatches at best, of his tales about our prewar diplomatic corps.

The purges of 1937–1938 struck our diplomats with particular force. The chief crime of those years was connections abroad, and the diplomatic corps was marked for Lubyanka by the very nature of their work. The relentless scythe of blind terror devastated the ranks of what was then called the People's Commissariat of Foreign Affairs. Nearly 80 percent of all diplomatic posts were left vacant, and it wasn't clear how to fill them until the party, in its perspicacious way, issued a call: "Stakhanovites to the diplomatic service!" No sooner said than done. Heroes of labor from all over the country were sent to Moscow to take special crash courses in which the future Soviet diplomats acquired the basic skills of that delicate profession—wearing a tie correctly, not blowing your nose into the tablecloth at dinner, and so on.

Hitler had often expressed displeasure that an unquestionably Jewish diplomat, Yakov Suritz, was serving as Soviet ambassador to Berlin. Stalin decided to humor the Führer, and in the spring of 1939 Suritz was transferred from Berlin to Paris. This was perhaps the first inkling of the Soviet–German pact which stunned the world a few months later. Late that summer a crash-course graduate named Shkvartsov, the former director of a textile institute, was appointed Suritz's successor.

In the diaries of Foreign Minister Joachim von Ribbentrop, who was hanged at Nuremberg, you can read a most curious entry, dated November 1939: "Yesterday I was at a reception for the new Soviet ambassador. He pretends to be an idiot, but he can't fool us!" Even that slyest of diplomatic foxes was bewildered by the shocking appointment and viewed it as a subtle feint in Stalin's foreign policy. When Molotov visited Berlin in November 1940, he quickly realized that the representative of Soviet power was a blockhead and had Shkvartsov recalled.

Of all Turok's stories, the tragic odyssey of Nikolay Ivanov made the strongest impression on me. There are a few lines about his fate in Ehrenburg's well-padded memoirs, but Ehrenburg could have afforded to be more generous—after all, as he says himself, Ivanov saved his life.*

Nikolay Ivanov was far from being a hero of labor. The son of a well-known professor of medicine, he received an excellent upbringing at home and knew two or three foreign languages— and that in the end brought about his downfall. He became a Young Communist and then a party member. Until 1939, when blind chance played a terrible trick on him, he taught political economy at a Moscow institute. Turok's version of the story is that in mid-1938 Ivanov was suddenly offered a minor diplomatic post in some impoverished Near East state (Yemen? In those days there were hardly any independent states in the region).

Ivanov reacted with indignation. "What kind of diplomat am I? It's some ridiculous mistake! I'm not going anywhere!"

A few months later the offer was renewed. Ivanov probably assumed that there had been a foul-up somewhere. "Why should they want to make a diplomat out of me?" Later he realized that he was picked out because he had conscientiously noted his language skills in his party dossier. And, besides, he had such a nice proletarian name.† A polished Ivanov, just the ticket!

Ivanov was summoned again, this time by Georgy Malenkov, the man in charge of party cadres, who was a tough character despite his womanish face (in high party circles he had the female nickname "Malanya"). "I don't want to see you here again!

---

*[Ilya Ehrenburg, *Memoirs: 1921–1941,* Tatania Shebunina, tr., with Yvonne Kapp (Cleveland: World, 1964), pp. 485–488).]
†[The equivalent of Johnson.]

Go on over to Kuznetsky and get your appointment. Shoo, get out of here!"*

When Ivanov arrived at the Commissariat of Foreign Affairs with Malenkov's note, a functionary discovered that the vacancy intended for the poor devil had been filled, but since they couldn't let Malenkov find out about the chaos reigning in the commissariat, he had to find a post for Ivanov. With no time for reflection, the functionary scribbled something on a piece of paper and politely invited Ivanov to go to a room that turned out to be a section of the West European division. There he received an assignment which he signed without a murmur. Ivanov had been appointed first secretary of the embassy in Paris with orders to take up the post immediately.

It was the spring of 1939. Before Ivanov got his first look at Paris, the newsreels were showing a fleeting glimpse of Ribbentrop's leather-clad back as he climbed into a luxurious car at Vnukovo airport. The Soviet–German pact radically altered the political situation in Europe. A flood of congratulatory telegrams poured into the Kremlin from all over the Soviet Union with fulsome praise for the great genius and sagacity of Stalin, who for the nth time had frustrated the machinations of the imperialists.

Just then Yakov Suritz, our ambassador in France, came down with flu. Since Ivanov hadn't yet taken up his post, the second secretary was left to run the embassy, and he, as knowing people said, was not on the diplomatic payroll but worked for the security apparatus instead.†

Lording it over the embassy, the second secretary decided

---

*I recall those exact words from Turok's story.
†Regular diplomats fear and disdain such types. Many years after the events described I ran into this phenomenon myself. The papa of a congenial kid named Oleg Generalov, who worked in my group as an engineer, had been our ambassador to Australia. I asked Oleg what his father thought about Petrov (a Soviet "diplomat" who defected to the Australian authorities with all our codes). "He's not ours, not from the Foreign Ministry—you can expect anything from those bastards," gloated the elder Generalov.

that that Soviet establishment should join the chorus of spontaneous expressions of deepest gratitude to the Best Friend of
Soviet Diplomats. A telegram to Stalin with the traditional word-
ing was quickly composed. The ailing Suritz asked his wife to
read and sign it. In their stupidity, she and the second secretary
forgot to encode the epistle, and the next day it was published in
the Paris press. A political scandal broke. The French government, which regarded the Soviet–German pact as a knife in the
back, declared Suritz *persona non grata* and ordered him out of
Paris in twenty-four hours. The new first secretary Nikolay Ivanov was left in charge.

Ivanov, a far from stupid man of strong character and a communist of the old school, found himself in a tough situation after
the Fascists occupied Paris. He found it unbearably difficult, for
instance, to be furnishing Soviet passports to interned Spanish
Republicans in mortal danger (he saved the lives of many thousands of people) and at the same time sitting in meetings with
the German military commander General Otto von Stülpnagel
and the ambassador, a scoundrel named Otto Abetz—"our
sworn friends," as it was put at the time. In those terrible
months prominent antifascists including Ehrenburg took refuge
in our embassy.

Ivanov was among the first to warn Moscow of the impending
German invasion. A true patriot, he did his duty under incredibly
tough conditions. The second secretary, on the other hand,
served the Soviet–German pact with faith and fidelity and soon
found a common language with the German administration and
the Gestapo. The first and second secretaries of our embassy
came into sharp conflict over matters of principle, and Ivanov
was suddenly recalled to Moscow in December 1940. It must be
assumed that his enemy had a hand in it.

When he got back to Moscow, Ivanov went straight to
Molotov's office. Molotov received him quite amicably. "I
see you're very tired, Comrade Ivanov—nerves, nerves. And
besides, they tell me you can't manage to work with the

Germans. Have a good sleep, and tomorrow we'll see about it."

Ivanov was arrested that night and sentenced the following September—when the Germany army was at the gates of Moscow!—to five years on a charge of anti-German propaganda. He tried in vain to obtain a review of that absurd and monstrous verdict. In 1946, having serving his time down to the last minute, Ivanov was released and got a job at a provincial institute teaching political economy as it had been retouched by Stalin's latest "research" in the field.

Our Soviet Rabbi

... We grow older day by day,
We come closer to the ashes.
—What can I tell you? I was a Jew
Who lived in times like those.
                    —*Unknown poet.*

I FIRST met Mates Agrest in September 1938. We were
among the half dozen young men lined up in chairs
outside the office of Comrade Kozhushko, an inspector
in the People's Commissariat of Education. The line
advanced slowly, but we were willing to wait. All of us
had pretty much the same problem—getting exempted
from the two-year work assignments that the commissariat doled out to students graduating from institutions
of higher education—and our fates were being decided
behind Kozhushko's door. I had just graduated from the
Moscow University physics department and been assigned to the Beryozovka district just east of Krasnoyarsk, deep in the swamp forests of Siberia. Being by
nature both fatalistic and lazy, I would have resigned

myself and gone, but I had a wife and, more important, a new-
born daughter.* I had to think of my family. The physics department didn't keep me on—although I swear to God that I wasn't
a bad student—and I spent the summer desperately scouring
Moscow for a graduate program that would take me. Fantastically improbable as it may seem today, I found two suitable
positions. One was at the Karpov Institute of Physical Chemistry. I took the application form, but I didn't like the atmosphere
at that reputable establishment.† An announcement in the Moscow evening paper directed me to the other program, at the
Shternberg Astronomical Institute. I entered an old-fashioned
courtyard overgrown with grass and crossed the threshold of
the small wooden building into which the pitiful rooms of the
institute were crammed. In the office a pretty woman greeted
me with a rare kindness that made up my mind for me: I decided
to become an astronomer—as I thought, for the time being, and
as it turned out, for life.**

That year it was decided that more physicists were needed to
augment the ranks of astronomers, and I wasn't the only alum-
nus of my department accepted at GAISH. In two months I
learned general astronomy, refreshed my bad German, and
passed the qualifying examinations. Then the Commissariat of
Education came between me and my choice, forcing me to follow
the law by taking up my assignment in Siberia. The interview
with Comrade Kozhushko was only one stage on the rocky road

*She is now a senior research associate at the Joint Institute for Nuclear Research at
Dubna and a grandmother.
†Two years later, an order was posted at the Karpov Institute containing the following
memorable paragraph: "4. Associate of the Electrochemical Laboratory Comrade
Morokhov is hereby reprimanded for applying to the Karpov Institute a word that in the
language of poorly educated people is used to denote a house of prostitution." It was
signed by the director of the institute, Academician Bakh himself. A month afterward a
new order appeared, revoking paragraph four and thereby confirming Comrade Morokhov's diagnosis.
**That same splendid Elena Andreevna still reigns over the main office of the institute;
we've been friends throughout the intervening forty-three years.

to science. In the end, all of us got exemptions and made it into graduate school, but we sweated blood in the process.

Two hours outside Kozhushko's office had made me hungry. Getting up from my chair, I told the fellow ahead of me that I was going to the lunchroom.

"Buy something for me, too, please—I'm afraid to go myself, I'm next to see Kozhushko!"

"Fine," I said, and suddenly I remembered the young man. He was from Leningrad and had taken the qualifying exams in celestial mechanics at the Shternberg Institute while I was passing mine in astrophysics.

I came back from the lunchroom and handed my colleague a salami sandwich. To my great amazement, the fellow mumbled something and turned it down. "It's perfectly good salami, you know," I announced perplexedly. Just then the door to Comrade Kozhushko's office opened, and the strange little fellow beat a hasty retreat.

"He must be a vegetarian," I thought blankly, chewing on his salami.

He came out of the office, and I went in. The bureaucrat from the Commissariat of Education spent a long time badgering me. When I finally left, I wasn't surprised to find the Leningrader waiting for me; since we had both been admitted to the Shternberg Institute, exchange of experience would be useful.

We walked out onto the street together, and after we had quickly disposed of our common business, I asked him, "By the way, why didn't you take the sandwich? You asked me to bring you something."

The answer amazed me: "Eating salami is against my religion." I looked suspiciously at the young man, but he was serious.

Memories of my boyhood swarmed through my mind. I grew up in a traditional Jewish environment in a small Ukrainian town, studied the ancient language of my ancestors, and went with Mama to the synagogue. For some reason although we were all desperately poor, I can still remember the special *aroma* of our holidays. Then came seven years which split my consciousness between Jewish home and Soviet school. In 1930 my family left our native Ukraine, and after that I lived in Kazakhstan, on the Amur River, in the Maritime region, and finally in Moscow. My Jewish childhood was left behind in the irretrievably distant past. I had become a modern Soviet youth.

This living relic from Leningrad stirred up memories that stabbed me to the quick. I began questioning him greedily: how could he have remained a real Jew all through the period which has been called, all too mildly, "the era of reconstruction"?

The boy, whose full name was Mates Mendelevich Agrest, was only a year older than I, and he too had been born in a small town—not in Ukraine, however, but in Belorussia, in the Mogilyov region. From then on our fates differed totally. At the age of five he was enrolled in a *cheder*—a Jewish religious school, where he studied at the expense of the community. After the *cheder,* he went to a *yeshiva*—the equivalent of the Orthodox religious seminary. For him and his contemporaries, time stood still. Outside raged the storms of the Civil War, banditry, the New Economic Policy (NEP); the five-year plans began; an ancient way of life was crumbling. But the hard-working boys, pale as shadows, kept stubbornly studying the medieval lore of the Talmud ten to twelve hours a day. There was relative rest on the Sabbath, but even then there were prayers to be recited. At fifteen he graduated from the *yeshiva* and became an *ordained rabbi.* But "what millennium, my dears, lies outside the door?"* It was the stormy year 1930—the Year of the Great Turning Point.† There was no job for a newly hatched rabbi. Mates ended up in Leningrad with practically no means of existence and no knowledge of the Russian language. You can imagine how difficult it was. Hunger and a homeless life weren't his main

*[Boris Pasternak, "About These Poems," *My Sister Life* (1917).]
†[The year that forced collectivization of agriculture began.]

woes; his real problem was the absence of perspective. What should he do? How could he find himself in this frightening new world and still remain true to himself as an Orthodox Jew of high spiritual rank? He managed to do both.

He decided he would study for the entrance exams to the famous mathematics and mechanics department of Leningrad University. In the religious schools, beginning arithmetic was the *only* "secular" subject covered, so he knew nothing of what we call education, and he had to study in snatches while working at various odd jobs to feed himself and send at least a few crumbs to his parents. Under those unimaginable conditions it took him a little over a year to prepare for the university. How can a phenomenon like that be explained? First of all, he undoubtedly had a capacity for abstract thinking hypertrophically developed by his traditional Jewish education. I would guess also that after the Talmud and the commentaries to it, learning physics and history didn't seem that hard. He passed all his exams brilliantly and . . . flunked Russian. Nevertheless—pay close attention, comrades—Mates was accepted by Leningrad University as a Jew, for whom Russian was a foreign language. In our brutalized times those who read these lines will find them funny. I ask you to stop and think a minute: whom and what are you laughing at?

In his student years at Leningrad University, Mates found the perfect job: at the public library he deciphered medieval Jewish manuscripts from the Cordova caliphate and became an expert on the amazing Jewish-Arabic culture that flourished in southern Spain ten centuries ago. So there I was, walking the streets of Moscow with a highly learned rabbi just my own age. I was twenty-two.

At the Shternberg Institute we became fast friends, and our friendship has lasted ever since. During that entire period Mates has scrupulously followed the dictates of Jewish law, which in our country was (and is) not simple. Before the war he married a Jewish girl from a traditional family of the type already rare. The young couple lived near Moscow, in the Jewish suburb of Udel-naya, with a father-in-law who was an Orthodox Jew and a mother-in-law just as devout. In the Soviet period this was an astonishing relic of Sholom Aleichem's Kasrilowka. I enjoyed visiting them and reveling in their happiness and the specific microclimate, like an echo of my childhood, which they managed to create. In the electric train the illusion of a Jewish village rapidly dissipated, and by the time I got back to Moscow the harsh climate of the graduate student's impoverished, unsettled life surrounded me again.

When the war started, our fates once more diverged. A healthy, thriving, red-cheeked lad, I was turned down by the army (myopia of minus ten diopters), and Mates, small and far from martial in spirit, was immediately commissioned. At first he had a good position commanding a squad of barrage balloons in the anti-aircraft defenses of the city of Gorky. One day, how-ever, Mates launched his balloons just as a storm struck, and two "sausages" caught fire. Regulations required that he be given a warning from the local meteorological station the day before a storm was expected, but due to the negligence of the local meteorological bosses, the warning hadn't come. Mates was court-martialed. The situation was dramatic: the head of the weather service was Captain Pavel Parenago, who had been our professor at the Shternberg Institute and was well acquainted with graduate student Agrest. To the religious lieutenant's hor-ror, Captain Parenago brazenly maintained that he *had* sent the storm warning. As they say, your own skin is closest. Mates Agrest was demoted and sent to the front with a penal battalion. It's a miracle that he came back alive and largely whole.*

When I saw my friend again after a separation of almost five years, he was lame (from a wound) and walked with a cane. Once I asked him whether he had observed the prescriptions of Jewish law at the front (for example, resting on the Sabbath). He

---

*[Parenago (1906–1960) headed the department of stellar astronomy at Moscow University from 1940 until his death.]

answered seriously that the Talmud provided moderated variants of behavior for such situations. His entire family—parents, brothers, sisters—had been brutally killed by the Germans in Belorussia, and overall Mates found it difficult to adjust to the complexities of peacetime. I tried to give him whatever moral support I could. He pulled himself together and defended his dissertation—something about the system of Saturn.

In that "cheerful" year of 1947, his status as battlefield veteran didn't count—nobody would risk hiring a Jew. It became his lot to see the sheepish, furtive smiles which accompanied various forms of rejection. In this critical situation he came to me for advice. He had been offered a strange job—he would go off to the end of the world, God only knows where, and be deprived for a number of years even of the right to correspond; in exchange he had a chance to participate in interesting and important work. It was all strange and unexpected.

"Take it," I said decisively. "There'll be no life for you here."

Once more Mates disappeared from sight for almost four years. In 1951 I got an unexpected telephone call telling me that he was back in Moscow. I had trouble finding the address Mates gave me, and when I did, I was stupefied by the luxurious house in which he and his family were camping. Our reunion was joyful. His Rita had grown appreciably rounder; Mates himself exuded well-being. Best of all, in a well-appointed bedroom three little boys were sleeping side by side. From half-hints (he never, then or afterward, told me the name of the place where he had worked, and I didn't ask—it was clear anyway) I gathered that he played the important role of mathematician-calculator at the epicenter of our nuclear program. Don't forget that back in 1951 there were no computers: difficult mathematical problems had to be solved with desk calculators and *quickly* at that. All the eminent physicists who ended up insuring the Soviet nuclear potential worked directly with him, and he was well respected. But suddenly, for reasons I'm not sure about even now, he and his family were evicted from the site literally in twenty-four hours (it could have been worse—Beria himself headed the nuclear program) and sent to a splendid new institute in Sinop, on the outskirts of Sukhumi on the Caucasian coast of the Black Sea. The Moscow house where we met was a stopover on the way.

During the last thirty years I've been to Sukhumi often, and sometimes I've stayed in my friend's splendid apartment on the edge of a subtropical park. The children, mere mites in 1951, have become scientists themselves. His wife's parents have died, but the overall traditional spirit of the family remains immutable. Every morning Mates puts on his *yarmulka,* throws on his *tallis,* winds the *tefilin* around his naked arm, and recites his prayers, and every Friday evening in his home the Sabbath candles are lit.

Once I asked him, "It can't have been any easier to observe Jewish customs and laws at the site than it was during the war, can it? After all, the 'mitigating' wartime circumstances foreseen by the Talmud could hardly apply."

"Yes, it was tough," my old friend said, and he shared a dramatic story with me.

During all his years at the site, Mates never worked on Saturdays. But what is meant by "work"? The Talmud defines it precisely. Writing is work, but reading or carrying on conversations and discussions isn't. And so, on a routine Saturday, Mates Agrest, the head of the computing laboratory, was seen and sensed by all his colleagues to be working actively from morning on: he issued instructions, studied reports, glanced over calculations, and gave guidance and instruction. But in the Talmudic sense he wasn't working. His pencil never traced a single figure, and he made no marks on his co-workers' calculations. You'd think that nobody would catch on, but one man did spot that elusive trait of Mates's otherwise irreproachable activity.

That man was Yakov Zeldovich, a very important person at the site.* One Saturday he sent for our rabbi and casually men-

*[And himself a Jew.]

tioned that a few details of a calculation the laboratory had made the day before were not clear to him. Mates began explaining it in comprehensible and obvious terms to the future academician. "But I don't understand this spot here. Please write the formula for me. . . ."

The ordeal went on for two hours. Zeldovich displayed sadistic inventiveness and extreme perseverance. Poor Mates was in a sweat. He resorted to the most improbable dodges to explain to his tormentor "on his fingers" that there was no mistake, that the calculation was correct. All in vain! For the first time in his life poor Mates was forced to violate his law.

The start of the space age in 1957 and the idea that humans would literally begin storming the heavens staggered my old friend. Mates reacted the way you would expect from a learned rabbi: he began searching the Old Testament for references to the appearance of newcomers in space. With enormous enthusiasm he wrote a commentary on obscure passages in the book of Enoch. The terrible fate of Sodom and Gomorrah drew his attention. He was fanatically rapt in his research and even today has a rabid belief in his interpretation of the ancient myths. Blessed is he who has faith! Mates Agrest is that rare thing in our terrible age: a happy man.

The Passengers
and the Ship

IN 1947 the Soviet Union—a country still famished and overtaxed by a devastating war in which nearly every second adult male perished or was crippled—equipped a blindingly white beauty of a steamship with a load of scientists and equipment and sent it across the Atlantic on a southwest trajectory to observe a total solar eclipse on the far side of the earth. The path of totality on May 20 passed over Brazil from the southern Parana state to Bahia, an Atlantic port in the northeast part of that huge country. Bahia is famous in the history of science for the months young Darwin spent there on the world-circling voyage of the *Beagle*. The voyage of the *Griboedov* was also a landmark in the history of science—the new science of radio astronomy, which was just beginning its triumphal march. Eclipse observations carried out in Bahia harbor from that splendid ship proved decisively that the source of the Sun's emission in meter waves is the corona, as two young theoretical astrophysicists at the start of their careers, Vitaly Ginzburg and I, had independently predicted a year earlier.

Astonishingly enough, both Ginzburg and I took part in that expedition. The authorities automatically approved the entire staff of the expedition as proposed by its leaders. In our extreme inexperience we all took that approval for granted. Looking back, it is apparent that the various party cadres, foreign sections of institutes, and, of course, the visa commission which ruled them were still taking their first timid steps. During the next few years they rapidly came to realize that their basic task was "to hold on and not let go"—to hinder contacts between real Soviet scientists and world science. Most of the people who traveled abroad after that were bureaucrats, open and not-so-open collaborators of the Ministry of Love.*

Our expedition nearly ended before it got under way. For almost two weeks we languished in idleness on board the *Griboedov* in Libava—to our woe, that ice-free port had frozen over for the first time in many years.† Time was running out by the time the icebreaker *Ermak* led us literally into "clear waters" on April 13, a mere five weeks before the moment of eclipse. We had a twenty-two–day Atlantic crossing ahead of us, followed by the journey to the site in the interior of the country, the resort hotel Agua de Araxa near the village of Barreiro, in Minas Gerais state. Once there we would have to set up our instruments for optical observations on special brick piers that had yet to be laid. With this deadline facing us, we rushed straight to our distant goal with no routine stops to pick up incidental cargo. We did spend twelve hours in the small Swedish town of Karlshamn getting the ship's hull demagnetized, a necessary measure for crossing seas still sown with mines left over from the war, and we also stopped in Southampton to pick up some British-made Ilford photographic plates.**

---

*[Shklovsky's ironic name for the NKVD, whose security functions were merged into the KGB in 1954.]

†[Libava (in German: Libau) is the pre-1917 name of the Latvian port of Liepaja on the Baltic.]

**[The USSR did not produce satisfactory photographic plates.]

Today in the era of the scientific-technological revolution, there are no more voyages like that one. In the mouth of the English Channel a terrible equinoctial storm struck us. Our cargoless 5,000-ton shell lost its steering. At each pitch we listed by forty-five degrees, and waves of cold, salty water rolled across the deck. I turned out to be immune to seasickness. With a childlike curiosity, holding on to guardropes, I fought my way to the bow, where the amplitude of the pitching was at its highest. There was something desperately merry about looking at the dancing horizon as it rose above the mast and then sank into the abyss. Three-fourths of the sailors were flat out with dry heaves. How young I was! I got the crazy idea of going to the saloon for dinner. The problems were far from trivial. For instance, how do you go down a ladder that has a negative angle of inclination to the horizontal plane? The captain, a real sea wolf, was sitting alone at the table, which had been covered with a wooden grid to keep dishes from sliding into diners' laps. A suffering, seasick waitress served the two of us. Watching her bring bowls of soup was a real circus number, and swallowing it was no simpler. Copying the captain, I picked up the bowl on my palm and kept my eyes fixed on the level of the soup. Even the most ferocious pitching has a rhythm, and I got the soup down safely.

The captain saved the ship from destruction by turning back and, with a display of great skill, steering pilotless into the narrow mouth of Plymouth Bay. Afterward I found out that our radio operators received six separate SOS signals that terrible night. In those years after the war shipwrecks were common. The hastily built, welded Liberty ships could be snapped in half by a high wave.* Our *Griboedov,* durably riveted together in the old-fashioned way by Swedish shipwrights, came through that cruel ordeal splendidly.

---

*There is a bitter sailor's joke from war days to the effect that the longest ship in the world is the *Dvina:* its bow is in Sevastopol, and its stern in Constantinople—the ports to which the pieces of the ill-starred ship were towed.

After ten hours in Plymouth Bay, the ship continued its much delayed journey. The captain decided to gain time by taking the ship directly by the great circle route instead of along established sealanes. We had wonderful sunny weather throughout our twenty-two days at sea. The ocean was as empty as in the times of Christopher Columbus—we didn't meet a single flag. Flying fish flopped onto the deck. Southern constellations with exotic names came into sight. We crossed the equator and had a raucous celebration of the festival of Neptune. To the traditional question put by a sailor disguised as the ruler of the seas (a hempen beard, a trident, and a cardboard crown) and surrounded by "negroes" smeared with soot: "What ship is this, what cargo are you carrying, whither do you set your course?" the captain from the heights of the bridge answered (I remember it word for word): "Our ship is a merchantman, our land is Soviet. And we carry learned men to observe the eclipse of the Sun and enrich science."

Neptune found the captain's answer totally satisfactory and proposed "to salt those who are not yet salty." And then the fun began! The sailors dragged out hoses and started dousing each other with seawater at terrible force. The "men of science," dressed for the festive occasion in their best suits, were assembled on the upper deck. A moment finally came when the gaiety was beginning to fade, since the half-naked sailors were obviously reluctant to salt the clean audience. Having previously locked the exit to the area where the cabins were located, I undressed, ran down the ladder, and begged them to salt me. Then a sailor friend and I dragged the hose up to the upper deck. My God, that was a sight to behold! Notwithstanding the howls of "Hooliganism!" from the still dry passengers, nobody who had not previously crossed the ocean equator escaped the seawater christening. A curious phenomenon could be observed: a man once drenched immediately joined the camp of the drenchers. Our oak, the deputy political officer, held out longest of all. Howling, "You won't get away with it! This is ideological sabotage!" he locked himself in his cabin. Under the spell of "bourgeois ideology," the sailors, led by the senior mechanic, thrust the hose into the cabin through a porthole and started flooding it. After a few minutes the political officer ran out howling wildly and was at once knocked off his feet by the powerful jet from the firehose. I had never seen such an unrestrained outburst of popular emotion, and I found the raging mob I had set loose terrible to behold. Everything soon returned to normal, however, and the holiday ended with a banquet washed down with lots of wine.

More long, marvelous, but also monotonous days passed. Toward the end of our voyage across the Atlantic we were all starved for the sight of even a bit of dry land. At last the first Brazilian territory, rocky islands covered with tropical forest and bearing the melodious name of Fernando de Noronha, came into view. Even though I know my geography, I had never heard of them. Two days later we arrived in a port bearing the sonorous name of Angra dos Reis. The town was approximately one hundred miles south of Rio. Our leaders' choice of port and the complex route inland was mainly determined by the fact that Brazil hadn't yet settled on a standard gauge of railroad track: Angra was a spot from which we would be able to unload rapidly and put the optical party directly onto a train to our designated observational site at Araxa, 700 kilometers away. After the *Griboedov* finished unloading us, it set out immediately for the north, to Bahia, where the radio-astronomy observations of the eclipse on board would be so spectacularly successful.

The solemn moment came for mooring the ship at the wall of the wharf. The panorama of the bay rimmed with high mountains was entrancing. The white town was drowned in greenery. Far off we could see the ruins of the oldest monastery on American soil (sixteenth century) overgrown in unruly tropical foliage. We were the first Soviet ship ever to dock in Angra dos Reis, and colorful local inhabitants, mainly mulattoes, poured onto the wharf.

We passengers, proud and happy, feeling like heroic pio-
neers, lined up on the upper deck, wearing the white wool suits
especially made for the participants in the expedition by the
Academy of Science tailors. The only reason for equipping us
that way was apparently Ostap Bender's phrase about the white
trousers of the aboriginal inhabitants of the city of his dreams.*
It didn't take us long to realize that Ostap had made a bad mistake—only the Brazilian proletariat wore white trousers.

It was natural for the captain to want to show off Soviet skills
by mooring artistically: the ship had to touch the berth *at a single
point* and come to an instant halt as if rooted there. This is not
easy, but the captain, standing on the bridge in his snow-white
naval jacket, concentrated on the crucial maneuver and managed
it brilliantly. The crowd of experts on the pier would doubtless
have been impressed if there hadn't been an annoying occur-
rence. At that exact moment some reprobate on board the
Griboedov had an urge to use the head. And that was why, just at
the climax of the single-point mooring, a powerful stream of
seawater containing the wastes of the aforementioned reprobate's biological activity splashed all over the dazzlingly clean
wharf. Someone had forgotten to batten the hatches of the heads
before mooring. Small boys were the first to grasp and appreciate the paradoxical situation, and they burst into loud peals of
laughter, yelling something in the language of Camoens. Adult
gapers followed suit.

*[*The Twelve Chairs* and *The Golden Calf,* by humorists who wrote together under the
pseudonyms of Ilya Ilf and Evgeny Petrov, recount the adventures of unflappable con
man Ostap Bender, "the Bigtime Operator," who pursues various schemes to enrich
himself during the late 1920s. Bender became a sort of underground hero to indepen-
dent-minded Soviets during the years of Stalinist repression, and his adventures were
used as an Aesopian code for dangerous topics. The books were translated into English
shortly after their publication in the Soviet Union: *The Twelve Chairs,* John Richardson,
tr. (1928; New York: Random House, 1961); and *The Golden Calf,* John H. C. Richardson, tr. (1931; New York: Random House, 1962). In *The Golden Calf* Ostap Bender
dreams of relieving an underground millionaire of his ill-gotten fortune and escaping to
the unbridled capitalism of Rio de Janeiro, which he thinks of as: "A million and a half
people, and every one of them in white pants" (p. 25).]

There are situations when passengers cannot be separated from the ship. Pitiful prattling to the effect that "it wasn't me, I had nothing to do with it" was so foolish that nobody even dreamed of justifying himself that way. We all burned from shame and, although we were now able to go into the promised land for which we had so desperately longed, nobody went ashore. It was only the next morning that we began creeping timorously out onto the now deserted wharf.

I recalled this edifying story thirty-four years later when I attended a symposium on extragalactic radio astronomy in the exotic town of Albuquerque, New Mexico. Unlike years past, the bosses of the symposium treated us, to put it mildly, with less than warmth. Of course, we were not responsible for the Afghanistan business and Sakharov's illegal exile, but we felt just as sullied as the passengers of the *Griboedov.* * The problem of the passenger and the ship is not always unambiguous. I spent many days with my American colleagues during the dirty Vietnam War, and neither I nor other Soviet astronomers ever dreamed of connecting those passengers with the imperialist ship of the transoceanic superpower.

*[Andrei Sakharov and his wife Elena Bonner were exiled to the city of Gorky on January 22, 1980.]

7

Amado Mio, or "The Idiot's Dream" Come True

HOW could I have known that the 1947 eclipse expedition to the Tropic of Capricorn, to a faraway Brazil as beautiful as anything in a fairytale, would be the brightest and perhaps the happiest months of my complicated life? In that third postwar spring I was brimming with health and youth and an unshakable faith in an endless and happy future; I took it for granted that the expedition was just the beginning of soul-stirring days ahead. After my poverty-stricken boyhood and the suffering of the war years, the world had at last opened up to me, just the way I thought it would in my childhood in the little town of Glukhov as I nearly died waiting for the next issue of that marvelous magazine to which I subscribed, *The World Pathfinder.* Devouring it and other magazines like *Around the World* and *The World Tourist,* the volumes of Jack London's complete works in their striped brown paper covers, and Conan Doyle's adventure stories took me a thousand miles away from my native Chernigov region. The salt spray of the sea, the wind whistling in a ship's riggings, courageous people tempered by the tropical sun—that was the stuff of my dreams.

Even today I have a passion for geography and can't walk by a map with indifference. In my wretched and poverty-stricken youth, however, the muse of travel to distant lands faded into my subconscious. Living in distant Vladivostok, I shivered every time I looked at the map of my homeland, wondering how the devil I had ended up so far away. During the war the maps of the front lines evoked different emotions—at first fear and then hope.

After the war I found salvation from wretched reality in a greedy absorption in science. I was fortunate that the start of my scientific career coincided with the onset of the second revolution in astronomy, and I realized it with every fiber of my being. It was as if my childhood dreams of faraway lands had come true. Often I felt like an adventurer paving the way into an unknown, mysteriously beautiful land. That was real happiness. I am profoundly convinced that without those daydreams over the *The World Pathfinder* and the works of Jack London and Robert Louis Stevenson, I could never have accomplished what I did. As a scientist I was a strange mixture of artist and conquistador, a phenomenon possible only in eras when established conceptions are breaking down and new ones arising. That style of work is impossible today; now Voltaire's dictum that "God is always for the big battalions" is rigorously observed.

In 1947 "the idiot's dream" came true, and realization that I was actually going to South America flooded me with a warm wave of joy.* The muse of travel to faraway lands, so long dormant, awoke and captured me body and soul.

In Angra dos Reis, I was kept busy loading equipment and supplies from the boat onto the train inland. My fellow laborers in that line of work were technicians on the expedition, two

---

*["The idiot's dream" is another reference to Ilf and Petrov's *Golden Calf* and Ostap Bender's dream of escape to Rio de Janeiro.]

cheerful men with a zest for life. A local Armenian by the strange name of Dukat, who dreamed of repatriation to his native land and therefore helped us selflessly, made himself invaluable in contacts with the authorities. Without him the entire business would have been a mess—there was little more than a week left until the eclipse—and we faced numerous obstacles in transporting our equipment by rail to the observational site at Araxa.

Our guardian angel Dukat did his best to keep us from making the blunders inevitable in a foreign country. Once he made the following recommendation: "Remember, comrades, that the language of this country is Portuguese, which is completely foreign and unknown to you. Words that are completely decent in Russian can sound completely indecent in Portuguese. For instance, under no conditions, never under any circumstances, utter the words 'kuda' [whither] and 'pirog' [pie]." We were in too much of a hurry to ask him for a translation of those innocent Russian words, but I kept his recommendation firmly in mind—and it served me well in a bit of mischief later on.

The leaders of our expedition had decided that the participants would be living, if not in tropical rainforest, at least in savannah or pampas, but we ended up not using the tents and odds and ends we had brought along for an extended stay under difficult tropical conditions. Araxa was the site of a mineral spring famous all over Latin America where a super-modern luxury hotel, one of the best on that exotic continent, had been built shortly before our arrival. As we soon found out, ex-king Carol of Romania was in residence there, and a modest room cost twenty dollars a day, a fantastically high price in 1947. That was beyond our budget, but our hospitable hosts made the grand gesture of declaring us guests of Minas Gerais state. We stayed free and ate our sumptuous meals in the hotel.

An observation site had been set aside for us half a kilometer away, not far from the henhouse. We were on the edge of the impenetrable rainforest, from which specimens of local fauna trespassed from time to time onto the site. Hummingbirds, blindingly vivid little bundles of rainbow, flew past us. Misha Vashakidze told us ingenuously about the armadillo he encountered as he wandered off to a secluded spot to take care of private needs. We found out later that armadillos had a direct, if somewhat mysterious, connection to our expedition. The ship's doctor Baluev (a splendid card player and a worthless medic) had a secret mission: to collect parasites infesting armadillos, which, it seems, were absolutely necessary to the manufacture of preparation "K.R.," a supposed cancer vaccine which at the time was a cherished secret of Soviet science. Its promoters, microbiologist Nina Klyueva and histologist Grigory Roskin, were later accused of giving away the formula for the vaunted, but purely fraudulent vaccine to Anglo-American spies masquerading as scientists. They were condemned by a court of honor for this "unpatriotic" deed and stripped of all their scientific degrees, titles, and posts. That rigged trial was perhaps the first drop of rain from the approaching stormcloud of postwar Lysenkoist obscurantism.

I had another memorable contact with the local fauna. One day I was blackening a magnesium screen in a neglected shed on the edge of our site, while a local carpenter planed something at a nearby workbench. Suddenly I saw a blindingly beautiful snake, a meter and a half long, fiery red with black velvety spots, crawling across the dirt floor. "Jose!" I called my Brazilian namesake. He turned around and, like lightning, leaped aside, yelling something I couldn't understand. It was only when he grabbed a board and dexterously pinned the snake's head, keeping a respectful distance from the thrashing reptile, that I realized the gravity of the situation. I seized a stone from the floor and with a few blows smashed the snake's head. Jose's sweaty face was distorted with fear and repulsion. Carefree ignoramus that I was, I scooped up the snake on a shovel and set out for the neighboring hut, where our girls Zoya and Alina were hard at work. Smirking idiotically I thrust the shovel through the window and called Alina, who was sitting with her back to me. Her leap was even flashier than Jose's. When the uproar subsided, I found out that my namesake and I had killed a coral snake, one of the most deadly in South America.

After each working day, we returned to the hotel tired and plastered with red Brazilian soil, took showers, changed our clothes and, wearing the white wool suits tailored for us by the Academy, went to the dining room. The hotel management had placed our team at tables in the exact center of the room. The solar eclipse had been widely advertised as an attraction, and its highlight was the presence of the first Soviets ever seen in those parts. It was as if the war bathed us in its crimson light: unwittingly, we were in some sense, if not heroes, at least uncommon people. The hotel didn't do badly out of us; it was nearly empty when we came, and by the eve of the eclipse it was jammed. For their cruzeiros the rich guests wanted to see the novel visitors from overseas, so to speak, "with no deception," and at dinner they were given a good view.

Sitting under a crossfire of looks from idlers greedily gawking at you is far from pleasant. It was especially hard for me and the other young members of the team who had no experience of social events and didn't know the finer points of table manners. What fine points could I have picked up during the war, which chiefly steeled my character to the stoicism of carrying a make-weight bread ration home intact? I was always doing the wrong thing. My problems began with the menu, which was in French. My first strategy for overcoming this difficulty was sitting next to Aleksandr Mikhailov, the head of our expedition—not a simple thing to manage—and mechanically repeating his order.* I

---

*[Mikhailov (1888–1964) was director of the Pulkovo Observatory from 1947 until his death. A positional astronomer of note, he worked on the determination of the figure of the Earth and surface of the Moon, along with the theory of eclipses. Mikhailov's predictions of the length of totality were used at the total eclipse of the Sun which crossed the Crimea in 1961. Unfortunately, the eclipse ended several seconds before his predicted time, ruining the exposures of some of the instruments. The eclipse was cloudy, so no great harm was done.]

soon became convinced that this wasn't a good idea. Mikhailov was on a strict diet, and mimicking him deprived me of a chance to try the delicious broiled meats typical of Brazilian cuisine. I embarked upon dangerous individual initiative, appealing in critical moments to the director for consultation. I remember once picking unsuccessfully with my fork at an exotic fish.

"What are you doing?" sputtered Mikhailov under his breath.

"I'm trying my luck with a fork; you can't eat fish with a knife, after all," I babbled.

"That's exactly what you do, with the special fish knife lying to your left!" Live and learn.

Another time Mikhailov replied quietly but distinctly to one of my foolish questions: "More independence, Iosif Samuilovich. You should be guided by the basic principle that a man at table should be as far as possible from a dog. A dog eats like this"— Mikhailov bent low over his plate and, to the astonishment of those around us, started waving his hands back and forth—"and a man, like this—" he leaned back against the spine of his chair and held his knife and fork in almost fully extended hands. After that I never consulted Mikhailov again.*

We wolfed down our lunch under more natural conditions. Two uniformed waiters brought our food by car to the site. Dirty as imps, sitting on the expedition's packing cases, we savored Brazilian specialties and taught the nice boy waiters Russian words.

In those antipodes we had surprising encounters with foreign ways at every step. Once Zoya and I were waiting for the elevator beside a small group of glossy young "Brasilieros" of both sexes, who bore the hallmarks of being children of the rich. The

---

*A few weeks later, on our way to Argentina, I got revenge. In the saloon during idle talk after dinner I decided to demonstrate my erudition by citing from memory Anatole France's delightful aphorism: "In some respects our civilization is far behind the Paleolithic: primitive peoples ate their old men—we elect them to the Academy." Mikhailov, who was present at the time, didn't turn a hair—prerevolutionary upbringing tells—but after that his attitude toward me was always cool and guarded.

young men, all with identical black mustaches, were chatting animatedly with their girls and simultaneously scratching themselves with hands thrust deep into their trouser pockets. Zoya didn't know where to look, but the Brazilian girls didn't react at all. I think I've figured out their behavior. Of course, it wasn't that they needed to scratch themselves; they were immaculate. The gesture, which we found indecent, was a way of demonstrating what might be called their uninhibited natures.

In general, the concepts of what is acceptable and what is not are completely different from those we are used to. For instance, there are noble illnesses and indecent ones. In Europe tuberculosis is a sad and romantic disease which we associate with Chekhov and Chopin. Brazilians consider the disease shameful, because it is connected with the slum poverty of the *favela*. On the other hand, venereal diseases are accepted in Brazil and even have a certain aura of chic, especially when the sufferer is treated by famous doctors. Medical treatment is a mark of prestige, a graphic indication of a certain level of wealth.

Work at the site continued day and night; to use a chess term, the time pressure was awful. My roommate, Aleksandr Lebedinsky, worked frenziedly, exhausting himself in single combat with his overly complex spectrograph.* The local press printed a funny photograph of him wrestling with it over the caption: "This is Professor Sasha—the inventor of a machine with nine objective lenses." And, like every other eclipse, ours was adorned with the piers resembling huge girders which were part of Mikhailov's apparatus for observing the Einstein effect, the deflection of light from a star as it passes near the limb of the solar disk. By May 20 everything was shipshape, and a squad of police had arrived to maintain order at the sparkling clean site. Alas, although the weather was ideally clear for the entire month beforehand and many weeks afterward, a couple of hours

---

*[At eclipses, spectrographs were used to break up and analyze the light of the upper atmosphere of the Sun after the Moon blocked out the bright surface.]

before the eclipse storm clouds appeared out of nowhere.*

Our hearts clouded over as well, but we bore up. I still have a snapshot of Ginzburg and me playing a local game, something like tic-tac-toe, by drawing lines on the dusty ground. Somebody snapped it just at the moment of totality—eclipses are never as dark as most people picture them. By evening I had recovered from fate's blow, rationalizing that man doesn't live by eclipse alone and that, as Grigory Shain liked to put it, "man is not made for the Sabbath, but the Sabbath for man." Nevertheless, the tremendous labor of breaking down apparatus which had never operated and finding pieces which had got lost was no fun. In the midst of the work, we heard that the management of the hotel was planning a ball for its guests and the foreign expeditions—American, Finnish, Swedish, Czech. The Brazilians themselves hadn't mounted one; there was not yet any astronomy to speak of in that huge and rich land.

In partial compensation for the dirty trick played by the weather, the dance was planned on a splendid scale. With South American verve, the hotel guests were arranging an amateur concert, and the foreign astronomers were invited to take part. That gave me an uncommonly invidious idea.

Our expedition included a certain "exempt comrade," who was there to assure—how can I put it?—the ideological restraint of our behavior. He was a tall, skinny man called Mikhail Ivanovich with a far from scintillating intelligence, but he went about his business unobtrusively and could have been a lot worse. His one small weakness was a feeble tenor voice, and he loved to sing.

"It's a shame, Mikhail Ivanovich," I said to him ingratiatingly, "that our people aren't taking part in the amateur concert. They'll end up thinking that Soviet scientists are all drybones

---

*The weather at the eclipse in 1946 at Rybinsk, for which I served as a laboratory assistant, was also overcast. Clouds became a tradition of all the expeditions in which I ever took part.

and robots. Think what a pretext that could be for anti-Soviet propaganda."

"But we don't have anybody with talent. Who could appear?" Mikhail Ivanovich took the bait.

"How about you, for instance? You have a fine tenor!"

He was obviously tempted. "What could I sing for them?" he asked timidly.

"Something from the classical repertory. All those sambas and rhumbas are not our style. Why don't you sing Lensky's aria?" (I proposed this highlight from Chaikovsky's *Eugene Onegin* with Dukat's advice about the dangers of certain Russian words firmly in mind.)

The evening of the dance arrived. There was an incredible uproar over the elections for "Miss Eclipse." The voting was secret, but a clumsy, flat-faced young lady, the daughter of a rich local planter, ended up being elected. What can I say? They knew their own business, but they had so many beauties to choose from.

The concert began. I had warned close friends beforehand that it would be a circus. The preposterous lanky figure of our art lover appeared onstage in the severe black suit he had struggled into for the event. In a feeble goatish voice he began bleating Lensky's aria, which began with one of Dukat's forbidden words: "Whither, whither have you retreated? [*Kuda, kuda* vy udalilis'?]." The result exceeded my wildest expectations. The *senhoritas* instantly disappeared, and the *senhors* began neighing like stallions, yelling and applauding stormily. Mikhail Ivanovich took the din for stormy approval and raised his small voice. The uproar effectively put an instant end to the concert.* For nearly forty years now I have been intending to look into a Russian–Portuguese dictionary complete enough to tell me

---

*That this mischief cost me dearly cannot be ruled out. For the next eighteen years I was not permitted to travel abroad. There was a hitch of some sort in my dossier, and I can't think of anything else that could have been held against me.

what the words *kuda* and *pirog* mean in the language of Camoens.

The next days were given up to tourism. We visited an exotic little town with the fairytale-pretty name of Belo Horizonte, the capital of our host state of Minas Gerais. I recall the huge pyramids of ripe pineapples heaped up on the ground in the market—just like beets in my native Chernigov region—and the flowers and their heady odor.

We also organized a trip by road hundreds of kilometers away to see the deepest gold mining shafts in the world. Along the way I witnessed a memorable little scene. We were the object of fixed attention not only from our own political officer but from outsiders as well. Types who spoke good Russian appeared from nowhere and attached themselves to us with insistent offers of dubious services. A certain Ukrainian, representing himself as a professional singer and making no attempt to hide his connection with the local police, was the most blatant of them. His job seemed to be to protect Brazilian workers from the pernicious influence of Red propaganda. In the bus, by an irony of fate, this type perched next to our Mikhail Ivanovich. Sensing the piquancy of the situation, I sat right behind them and pulled Slava Gnevyshev down beside me. The two political types began chatting in Russian about their joint profession (I have in mind, of course, the vocal one).

"Do you have a lot of new songs now after the war?" asked the Brazilo-Ukrainian.

"Oh, yes," said our type with great satisfaction.

"And what song is the most popular?"

"I think it would be 'Wide Is My Native Land.' "

"I don't know it. Please teach it to me."

And the two representatives of one of the world's oldest professions passed the trip amiably singing. Their type had quite a pleasant baritone. The entire bus fell silent and, touched, listened as the two sang with great passion, totally oblivious to their ludicrous situation.

We weren't permitted to go into the mines. The English company that owned them also feared the Reds.

We finally got to Rio, flying there from Belo Horizonte in a
Douglas—my first airplane flight—and enjoyed all the delights
of tourism in that *cidade maravilhosa* (wonderful city). We
spent one entire day on Copacabana Beach, guided by a nice
chap named Kalugin, the local TASS correspondent. My God,
what a beach! It's not so much sand as golddust. Even in the
calmest weather a wall of breakers about 2 meters high looms 10
meters offshore; it's 4,000 kilometers across the Atlantic to the
African coast, and the ocean seems to be breathing in and out.
Once again we ran into surprising local customs. It turned out to
be against the law to approach the sea, take off your clothing
(except, of course, bathing trunks), and plunge into the ocean.
By local notions the *process* of undressing was improper. You
had to arrive at the beach already fully prepared to swim, but we
didn't see communal dressing rooms anywhere on the entire
gigantic beach. Brasilieros undressed at the homes of friends
living many blocks away, and on Sundays crowds of people of all
sexes and ages walked along the hot city asphalt wearing only
their trunks and bathing suits—and that was considered completely proper.

I found the young people, some swimming and others playing,
strikingly handsome in their spectrum of skin color from agate
black to rosy white. None of us ever noticed any sign of racial
discrimination in Brazil. The local boys played soccer right on
the beach. That's where they recruited Pele, Jardinho, and the
other Brazilian wizards who eleven years later rocked the sports
world at the championship in Sweden.

Lying on that golden beach, we discussed in detail the question of the businesses Ilf and Petrov's "Bigtime Operator,"
Ostap Bender, might have set up if his childhood dream had
come true and he had gotten to Rio. Some interesting notions
were advanced. He would undoubtedly have organized a chain of
dressing rooms at Copacabana, and he might well have opened

hair-straightening salons for the local population. We decided to take advantage of the rare opportunity to build a monument to Ostap Bender on Copacabana Beach in the presence of representatives of the Soviet regime (the first secretary of our embassy), press (the aforementioned TASS correspondent), and society (we passengers of the *Griboedov*), as well as the local beachgoers. We built a pyramid out of sand, invited some of the blackest Brasilieros to join us, made speeches appropriate to the occasion, and had ourselves photographed. I still have that photo and enjoy looking at it from time to time.

I loved wandering around the city, admiring the colorful crowds of Cariocas. At night near the hotel the incendiary music of the most recent pre-Lenten carnival was played—tunes like "Chica-Chica," "Amado Mio," "O, Brasil"—and people danced the samba right on the street. As I write these lines the rhythmic beat and ravishing patter of "Chica-Chica" still ring in my ears. I turned my dollars into cruzeiros and spent them on visits to cafés and the purchase of souvenirs. The best store in Rio for exotic curiosities belonged to an old Jew from Odessa, who was touched to the quick to have his first customer from the old country. I was dying to buy the shrunken head of an Indian from some cannibal tribe at the headwaters of the Amazon. The head-shrinking craftsmen remove the bones from a freshly severed head and then tan it for long months over a slow fire. I was particularly impressed by the eyelashes, which don't shrink in the smoking and seem huge on the tiny head (12 centimeters). The ex-Odessite, gripped by pangs of nostalgia, offered me the head at half price, $200. Alas, I didn't have that much money, and all my attempts to find a partner among my colleagues met with indignant rejection. It's a shame—today you can't buy a shrunken head at any price.

Our embassy arranged the customary reception for the Soviet expedition. At the height of that exercise in diplomacy, a middle-aged Brazilian introduced himself to me as the president of the Rio chess club. "This evening," he went on, "we are having the traditional Thursday blitz-tournament of the capital's masters." He had been given the honor of inviting chessplayers from our expedition to participate. The news that there were chessplayers in the expedition could have come from only one source: during our days in Araxa Misha Vashakidze and I used to slip off to town and jauntily whip dapper but unskilled patrons of the local café.

At the reception I was just tight enough to agree on the spot to the unknown *senhor's* flattering invitation. If Ostap Bender could pose as a grandmaster and offer to play all comers at the Four-Knights chess club in the town of Vasyuki (for money in advance, of course), why shouldn't I, in the city of Ostap's golden dream, repeat his immortal exploit? Unconsciously, of course, I was foolishly assuming that their capital masters played on the level of the Araxa amateurs. I suborned Lebedinsky and Misha Vashakidze (who, citing intoxication, balked fiercely), and the secretary of the embassy also joined our party. Under Mikhailov's disapproving stare, we left immediately for the Rio equivalent of Vasyuki's Four Knights.

On the way my enthusiasm cooled when I found out that our host, the president of the club, had just finished serving as referee of the first USSR–USA radio match in New York. "Now we've done it," I thought dejectedly, but the comic aspects of the situation kept me from being too downcast.

In the smoke-filled room of the chess club the local masters, all bald and sporting black mustaches, were lined up in ranks. I saw that their knees literally trembled—and with reason: the young Botvinnik was world champion, and the fame of Soviet chessplayers was at its peak. Before we cast lots, the president proposed that one of us should run through an unofficial game with him. I sat Misha down at the table. "Come on, I'm too drunk," babbled the future author of the discovery of polarized emission from the Crab Nebula (see Chapter 8).

"Play and don't fool around. We'll prompt you."

In a blitz, of course, you play against the clock, ten minutes for the first forty moves. The match began. The president was so nervous that his hands were shaking. We shamelessly prompted Misha's moves in Russian. The Brazilian master lost his bishop on the sixth move, but by the tenth he realized that he was playing a duffer, pulled himself together, and jauntily took the game from Misha. That was the beginning of the end: our quartet came in solidly last in the ensuing tournament. All three of my games ended in a draw.*

The next morning we traveled by train to Angra dos Reis, where the *Griboedov* was waiting for us. We had more days of tourism as our ship headed south to pick up cargo in Argentina. In La Plata Bay I was struck by the sight of masts of a sunken ship sticking out of the water, the remains of the famous German pocket battleship *Admiral Graf Spee,* which was sunk by its crew in front of a pursuing formation of English cruisers. We spent an evening in Montevideo, went to our embassy, and wandered around the enchantingly beautiful city. After Rio I found it somehow old-fashioned and European. Then we sailed the mighty, muddy, chocolate-colored Parana 400 kilometers upstream as far as Rosario. The sight of the Swift packing plant off in the distance reminded me of that delight of the war years, cans of stewed meat which opened with little keys.

The local police came on board the *Griboedov,* herded us into the ship's lounge, and handed us forms to fill out—in Spanish. There were only about ten questions, child's play in comparison to our Soviet forms. The questions were standard and, notwithstanding my ignorance of the language, I guessed at their meaning and answered as best I could. I hit an obstacle at the sixth line, however, and decided to see how my senior comrades were answering it. I came up to Yasha Albert just as he was carefully writing out "Greek Orthodox," and I filled in my own answer,

---

*A few months later I chanced to meet TASS correspondent Kalugin in Moscow. He informed me that the day after our chess debut, the local press ran huge headlines trumpeting: "Tremendous Victory of Our Chess Players Over Soviet Masters."

"Atheist." Afterward I had a lot of fun teasing Yasha about that "Greek Orthodox." For about ten years now Professor Yakov Albert has been a refusenik waiting for an exit visa to Israel.

While the *Griboedov* loaded up with millet for Switzerland to transit across Holland, we took the *El Rapido* express on a four-day trip to Buenos Aires. It was winter in Argentina (something like late September rains in the Moscow region). I spent three days in Baires, as the Argentinians call their capital. We made a trip to the La Plata Observatory, and Mikhailov, navigating by city map, got us lost on the way back because he forgot that in the Southern hemisphere the noon sun is to the north. Overall Argentina, obviously "northern" in spirit (if not, of course, in geography), makes a striking contrast to "southern" Brazil.

In Rosario again, we made ourselves at home on the familiar, cozy *Griboedov,* which set out on the return trip that same day. We passed Rio in the inky, tropical night. It was about two o'clock in the morning, and the watch and I were the only people on deck. As the painfully familiar lights of the unforgettable city slowly receded, a thought, simple to the point of horror, pierced my being like a sharp pain: *I would never see it again!* Of course, even at home I've often been in places to which I've never returned—for instance, Vladivostok, where I spent my youth. But this departure was as irreversible as death, and I felt lonely and hollow at heart.

The last light onshore, a lighthouse, faded from view, and there was only the empty Atlantic ahead.

Before the Thaw

PROPERLY speaking, it all started well before January 13, 1953—the day major newspapers published the editorial denouncing "doctor-poisoners" which stunned and horrified the world.* For instance, in late 1951 some of my Jewish colleagues and I were dismissed from our own Shternberg Institute (see Chapter 10). Of course, my fate is an infinitesmal drop in the ocean of the calamities of the Judaic people, but it was a very typical story—many, many thousands of Soviets of Jewish nationality experienced the incomparable anguish of the obtuse, cruel, and profoundly insulting procedure of *exclusion* from a society of which they had considered themselves from birth to be citizens with full rights. It's very strange: suddenly, with infinite clarity, you sense that everything that was yours by blood and birth—the air, the grass, the people in the electric train—has become alien and hostile.

*[The article announced the arrest of nine doctors, six of them Jews, on the staff of the Kremlin hospital-clinic and accused them of the murder or attempted murder of some of the Soviet elite among their patients.]

Even before that, in 1949, there was the repulsive campaign against "rootless cosmopolitans" and the howls in the press to "unmask pseudonyms" and much more that it's sickening even to recall. A year earlier, Mikhoels' murder and the ensuing bloody devastation of Jewish culture in the Soviet state had been sanctioned at the highest level.* When did it all begin? There were clear signs of impending disaster during the war. My late friend, Major of the Guards Lipsky, one of the first to force the crossing of the Dnepr, never received the gold star of Hero of the Soviet Union to which that exploit entitled him. The divisional commander told him straight out, "The thing is, you're a Jew, I'm a Jew—it wouldn't look right! As a communist, you have to understand things correctly!"

The bacillus of anti-Semitism in its latent form was at work even in the prewar years. The Soviet ambassador Yakov Suritz was transferred from Berlin to Paris in 1939 because Hitler didn't approve of his origins. Only people with a very keen nose could have sniffed it out then, but soon there was no need for a sensitive organ: more and more often you had to hold your nose.

We all know that nothing happens spontaneously in our country. Stalin's iron hand was felt everywhere. It was as if the surplus of Jewish intellectuals in the prerevolutionary Russian Social-Democrat party and their skill in polemic blathering had made an irritating negative lifelong impression on the Best Friend of All Peoples, Great and Small. Of course, there were more profound reasons. It seems as if the Jews, in their historically developed singularity, could never blend into the socialist society under formation in old Russia, no matter how hard they tried.†

---

*[The Yiddish-language actor and theater director Solomon Mikhoels was murdered in January 1948.]

†At about that time at one of Stalin's closed saturnalias, he is supposed to have said, "It's not true what they say in the famous song: '. . . everybody's welcome at our table.' Some people aren't welcome—you know who I mean."

On that cold morning of January 13, 1953, the now famous academician Vitaly Ginzburg and I were at the Astronomical Council on Bolshaya Gruzinskaya Street working out the program of the forthcoming All-Union Conference on Radio Astronomy. Both of us had seen and been stunned by the *Pravda* editorial about "doctor-poisoners," but we were too depressed to exchange even a word of comment. The work wasn't getting anywhere; we sat passing our pencils vacantly over our separate pieces of paper in an unbearable leaden silence. I remember that the tiny dank room accentuated the gloomy desolation of the atmosphere.

"There's no point in sitting it out here," said Ginzburg. "We'd do better to go to the zoo."

The idea of going to the Moscow zoo nearby was fantastic. In midwinter, after school holidays and before the universities let out, it was virtually deserted. The weather was bitterly cold. For a long time we wandered the snow-covered, deserted grounds in total silence, until at last, chilled to the bone, we decided to warm up in the hot and humid elephant barn. Inside the huge enclosure stood the elephant family—papa, mama, and their lop-eared offspring—ignoring us as they munched their hay in measured rhythm.

After we had watched the idyllic scene for a while, Ginzburg broke our extended silence. As if to himself, he said, "It's nice for the elephant—he has his wife with him." Of course, he was thinking of his Nina. The future academician had every reason to envy the elephant and his mate: Ginzburg's wife couldn't live under one roof with him. She was in administrative exile in a village near Gorky on trivial grounds amounting to no more than idle student talk.* Nina worked in the city which has since become notorious as the site of the Sakharovs' exile. The young

*[Nina Ermakova was arrested in 1944 for supposedly plotting to kill Stalin; the accusation did not hold up, but she was sentenced to a labor camp and then exile anyway. See Ginzburg, "Notes of an Amateur Astrophysicist," *Annual Reviews of Astronomy and Astrophysics* 28 (1990):18.]

and brilliant doctor of sciences Vitaly Ginzburg met Nina at a seminar he gave in Gorky—heaven only knows why she showed up there. He fell deeply in love with her. Ginzburg was married to a fellow student and had a small daughter to whom he was greatly attached, and he was a party member besides. He displayed a courage rare in our times and our country by getting an honorable and open divorce and marrying a woman in exile with no civil rights. He went through hell, because his "legal" wife didn't want to divorce him. It's dreadful just thinking about the smears he suffered from the party and local committees.

He overcame those insuperable obstacles and was, of course, happy. I recall that on our expedition to Brazil in 1947 he moped the entire way, thinking only of his Nina during their first extended separation. I tried in vain to divert him from a mood which is, alas, beyond my comprehension by pointing out the unprecedented beauty of the tropics. He refused to be consoled.

Afterward, back in Moscow, one November day, he got word that the old, grossly overloaded ferry on which Nina and other hard-working commuters crossed the Volga every day to Gorky had overturned in the middle of the great river. Sludge ice was going down the river, hundreds of people perished, and only a mere handful survived.* For three dreadful days Ginzburg thought she was dead; I don't know how he got through them. Nina, a fine athlete, swam the icy Volga at its widest spot, and once she got ashore strangers gave her refuge and warmed her. It's impossible to imagine Ginzburg's emotion when he saw her apparently resurrected. On that terrible day in 1953, with hard times ahead, it was natural for him to want to be with her. From the wintry zoo, without ever talking, we went our separate ways home.

Grim days crawled by. The situation got worse every week. I recall taking the electric train at night to Losinka, where my

---

*[The accident occurred on October 29, 1949. Ginzburg says that his wife was one of a dozen survivors out of some 250 passengers.]

poor mama lived crammed into one wretched room. Teen-agers sitting opposite me started calling me loathsome names of which "yid" was the least odious. The numerous passengers looked on, enjoying the diversion. Some of them even joined in the yelping. The boys were just ordinary workers, and I found it strange to see them transformed so unexpectedly into a pack of malicious wolfcubs. I remember the repulsive, shameful fear ripening and spreading somewhere inside me—the ancient Jewish fear in the face of a pogrom. That occasion was far from unique. A well-organized "wave of popular wrath" directed from above grew and took on force exponentially.

During those weeks in the winter and spring of 1953, emotions and relationships between apparently close people underwent severe tests. Noticing my depressed state, one woman friend remarked in irritation, "But in our country they can't have arrested people who aren't guilty of anything. There's no smoke without fire. Your doctors can't be such meek lambs." Not all my friends talked that way—at least, not to me—but many of them had the same thoughts.

Dark rumors circulated that barracks were under emergency construction in camps in the Far East to hold the three million Jews of the Soviet Union for protection from the indigenous population's "righteous wrath." A journalist by the name of Olga Chechetkina published a huge article in *Pravda* under the title, "Lidia Timashuk's Mailbox," filled with traditionally anti-Semitic hysterical howls and appeals from "simple Soviet people."* In every issue the nation greedily read accounts of the vile embezzlements and other loathsome crimes committed by people "who sat out the war in Tashkent." The accounts were accompanied by appropriate commentary. The stink of organized pogrom in the air made it difficult to breathe.

At that point a miracle occurred. They say that Stalin

---

*[Lidia Timashuk was an elderly electrocardiographer at the Kremlin clinic who was given the Order of Lenin on January 20 for denouncing the doctors.]

breathed his last on the Jewish holiday of Purim.* I've never gotten around to verifying the date, but I'd like to believe it. My memories of the days of Stalin's funeral rites, which were filled with painful anxiety and collective hysteria, are vague and out of focus. Oppressed by the question of what would happen next, I felt no relief.

Life soon settled down. Order was restored in the country. Articles about the Great Deceased often appeared in the newspapers, but his shade faded inexorably into the past and, after a lapse of some months, I was once again absorbed by deliberations on the still mysterious sources of cosmic radio emission. I was young and ready in the most literal sense to storm the heavens.

For over two years I had been agonizing over the nature of the now famous Crab Nebula, one of the brightest sources of radio emission. I was trying to explain that emission as an "extension" of its optical radiation. At the time nobody doubted that the latter could be traced to the long known thermal radiation of the hot gases forming the nebula. All gaseous nebulae identified by astronomers had exactly that kind of emission. Alas, my attempts were a fiasco: the Crab's radio emission was too intense to be an extension of its optical radiation.

On the eve of that forbidding new year, I decided to forget about the Crab's optical radiation for a while and work at understanding the nature of the radio emission. The crux of the matter was in the cosmic rays with which the Crab is literally "stuffed" and, more precisely, in the electrons of super-high energies which, moving through the nebula's magnetic fields, should emit electromagnetic waves. I managed to get that article published before the gloomy period of the doctors' plot. In those wintry months I was in no mood for science.

But the storm clouds dispersed. On the afternoon of April 5, 1953, I was standing on Pushkin Square, waiting for tramway no.

*[Stalin died on March 5, 1953.]

17 to take me back to the Ostankino barracks I called home. The tram didn't come for a long time and, with nothing better to do, I wandered over to the newsstand. There I spotted a short notice that the doctor-poisoners had been rehabilitated and all accusations dropped. I will never forget the intense hot wave of joy that nearly knocked me off my feet. My tramcar, crammed to capacity, arrived just then and I managed to jam myself onto it. I hung from a handrail in the incredible crush, my every cell singing with happiness. And suddenly a thought with no apparent connection to the rehabilitation of the doctors flashed through me like lightning: If the Crab's radio emission can't be explained as an extension of its thermal optical radiation, why can't I explain the optical radiation of the nebula as an extension of its radio emission? By then I was quite sure that the latter was nonthermal in nature and, if that was so, the optical radiation could also be nonthermal and originate in "relativistic" electrons, but at energies some hundreds of times greater than those producing the radio emission.

The tram took forty-five minutes to get to Ostankino. I was in a state close to somnambulism. In that short time I mentally carried out the entire theoretical calculation for the radiation. At home I immediately wrote an article for the *Transactions* of the Academy of Sciences without a single correction, and Grigory Shain submitted it a week later.*

I think that was my best work. It caused an explosion of

*[If the Crab's radiation were from a normal nebula, the radio-emitting particles would produce little optical emission, but "synchrotron emission" by high energy electrons spiraling in magnetic fields can be just as strong in optical as in radio frequencies. In that case, as Shklovsky predicted in his 1952 article, the light would be polarized. In 1953 V. A. Dombrovsky, working at Byurakan, discovered strong polarization in the Crab's emission. The following year Mikhail Vashakidze measured the polarization at Abastumani, and in 1956 the Dutch astronomers J. H. Oort and Th. Walraven published a beautiful compendium of polarization maps and description of rapidly moving wisps in the nebula. Later a pulsar was discovered at its center, presumably the remnant of the supernova explosion recorded by the Chinese in A.D. 1054.]

further research in many countries, and the waves from that explosion are still expanding to the present time.

A week or two later I met the same woman friend, whom I hadn't seen for three months, and she said with a smile, "You see, here you were all in a sweat for nothing! They've let your doctors go—they're innocent. It's in the newspapers." What could I say?

The Moscow working class made haste to respond to the *Pravda* item. In the suburban electric train I heard with my own ears a song dedicated to that notable event; it was sung to a tune popular in those years: "It's hard, my friend Pestrukha, to live in the world alone . . ." I can still remember almost all the words:

> I read the daily paper—to grasp it still I fail:
> What can the story mean? And who is off to jail?
> My dearest Comrade Vovsi, for you I'm very glad.
> It's been explained away, and you did nothing bad.
> In frosty cell you languished without any reason—
> Against our Soviet state you clearly meant no treason.
>
> Oh, dearest Comrade Kogan, doctor of renown!
> Though you've no cause to cry, the whole thing got you down.
> A candidate of science, you reached a nervous pitch,
> All thanks to Timashuk, a stinker and a bitch. . . .*

Alas, the last line has vanished from my mind. I only remember that the song ended on an upbeat. With a bit of imagination, its mocking and even mischievous tone can be seen as the contemporary equivalent of the Purim-spiel, the traditional merry miracle play with which the holiday is celebrated. At any rate, it reflects the Russian national trait of being quick to forgive and forget.

---

*[Kogan died under torture in prison. Lidia Timashuk's Order of Lenin was revoked on April 4.]

The song was a precursor of the thaw. It foreshadowed the era of bards and minstrels; the uproar of the 1960s was imminent.* Alas, everything comes to an end, and that era, too, is long past.†

*[One mark of the comparative freedom of speech of the Khrushchev epoch was the appearance of a remarkable generation of poets—Bulat Okudzhava (b. 1924), Vladimir Vysotsky (1938–1980), and Aleksandr Galich (1919–1977)—who sang their tough, mordant verses to their own guitar accompaniment. See Gerald Stanton Smith, *Songs to Seven Strings: Russian Guitar Poetry and Soviet "Mass Song"* (Indiana University Press, 1984).]

†[Shklovsky is reflecting on the Brezhnev years of "stagnation," which a Soviet writer recently described as being less harsh than the Stalin epoch, but desperately boring and empty.]

Yura Gastev and Cheyne-Stokes Respiration

I FIRST met Yura Gastev late in 1941 in the exotic city of Ashkhabad, where we had ended up in evacuation with the Moscow University convoy. Yura stood out among the motley throng, primarily students, because he was so young, only fourteen, and still looked like a puny kid. Of course, Yura wasn't a student; he had gone into evacuation with his older brother Petya, who was in his second year in the department of mechanics and mathematics (mech-math). A few months later Petya was sent to military school, graduated as a junior lieutenant, and then went to the front and the quick death that awaited 97 percent of the young men his age who served in the army. The Gastev brothers were the sons of Aleksey Gastev, one of the first proletarian poets (of the "Smithy" group) and later a prominent political activist, the founder of the Soviet system called "Scientific Organization of Labor" or NOT. Like many famous figures in our history, Aleksey Gastev perished before the war.*

*[He was arrested in 1938 and died in prison in 1941.]

And so, since his mother was in exile as an "enemy of the people," in Ashkhabad Yura became to all intents and purposes an orphan. Just as during the war an orphaned boy would become a "son of the regiment," fed and raised by a troop detachment, Yura could be called a "son of the mech-math." The department of mechanics and mathematics took the place of Yura's family, and he absorbed the philosophy, ways of thinking, folklore, love of music, and many more of the traits that distinguished the alumni of that most noble of Moscow University departments.

After Ashkhabad I didn't see Yura again for two years. In September 1942, I moved on to Sverdlovsk, where my own Shternberg Astronomical Institute was in evacuation. I returned to Moscow and defended my candidate's dissertation in the spring of 1944, and in August of that year the mech-math sent me to Krasnovidovo outside Mozhaisk, the site of the university's suburban farm, which was supposed to be growing produce to supplement the scant rations of the university dining halls. Students were assigned to work at Krasnovidovo, and I was dispatched there as a "senior comrade" with the task of maintaining a suitable level of labor discipline.

I found the Krasnovidovo farm in a monstrously muddled and neglected state. All the grain fields and arable lands were so overgrown with impenetrable weeds that no worthwhile plant could possibly sprout. The war was still on, and the workers were mostly girl students and a small contingent of boys with draft exemptions. Among them I was overjoyed to see Yura; he still looked much the same, even though he was now a student himself.

Our first problem in Krasnovidovo was the gnawing hunger that makes it impossible to think of anything but food. The farm director, Comrade Bocharskaya, an old party worker, was a loud, fat woman who had occupied various administrative posts and a few years later became the deputy director of my astronomical institute. I don't have to say that she knew as much about agriculture as she did about astronomy. Thanks to her complete incompetence and helplessness, we were in effect reduced to grazing. Supplies of provisions manifested themselves only in the form of two bowls of oatmeal jelly, one in the morning and the other in midafternoon. I still shudder every time I think of that, if you'll accept the word, "food." No matter how young and hungry we were, we couldn't manage to swallow more than a spoonful of the cold, loathsome mass. Only one fellow, to all appearances a downright simpleton, could get through a bowl of that abomination. To this day I remember the feeling of revulsion he aroused in the rest of us.

Something had to be done, and under my astute leadership we found that the only solution was—young potatoes. Alas, there wasn't a trace of that root crop at the university's Krasnovidovo farm. The situation was not much better on neighboring state farms or in the fields of the collectives, where weeds were the only crop that flourished. The only thing left to do was to steal potatoes from the private sector.* Aside from the ethics of the question, potatoes were everybody's basic source of nourishment, and this occupation was not without risk. In the dead of night our small masculine band would set out on a dangerous hunting expedition. We posted one person as lookout, and the three or four other members of the group, Yura and I among them, collected our booty. I became especially proficient in digging potatoes two-handed, following the method of the girl Mamlakat, who is celebrated in our school readers.† As the comrade in charge, I tried to ensure that the loss to each individual proprietor was minimal and kept changing our field of action, often at the price of grumbles from the team.

Our poor, hungry group of girls was fed on the potatoes procured at that risk. This filled our hearts with pride and had one

*[The individual plots of collective and state farmers and the summer cottages of city folk.]
†[Mamlakat Nakhangova was a little Uzbek girl who became a national heroine of labor for picking cotton with both hands.]

amusing consequence. We slept on the floor on the upper story of our building, the girls occupying a large room and the young men a small adjacent anteroom. The girls had to pass through our room to get out. Every morning the fun began. There would be a timid knock on the door and a little girlish squeak, "Boys, can we come through?"

This natural request was met by Yura's traditional question, "And who are we?"

The ritual dreamed up by the resourceful Yura required the girls to answer in amicable chorus, "You are our true benefactors!"—meaning that we fed them.

Girlish pride, however, didn't permit our neighbors to utter that phrase. "Phoo, that's enough!" "Stop being such hooligans!" "Cut out the horseplay!"

"Certainly," we answered. But the girls were in no hurry to come out of their confinement, since we were lying on the floor with no covers—so to speak, in our natural aspect. Sometimes a desperate maiden, squinting her eyes, would try to break through, but such attempts brought only shame. At last, after ten minutes of wrangling, the girls would chirp the required phrase in unamicable chorus. Often we forced them to repeat it with greater conviction. Then we covered ourselves with our torn blankets, and the girls, eyes averted, aflame with hatred, came through in single file, stepping over our bodies.

The same scene took place every morning. To avoid misunderstanding, I should note that this was a totally innocent amusement, and there were the closest of comradely relations between the boys and girls.*

I still have fond memories of the three weeks I spent with those glorious kids in Krasnovidovo. Yura kept us all amused by reciting without mistake several pages of Ilf and Petrov's *The*

---

*Some twenty years later I was on vacation on the Caucasian coast of the Black Sea when a respectable-looking lady flabbergasted me by remarking, "I know who you are— you are our true benefactor!"

Twelve Chairs and *The Golden Calf* and identifying on demand the books' most obscure characters. He had a phenomenal ability to repeat each morning's radio news from the Soviet Information Bureau. This was far from easy in those days when our troops were wresting from the fascists dozens of populated points with hard-to-pronounce Belorussian names like Dedovichi, Belokopytovichi, and so on.

How can I forget the day when I was in Moscow on business and heard that the Allies had taken Paris? I returned at once to Mozhaisk and ran nearly the entire 18 kilometers to Krasnovidovo to share the joyous news. Even now I occasionally meet boys, now grown old, from that unforgettable summer, the last of the terrible war.

In Moscow Yura and I didn't see each other. Our interests were too different, and the eleven-year gap in age too substantial. I didn't hear about Yura's sad fate until a full year after our cheerful stay at Krasnovidovo. He got into trouble during the winter examinations in February 1945. At that time the mechanics-mathematics and history departments were both located in the "new" university building on Mokhovaya Street (no. 11). Picture the scene: Yura has just passed his exam in analytic geometry and is rolling down the stairs like a loose screw, textbook tucked under his arm. A small group of historians who have also just taken exams are standing at the bottom. One of them grabs Yura, seizes his book, tauntingly reads its title, and pronounces with corporative contempt, "Just imagine, Muskhelishvili!"

Never at a loss for a comeback, Yura makes exactly the same motion, grabbing the historian's textbook from under his arm and saying on the same note, "Just imagine, Dzhugashvili!" (The textbook must have been Stalin's notorious *Short Course*.)*

---

*[Nikolay Muskhelishvili was a prolific author of mathematics textbooks. The *Short Course* referred to a history of the Bolshevik party published in 1938 and ascribed to Stalin.]

Yura's quick wit cost him dearly: someone in that small group of historians denounced him, and Yura was arrested and sentenced to four years in the camps. They may have held other sins against him, but his arrest most certainly originated in the Mus-khelishvili–Dzhugashvili clash.

Yura finished his sentence in the dangerous year of 1949, but I didn't see him then. When I did meet him for the first time in sixteen years, he had an interesting story to share. In early March of 1953 Yura was in a tuberculosis sanitarium somewhere in Estonia when Stalin, the Best Friend of Mathematicians, he who was also the Great Leader and Teacher, came down with his last illness. The whole country, the whole world—and Yura was no exception—strained to catch the sparse bulletins on the state of his health. He asked his neighbor in the ward, a gloomy and taciturn Estonian doctor, the meaning of the words "Cheyne-Stokes respiration" used in the latest bulletin.*

The doctor rubbed his hands and said in a businesslike way, "Cheyne and Stokes are very serious comrades. Let's have a drink!"

Notwithstanding the late hour, as the youngest resident Yura was sent out for vodka. All the stores were closed, but when Yura shared the earthshaking news, a completely unknown Estonian sold him the vodka. Since then Yura has drunk the health of those remarkable Britons, Cheyne and Stokes, every March 5th, and he has not limited his respect to memorial toasts. For instance, around 1970, when he defended his dissertation for the candidate's degree (in philosophy, I think), in the concluding words where it is customary only to "make one's bows and curtsies," he expressed his profound gratitude to the eminent British scientists James Cheyne and Jonathan Stokes, "without whose indirect assistance this dissertation could hardly have

---

*In the early eighteenth century Scottish doctor John Cheyne and Irish doctor William Stokes identified a pattern of irregular breathing connected with heart failure and other than fatal conditions.

been defended." Of course, Yura invented those first names for the venerable Britons out of thin air. None of the erudite philosophers on his committee caught on, and the defense went well.

Yura's marks of esteem for the Britons reached their apogee in 1975, when he wrote a complex, specialized, purely mathematical monograph, *Holomorphism and Models.* In his foreword to this fundamental work, besides thanking a large number of colleagues who inspired the author in his labors, he didn't forget to express particular gratitude to Professors Cheyne and Stokes, without whose assistance the book could never have seen the light. (He was absolutely right: there are any number of scientific and cultural figures in our country who should second Yura's gratitude. For some reason, however, they have failed to do so.)

Yury Gastev's monograph included a detailed bibliography (232 references in all). I find item no. 55 enchanting: "J. Cheyne and J. Stokes, 'The Respiration of Death Marks the Rebirth of Spirit,' *Mind,* March 1953." I think that was overdoing it: the deferential thanks to the English doctors expressed in the foreword would have been adequate.

One way or another, soon after the monograph was published a great scandal broke that had serious consequences for Yura and several employees of the editorial offices which had been so disgracefully lax. The most remarkable thing about the entire affair is that the tributes to the British doctors went unnoticed. Yura got into hot water over all too genuine references to "unreliable" mathematician-friends and, above all, to the "notorious" Alik Volpin-Esenin.* Since then Yury Gastev has held no permanent job and subsists on paltry chance earnings.

*[In 1968 the dissident mathematician Aleksandr Esenin-Volpin was freed from forced confinement in a psychiatric ward after nearly a hundred eminent Soviet scholars signed a vigorous protest petition; soon afterward Esenin-Volpin emigrated to the United States, where he remained active in monitoring repression in the Soviet Union.]

Anniversary Arabesques

IT was mid-1981 when I heard that amateurs of anniversaries had discovered that the old Moscow University Observatory, one of the forebears of the Shternberg Astronomical Institute, my beloved GAISH, first saw the light of day in 1831. Plans were under way for a formal celebration of the sesquicentennial.

My whole life is connected with the Shternberg Institute. I can still remember every detail of the July day in 1938 when I first walked into the small courtyard of the observatory. It was flooded with sunlight and looked like Polenov's "Moscow Yard."* The dome of a small church loomed across Pavlik Morozov Street, and the old astrograph tower rose above the yellow, peeling observatory building.† A nearly transparent old man with a

*[A painting by Vasily Polenov (1844–1927) of scraggly wooden buildings in an idyllic pasture-like setting with Kremlin domes and towers behind them.]
†[In the mid-1950s the institute moved to a new building in the Moscow University complex on the Lenin Hills west of the old city. Pavlik Morozov (1918–1932) became a Soviet martyr of the forced collectivization campaign after he was killed by indignant peasants for denouncing his parents as "kulaks." With glasnost the street may have resumed its old name of Bolshoy Nikolsky.]

short wedge-shaped gray beard sat on a bench not far from the courtyard gate, resting his hands on a cane and looking remarkably in harmony with the archaic nineteenth-century landscape. I learned afterward that he was Sergey Blazhko, the patriarch of the institute.*

It's hard to believe, but I've been connected with the institute for nearly a third of its 150-year existence. Aleksandr Pushkin might have visited it if he had been interested in the physical and mathematical sciences. The famous revolutionary Aleksandr Herzen was one of the first students to graduate from the Moscow University astronomy department. On June 26, 1833, he defended a dissertation entitled "An Analytic Exposition of the Copernican Solar System." Today we would consider the topic more suitable for a senior thesis, but, in any case, Herzen was disappointed to receive the silver medal in his class, while the gold was awarded to his classmate Aleksandr Drashusov, later professor of astronomy at Moscow University and director of the observatory. Herzen also knew the observatory's first director, Dmitry Perevoshchikov.†

---

*[Blazhko (1870–1956), the deputy director of GAISH, wrote many works on variable stars, meteors, and other astronomical topics.] Blazhko was a legendary figure, and there are all sorts of stories about him. I recall an anecdote from about the time I first saw him. One of the periodic campaigns to raise working discipline was on, and attendance at lectures had been made obligatory. The old man gave the physics department course in general astronomy to several hundred students in the Lenin Auditorium on Mokhovaya Street, where the benches were arranged in an amphitheater. His inaudible murmur didn't carry beyond the first two rows, and students sitting farther up kept busy as best they could. One day two of them settled in the top row and, crouching down surrounded by fans, played a chess match for the department championship. A critical situation developed on the board, and one player made a crude wrong move that broke up his game. His partner, oblivious to everything else, bellowed joyfully to the entire auditorium, "Balls to you!" Blazhko took this heartfelt cry as an inquisitive youth's expression of doubt as to the truth of the theorem he was demonstrating. Breaking off the proof, he suddenly chirped, "What do you mean, balls? That's a law of nature, not balls!"

†In his famous memoir, *Out of My Past and Thoughts,* Herzen records the following curious conversation. *Perevoshchikov:* "It's a shame, really a shame, sir, that circumstances kept you from working seriously—you had fine capabilities." *Herzen:* "Not everybody can aim for the stars. We down here on earth have work to occupy us too."

Probably the most eminent astronomer ever to work at Moscow University Observatory was the lively and irascible Fyodor Bredikhin. In his charming, well-written account of the history of Moscow Observatory, Blazhko describes with gripping directness the circumstances under which Bredikhin left the future GAISH:

> There is no longer any need to keep the affair secret. . . . Bredikhin had a small son. One day when he was playing in the observatory courtyard, [observatory director] Shveytser's rooster pecked [the boy] good and hard. Bredikhin grabbed an old saber he owned, chased and caught the rooster, and cut off his head. That was the start of a misunderstanding which resulted in Bredikhin's quitting the observatory.*

Isn't that delightful? I have a vivid picture of the ferocious author of the mechanical theory of comet forms chasing the unlucky rooster around the familiar GAISH courtyard.

The most heroic figure in our institute's history was undoubtedly Pavel Karlovich Shternberg. As a scientist he was of less than commanding stature—a most ordinary professor of German stock. But on the other hand, what a life he led! None of his co-workers at the observatory, including Blazhko (who was only five years younger), had any idea that Shternberg was more than just an astronomer. From 1905 he was an underground Bolshevik, working directly toward the October revolution. Up to 1917 the observatory building was the main meeting place for the central committee of the Bolshevik party, through which Lenin directed its underground Moscow organization. The com-

---

Perevoshchikov: "Spare me! How is that possible, sir? What kind of occupation is that, Hegelian philosophy? I've read your articles and I couldn't understand them—bird-brained language, sir. What kind of work is that? No, sir!"
*Blazhko's history appeared in the university *Bulletin* [*Vestnik MGU*], vol. 18 (1940). [Bredikhin (1831–1904), known for his work on comet tails, in 1873 himself became director of the Moscow Observatory.]

Iosif Shklovsky with his "catch of the day" and Igor Novikov.

OPPOSITE, Shklovsky and Nicolai Kardashev.

ABOVE, Shklovsky and Herbert Friedman in the library of the Herzogenburg Monastery, Austria, July 1, 1984. Courtesy T. M. Donahue

BELOW, Shklovsky with Gertrude and Herbert Friedman at the Hallstätter See, an idyllic, pastoral basin in Austria, July 1, 1984, Shklovsky's sixty-eighth birthday. Courtesy T. M. Donahue

Поздравляю
Вас с новым годом

И. Шкловс

OVERLEAVES, Shklovsky, a talented caricaturist, sketched these Russian ethnic characters between 1960 and 1970.

"Congratulations for the New Year"

mittee gave Shternberg the long-term task of combing the records of the Moscow City Council (of which he was a member) to prepare a detailed plan, a city map showing every connecting courtyard and alley, an indispensable aid in street battles. Shternberg's split personality reached phenomenal limits: he had two wives, one legal, a professor who was still living in my time; and the second, a comrade in the underground, whose fate I don't know. After the October revolution, Shternberg appeared transfigured before his stunned colleagues. He was the first director of the college-level institute of the newly created People's Commissariat of Education and, as a political commissar on the eastern front, played an active part in the defeat of Kolchak.* Shternberg's life was prematurely cut short by typhus early in 1920.

I often stop to admire the portrait of Shternberg which hangs outside the conference room of the new GAISH. He is depicted in command of an artillery battalion firing from the Sparrow Hills (not far from the present institute) on the Kremlin, where junkers were holding out. I guess he was lucky at that: if the typhus-carrying louse hadn't got him, he would have had trouble surviving the difficult years ahead. Trotsky was in operational command of the eastern front, and Shternberg must have known him well. Had he been purged, our institute wouldn't bear its present name.

When I became a graduate student at the Shternberg Institute in 1938, the director was Vasily Fesenkov, a bright and distinctive personality. Now, across the shroud of years, I see him in human scale as a typical representative of prerevolutionary Russian science who managed to cross the boundary of 1917. The general level of physical and mathematical sciences in our country was low before the revolution, and the lag behind Europe and America kept increasing afterward, although individual talents, of course, always crop up. Fesenkov (or, as we called

---

*[Admiral Kolchak became "Supreme Commander" of all the military forces fighting the Bolsheviks in the Civil War.]

him for short, Fess) had a characteristically slapdash style.*
There was something about him of the autodidact, a capricious
combination of broad nature and primitive, even childlike, ego-
tism, but he had one quality now rare among scientists: a lively
feeling for real nature, combined with a mistrust of its visible
phenomena. The slight ironic smile which played constantly
across his face is fixed in my memory.

In my student years I silently admired Fesenkov's monumental figure and revered him. He treated us small fry with kindly
condescension. For instance, I remember setting two of my fellow graduate students the famous problem which the high
school tutor in Chekhov's story gave to Petya, the merchant's
son. The conditions of the problem begin with the traditional
phrase: "A merchant bought . . ." I demanded that they solve it
without *x*—after all, Papa the merchant shamed the tutor by
working out the answer on his abacus.† Fess happened to cross
the lecture room while the graduate students were struggling
with it; I screwed up my courage and asked him to solve the
problem. You should have seen the childlike zeal with which he
set about it. And solve it he did, putting the overstudied graduate
students to shame.

Fesenkov stepped down at his own wish—a rare phenomenon

---

*My colleague Vasily Moroz told me a delightful story about him. Fess, then director of
Alma-Ata Observatory, was inspired by a trip abroad in 1954, three years before the first
Sputnik and the launch of various living creatures into space, to use the modest means at
hand to direct the building of an apparatus in which mice would be subjected to high
acceleration. The goal of the experiments was to investigate the small animals' reactions
to space flight. The work went at full blast, and the instrument was quickly slapped
together. After a difficult ordeal, the first victim of space medicine seemed to be breathing. Fess called an urgent meeting of the observatory's scientific council, brought in
invited guests, and reported the results of the experiment in optimistic terms. To make
his point as graphically as possible, he invited the audience to inspect the mouse. Unfortunately, the poor beast chose that exact moment to expire. Fesenkov gave up space
research.

†[In Chekhov's humorous sketch, "The Tutor" (1884), Petya's teacher sets him the
problem: "A merchant bought 138 arshins of black and blue cloth for 540 rubles. The
question is: how many arshins did he buy of each kind, if the blue cloth cost 5 rubles per
arshin, and the black, 3 rubles?"]

in those days—and Nikolay Moyseev, the head of the department of celestial mechanics, became director of the Shternberg
Institute. He was a colorful figure, somewhat reminiscent of
the mad Emperor Paul. A cripple who flourished his crutches
with bravado, Moyseev wore the colonel's uniform to which his
joint position at the Zhukovsky Air Academy entitled him. He
had a venomous, malicious wit. His descriptions of co-workers
were distinguished by their striking accuracy. I'll never forget
the classification of fools I chanced to overhear: "There are two
types of fools—*round* (typical specimen, Professor Parenago)
and *triangular* (typical specimen, senior lecturer Severny)."
Amazingly apt! Of course, everybody realizes that a triangular
fool (gloomy, awkward) is something completely different from
a rosy, optimistic, round fool.

Under Moyseev hard times set in at the institute. It began in
the usual way—with a tightening of the regulations about working hours. Two friends of mine and I were among the first to
suffer. Since our wretched living quarters had no bathing facilities, every Saturday afternoon we left work and went to the
Presnensky Baths next door. Saturday was a full working day,
and the baths became impossibly crowded afterward. This bless-
ing came to an end soon after Moyseev's accession: one of our
co-workers squealed, and a menacing order appeared on the wall
at GAISH forbidding the three of us our Saturday excursions.

Another whim of the Shternberg Institute's new sovereign
was tightening up on ideological-educational work. The climax
came after the war, when the global drop in political temperature
was matched by the creation of a super-ideological seminar at
GAISH. Moyseev, no longer director, was its frenzied leader. I
recall scholastic vigils on the Hegelian topic of "science as system and science as method" which went on for days, but I've
forgotten what put an end to those fatuous vibrations of the air.
Under Moyseev's leadership the celestial mechanics department fruitlessly elaborated a strange pseudoscience called "dynamic cosmology." I recall that after every department session,
its leaders, headed by Moyseev, went to a little store nearby and

passed around and killed a bottle of Moskovskaya on the spot. "Somehow celestial mechanics makes me thirsty for vodka," the chief liked to say. I guess if I were asked to name our institute's fundamental achievements, I would have to include the now established custom of three men clubbing together to buy and split a bottle.

When the war started, Moyseev moved into the observatory and drank heavily. When the fascists were deluging the district with incendiary bombs in the stifling July nights of 1941, he would pace the courtyard in a luxurious bathrobe, declaiming lines from the French poet Alfred Musset—I saw him myself. After the war he went mad over the scientific researches of Comrade Stalin, Coryphaeus of All the Sciences. Moyseev's last illness and heroically borne, unimaginable physical sufferings occurred late in 1955, just before Khrushchev's unmasking of the cult of personality. He couldn't possibly have survived that "outrage."

Moyseev was deposed during the Shternberg Institute's evacuation to Sverdlovsk (I don't remember what brought it on—as a mere laboratory assistant, I wasn't in on the affair). The new director was Sergey Orlov, who was a dear old fellow but no astronomer. His position apparently depended on his imposing and uncommonly noble appearance. In the good old days he would have been a high school teacher, but instead he became a scientist and an epigone of Bredikhin's mechanical theory of comet forms. Orlov was a kind, innocuous person, and for that we owe him thanks.

Orlov's reign, which lasted until late 1952, was a difficult period in the history of our country. Along with many of my contemporaries, I had a chance to appreciate fully Ostap Bender's famous explanation of the phenomenon of atmospheric pressure.* Late in 1951 my old friends from graduate student years,

*[Ilf and Petrov, *The Golden Calf,* p. 373: " '. . . the atmosphere exerts a pressure of four hundred and seventy pounds on every citizen. . . . It's a scientific fact. And it's been depressing me of late. Just think! Four hundred and seventy pounds. Twenty-four hours a day. Especially at night. I sleep badly.' "]

Sasha Lozinsky, Abram Zelmanov, Valya Berdichevskaya, and I—all of us "disabled veterans of item five"—were dismissed from the Shternberg Institute. Of that category only the war veterans Lipsky and Kosachevsky were kept on.* We were fired under the pretext of "staff reduction." I recall Kulikov, the deputy director of the institute—our "Uncle Kostya"—looking gloomily at me. "There's nothing to be done. Heads are rolling!" he droned in his northern accent.

I was astonishingly calm: I had already realized what was going on and was prepared for much worse. I drew my pay and, with a pocket crammed with 5,000 old rubles, invited my friends and colleagues at the institute, Grigory Sitnik and Yury Lipsky, to a farewell dinner at the restaurant in the Hotel Moskva. Unlike today, when, after the longest interval of peace in Russia's history, there are persistent shortages, postwar Moscow was fairly oozing with abundant, choice foods.

At the Moskva I got blind, stinking drunk, to the point of blanking out, although apparently I didn't show it. I remembered two things distinctly: (1) the last electric train to Losinka, where my poor Mama was living, left at 1:20 A.M.; and (2) the metro stopped working at one. Settling up (too generously!) with the waiter, I said goodby to my friends and, taut as a violin string, got past the ticket collector in the metro (in those days there were no turnstiles). Then I went limp, and it took me a long time to figure out why the escalator was dancing under my feet and I was taking so long to get down the damned thing. I noticed a laughing girl descending on the parallel line. "At this late hour the two escalator lines can't be going in the same direction," I decided logically, and just then the rising escalator, on which I was trying in vain to go down, threw me off at the top. Fortunately, I was out of sight of the ticket collector.

I came to in the wintry electric train, where, huddled in a

---

*[Item 5 on the Soviet internal passport categorizes its citizens by one of sixteen nationalities: those of the fifteen constituent "republics"—and Jews.]

corner, I heard: "Mitishchi. Next stop Stroitel." For the first time I had missed my stop at Losinka. The deserted platform at Stroitel was white with fresh-fallen snow. I knew enough to cross over to the opposite platform, where, still far from sober, I lay on a bench until 5:30, hundred-ruble notes spilling from my pockets and nocturnal shadows walking around me. It's strange that I wasn't robbed.

Two weeks later I was reinstated. My old chief Nikolay Pariysky interceded for me, and Ivan Petrovsky, the rector of Moscow University, managed somehow to help me. I'll never forget that night as long as I live.

In 1952 Boris Kukarkin became head of the institute. He was an unscrupulous man with a craving for power at any price. Before my very eyes, in a year or two he made a 180-degree turn. Just after the war he was calling for us young astronomers to publish only in British and American journals to affirm and propagandize the outstanding accomplishments of our national science. Two years later, with no less fury and in the name of that same national science, he was cursing the pitiful stateless cosmopolitans who published in foreign journals. There was something of the Jesuit about Kukarkin, and a good dose of the hysteric. However, he had talent, and although he was largely self-taught, he loved astronomy.

Kukarkin was deposed in 1956. I took a hand in the affair, but I would advise anyone against taking part in a palace coup: something more loathsome always comes along. Historically the Shternberg Institute had always been a nursery for directors of other astronomical establishments. Now for the first time an outsider from Kazan—Dmitry Yakovlevich Martynov, or, as we nicknamed him from his initials, Dyamka—was called to rule over us, and the long era of "dyamocracy" began.

Martynov's personality was determined by the fact that he had been a director since he was twenty-five years old and, at one time, even rector of Kazan, the third university in the country. A belligerent functionary who knew the bureaucratic ropes thoroughly, he was imbued with a sense of his own grandeur which completely turned his weak head. To say the least, Martynov and I took an instant dislike to one another. That would have been only a minor misfortune had his distaste confined itself to me personally, but, starting in 1953, I had slowly been creating a section of talented young people acutely sensitive to the revolution in astronomy. We arbitrarily called ourselves the radio astronomy section, although we ranged far outside that field. Personally I was in the middle of a long period of creative uplift—the goddess of fortune favored me. When the first Soviet Sputnik was launched and the space era started, I suggested the striking "artificial comet" method that made it possible to carry out optical observations of lunar rockets (see Chapter 24). I began meeting with Keldysh's group of theoreticians on Miussy Square, and my kids threw themselves enthusiastically into space research.

My relations with Martynov got progressively worse, and seizing his chance, he turned me down in a competition. I was forced to complain to Petrovsky about the petty tyranny of the GAISH director and his underestimation of the importance of space research. And again the unforgettable rector saved me. I ended up going directly to Petrovsky about all the affairs, great and small, of my group; this isn't a normal way to operate, but what else was I to do? Dyamka was indefatigable in finding petty ways to poison our existence. Finally, in 1968–1969, the basic, creatively most active part of GAISH's radio astronomy section (and I among them) quit the walls of our alma mater and joined the newly organized Academy of Sciences Institute of Space Research (IKI), where we gained more or less normal conditions of existence. One reason I left the Shternberg Institute was an active desire not to end up laid out on the large oak table in the conference hall. Over the years I've seen too many of my colleagues off to a world where you can be sure there will be no Dyamkas.

With the departure of our group, which served as a "fermentation enzyme," the Shternberg Institute lost any real prospect of further development. The fact that Solomon Pikelner worked at GAISH for almost twenty years was an important stabilizing factor. He was the model of probity, talent, and self-sacrificing service to science. His absurd death in 1975 substantially accelerated the process of erosion.*

The part of my section which remained at GAISH is still alive mainly because of the laboratory it set up at the great radiotelescope RATAN-600, near the Zelenchuk site.† Creation of the laboratory cost the institute almost nothing, and I'm proud to say that the initiative was mine.

Martynov retired in 1979. The result of Dyamka's reign was the loss of *connection between generations* and the destruction of the traditions that ensure the survival of any collective endeavor. At GAISH the collective disintegrated for all practical purposes into separate uncoordinated groups and subgroups. Dyamka's successor Evgeny Aksyonov is not from the younger generation, and he's not an astronomer—his field is celestial mechanics, and that's almost entirely mathematics. With his arrival, unknown characters crept out of the woodwork and immediately started giving orders.

"A sacred place is never left empty," and during those years relativistic astrophysics flourished—the brainchild of Academician Yakov Zeldovich, his uncommon energy, and his habit of keeping things "among friends." Their seminar meets on Thursdays in the familiar GAISH conference hall, where in the old days we held our exciting colloquium.

---

*[Pikelner died of botched care following the removal of his appendix.]

†[In the 1960s a great complex of instruments, the Special Astrophysical Observatory at Zelenchuk, rose in the northwestern Caucasus. The two major instruments were a 6-meter optical telescope, the largest in the world, and the RATAN-600 (the acronym stands for Radio Astronomy Telescope of the Academy of Sciences), a 600-meter–long array of partly steerable 20-meter panels. Neither has been particularly successful. Poor weather conditions, inferior detectors, and mechanical problems have hampered the optical telescope, and RATAN-600 has been eclipsed by modern synthesis arrays in the West. Lack of computer technology has also hampered Soviet instrumentation.]

Nobody can be against an important field of modern theoretical research like relativistic astrophysics, but there has to be some moderation.* The hypertrophic development of one organ at the expense of others is the first sign of a serious illness. Experiment and observation (in other words, real as opposed to fictional astronomy) is a demanding and, in our den of iniquity, insecure business, and today's young people are quicker at sizing up the situation than at seeing long-term prospects. They soon realized that they could be sure of expeditiously defending their candidate's degree in relativistic astrophysics, and for nearly ten years now there has been a steady suctioning off of capable and intelligent students into that field. The result of this uncontrolled propagation of qualified theoreticians whom nobody needs is that their chances of finding jobs are increasingly gloomy.†

A pathological development in a scientific collective is analogous to cancer, which begins with the uncontrolled propagation of a few pathological cells. From the point of view of the individual cell, everything is just fine, but for some reason the organism perishes.

This protracted disease is not incurable, but the cure demands a rational application of medical means, including surgery. But who's going to do it? There are still viable but uncoordinated cell clusters at the Shternberg Institute connected with the institute's observational stations. (To be fair about it, the creation of these stations, in particular the one in the Crimea, is

*[Relativistic astrophysics is the study of processes like black holes, the big bang, and the expanding universe in which relativity effects (very high velocities or strong gravity fields) come into play. With the exciting new ideas and concepts developed by Zeldovich, Stephen Hawking in England, Kip Thorne in the United States, and many others, this previously neglected field became the main goal of study of young astronomers everywhere, to the virtual exclusion of other subjects (stars, planets, Sun, even quasars).]
†[The situation in graduate schools which Shklovsky describes applies to the United States and other countries as well.]

perhaps Dyamka's only real contribution.)** Saving the institute as a whole, however, depends on the appointment of a new, *real* director—a leader of the collective, a fundamental astronomer, and preferably a somewhat younger man. But where are we to find him?

I was absorbed in these far from cheerful thoughts when my colleague Volodya Zabolotny, who lives in the old observatory building, came to see me. He had an amazing story to tell. On December 9, 1981, the 150th anniversary of the Shternberg Institute was celebrated with great pomp. At three in the morning of the next day, Zabolotny was awakened by a dreadful clanking and crashing. "It sounded as if we were being bombarded," said Volodya. When the din didn't let up, tenants of the building ran out into the courtyard, where a dreadful sight greeted them: in a cold rain mixed with snow, the rusted-out dome of the large astrograph was slowly rotating. The frightened woman on night watch was rushing around searching for the mislaid key—bad weather had kept people away from the tower for several weeks. There was something frightening about the dome's rotation, a strong odor of truly Gogolian deviltry. After twenty minutes or so, it suddenly stopped.

The next morning a natural explanation was found for the strange phenomenon: the knife switch which works the rotating dome was wrapped in a floor rag, and the rag soaked up dirty moisture from the almost continuous rain until it became conductive and closed the circuit. But to my mind there is a higher, symbolic sense to the fact that it happened on the night of the Shternberg Institute's anniversary celebration.

**[Because Moscow's lights did not permit modern dark-sky observations, several telescopes, including a 1.25-meter reflector, manned by a small Shternberg resident staff were installed at the Crimean Astrophysical Observatory.]

11

The Principle of Relativity

IT always makes me feel sad to hear the driver of Moscow trolley-bus no. 33 call out "Academician Petrovsky Street." I owe a great deal to the person for whom the former Exhibition Street is named. As I mentioned before (see Chapter 10), in 1952 Ivan Petrovsky, the rector of Moscow University, reinstated me in my post after several unfortunate Jewish colleagues of mine and I were fired from the Shternberg Institute.* A couple of years later he used his authority to give me, directly from the rector's fund, an unprecedentedly luxurious three-room apartment in the fourteen-story Moscow University building on Lomonosov Prospect, after my family and I had spent nineteen years crammed into a single room in a barracks in Ostankino. Petrovsky also enrolled my son in the university physics department, which was no easy matter. And I can't count the number

*[Petrovsky (1901–1973), a mathematician, began his academic career after working as an accountant and high school teacher. He was head of the mechanics and mathematics department of the university before becoming rector in 1951.]

of times he rescued me from the despotism of that malicious bureaucrat, GAISH director Dmitry Martynov. I was able to create a highly viable group within the institute and staff it with talented young people only thanks to selfless help from Petrovsky, who was constantly overruling the sluggish Dyamka's obtuse resistance. He found homeless young colleagues of mine places to live. With his *absolute instinct* (the equivalent of musicians' absolute pitch) for genuine science, even in an embryonic state, he was a great help to us at the beginning of the space age.

Petrovsky headed the most important university in the country for twenty-two years. It was the most precious thing in the world to him, both home and family, and for its sake he even gave up his beloved mathematics. A decent and honorable man, Petrovsky was never the absolute master in that home, however. Powerful feudal barons in the departments followed their own line, and often there was nothing he could do about it. I'm not speaking of the general line imposed by the party and government; to change the direction of that was clearly impossible. He always liked to say, "Remember—my power has its limits." He never made idle promises to his innumerable petitioners, but once he said, "I'll try to do something for you," there was no doubt that everything humanly possible would be done.

It's preposterous and strange, but some of my friends and acquaintances, highly educated people, were skeptical of Petrovsky's noble activity, to say the least. For example, I will never forget a conversation I had with the radically inclined, talented physicist Gabriel Gorelik.* He replied to my ecstatic praises of the rector by remarking sharply, "Your Petrovsky is the starry-eyed administrator of a bawdy house who sincerely believes that the establishment entrusted to his care isn't a brothel but just an innocent attraction with fancy dress." I pro-

*Gorelik's life was tragically cut short on the rails at Dolgoprudnaya Station.

tested categorically against this blasphemous comparison, but Gorelik was not to be convinced—that's the maximalist temperament of our native radicals for you!

Gorelik wasn't the only skeptic. To this day I can't forgive Andrey Sakharov for the sharp rebuke he delivered to the poor rector following the illegal dismissal of Sakharov's stepdaughter, a sixth-year student, from the university.* In that situation there was no way Petrovsky could have helped any student. A few hours after the "chat," Petrovsky died suddenly on the premises of the Ministry of Higher Education, where he had received another dose of humiliating abuse from the opposite flank of our native ideologues. Surprisingly, even a few months later Sakharov still didn't feel any guilt, as he himself told me when other circumstances brought us together at the Academy of Sciences hospital (see Chapter 23).

Petrovsky's fate was the old tragic story of a good man in a difficult position in cruel times. You have to understand how hard it was for him. I personally witnessed dozens of good deeds that remarkable man did. And from this, using a working knowledge of statistics, I can affirm with complete assurance that the total number of good deeds over the years he served as rector must have been on the order of 10^4! How many people are there among us with a lifetime total that high? Our radicals need to assimilate the simple truth that there's nothing worse than "unpadded" abstract good. Good must first of all be *specific*. It would be no more than justice to carve a simple inscription on Petrovsky's headstone in Novodevichy Cemetery: "Here rests a man who performed 10,000 good deeds."

Living and performing those good deeds at Moscow University couldn't have been easy. I'll never forget a conversation fraught with drama I once had with the rector in his small office in the new university complex on Lenin Hills, a room adorned by Nesterov's magnificent painting of "Pavlov at Koltushi," which

---

*[Striking at relatives was a common punitive measure against dissidents.]

depicts the great physiologist limbering up by stretching his arms over his desk. This time my business with Petrovsky (whom I rarely went to see) was a simple one, although important for my section. The audience couldn't have lasted more than three or four minutes (I recall his making a phone call on my behalf), but afterward, instead of seeing me out, Petrovsky started asking me animated questions about new developments in astronomy and then moved on to trivial topics. I realized that there was a more important reason for his behavior than the invariable benevolence he showed me personally: a group of uncongenial characters was sitting in line outside, waiting for the rector to receive them on business that Petrovsky found disagreeable. In no hurry to get on with it, he was using our light conversation as a brief "time out."

The relaxed nature of my chat with Petrovsky led some imp to goad me into the following pronouncement: "I often stop in the lobby of the main university building to admire the portrait gallery of great scholars which decorates it. It's an astonishing collection—for instance, there are two venerable Chinese elders, evidently eminent researchers, about whom I know absolutely nothing. It's all the more surprising that one quite eminent scientist is missing from the gallery."

"That can't be!" said the rector decidedly. "When the university was built, a commission of experts was put to work selecting the scientists whose portraits were to adorn the gallery. But then, Iosif Samuilovich, you have to keep in mind the substantial dose of subjectivity in any selection. For instance, X is a great scientist to one expert, and Y to another. But this sort of subjectivity doesn't apply to the most eminent. I'm afraid your candidate isn't suitable to fill the gap you've detected in the gallery. What's his name, by the way?"

"Einstein, Albert Einstein." As it's usually put, an uncomfortable silence reigned. And then I played a three-move combination with my beloved rector.

First I threw him a lifeline, saying quietly, "Evidently your commission was guided by the well-established principle of selecting only *deceased* scientists for the portraits. Einstein died in 1955, and the main building of the university was finished two years earlier."

"That's it exactly! I should have figured it out immediately—Einstein was still alive!"

I made my second move. "Of course, rearranging an already existing gallery is impossible—that would set a dangerous precedent. But we could certainly install a bust of Einstein in the physics department. True, it won't add anything to Einstein's reputation, which was a matter of indifference to him anyway. But it might do the department some good."

"Ah, Iosif Samuilovich," answered Petrovsky, obviously tiring of the subject, "you can't imagine how much money artists and sculptors charge for commissions like that! Back in the early 1950s they showered gold on us. Now it's hard even to imagine the amount we paid masters of brush and chisel for the university installations, and particularly for that gallery. Alas, times are different now! There's no money for the commission you're asking for."

And then I made my third move—as I thought, *checkmate.* "My brother is a sculptor, and I happen to know that there's a bust of Einstein stored in Konyonkov's studio which he modeled from life while he was living in America.* I think that if you, as rector of Moscow University, were to ask Konyonkov, who's quite old now, to donate that bust, the sculptor's a decent fellow and would be only too happy to do so."

Petrovsky got up from his armchair in a clear sign that the audience was over and he would rather receive the group of contentious troublemakers in the anteroom than go on talking to me. He saw me to the door of his office in silence and only then, shaking my hand in parting, said gloomily in his typical way, "Nothing

---

*[The famous Soviet sculptor Sergey Konyonkov (1874–1971) returned to the USSR in 1945 after twenty-one years in emigration.]

will come of it. Too many swine in the physics department. . . ."*

I dedicated my book, *Stars: Their Birth, Life, and Death,* to the bright memory of Ivan Petrovsky. What else could I do for him?

---

*Our obscurantists and louts take various attitudes toward the special and general theories of relativity. For example, a vile character named Tyapkin (who works at Dubna) "proves" that Einstein "stole the special principle from Poincaré and Lorentz," while the present rector of Moscow University Anatoly Logunov tries to show that the greatest physicist of all "didn't understand" his own general theory of relativity. It should be noted that the late Academician Fock was the first to propagandize this "idea." [Vladimir Fock (1898–1974) was a theoretical physicist known for his contribution to the Hartree-Fock method of modeling atomic structure and his work in quantum mechanics and radio propagation.]

12

Kaddish

EARLY in August 1956, I got a call from the permanent secretary of the Soviet *Astronomical Journal* telling me that my friend and mentor, Grigory Shain, was close to the end.* My eleven-year-old son Zhenya and I immediately went out to Abramtsevo, the Academy of Sciences summer colony, where the Shains had a dacha.

During the five days since Shain suffered a heart attack I had never stopped thinking of him, and in the electric train to Abramtsevo I was preoccupied with scattered and chaotic memories. I first met Shain in the summer of 1949, when I started working half-time at the Simeiz Observatory, of which he was then director.†

*[Shain (1892–1956) was an outstanding Russian astronomer, an expert on stellar spectroscopy and gaseous nebulae. From 1925 to 1945 he worked at the Simeiz station of Pulkovo Observatory and, after it became the independent Crimean Astrophysical Observatory, was its director from 1945 to 1952. According to McCutcheon, it was Shain who secured the review of Nikolay Kozyrev's case and his release in 1947 ("Stalin's Purge of Soviet Astronomers").]

†[Simeiz is a resort 20 kilometers west of Yalta on the south coast of the Crimea. The observatory was set on cliffs high above the Black Sea beaches.

It was the first time I had ever been in the Crimea. In those postwar days it was primordially depopulated: the native Tatar population was gone, and Ukrainian settlers from the Voronezh district had just begun to move into their empty houses.* Believe it or not, the famous Simeiz beach was as empty as in the times of the Tauri, whose rubbish-strewn burial grounds lay on the summit of Koshka near the observatory. Once in a while you came across solitary, unsociable vacationers, but the Simeiz sanatoriums, despoiled but not destroyed, hadn't yet reopened, and the town was still surprisingly deserted. The Crimea hadn't been that empty for hundreds of years, and I'd like to believe that it never will be again—but I have to admit that a Crimea without people was delightful.

Simeiz Observatory was a real oasis, bubbling with life. The older generation looked with disapproval on the young Moscow "touring company." Our merry songs and love of swimming shocked them. "Muscovite astronomical rabble!" grumbled old man Albitsky—who in those days was considerably younger than I am now. Every day during the lunch break I ran headlong down to the sea and, after a brief plunge, rushed back up. I never managed to cover the 360 meters in altitude in less than forty minutes. In a sweat and ten minutes late, I would cross the last rise in front of the observatory building, and the old fly-specked slogan hanging on the staircase never failed to tickle me: "There is no beaten path in science, and only the man who clambers up its stony byways with no fear of fatigue will reach the radiant heights."† At the observatory there was no control over working hours in the sense we now know it, but the example set by

---

After the war a new, more spacious observatory site was developed inland in the mountains west of Simferopol.]

*[The Tatars, descendants of the Mongol hordes who overran Russia in the thirteenth century, lived in the Crimea for 700 years, until they were expelled by Stalin in May 1944 on exaggerated allegations of collaboration with the Germans. Their homes and property were turned over to Russian and Ukrainian settlers.]

†Karl Marx—I reproduce it from memory, but I think that's pretty close.

Shain, who returned punctually to his tiny office on the second floor after the lunch break, was enough to maintain discipline.

I spent the summers from early June to late September at the observatory, and once or twice a season the Shains would invite me to their apartment. I found it fantastically luxurious after our Ostankino barracks. Pelageya Fyodorovna—Shain's plump, smiling, unusually "domestic" wife, herself a first-class observational astronomer—reigned over the household. The Shains fed us delicious food, and the surroundings were cozy and cultured. Classical music was usually playing on the radio phonograph; Shain's favorite piece was the Verdi Requiem. We didn't talk much about science—in general, he wasn't a man to waste words.

I spent four seasons in Simeiz, and they may well have been the best part of my life. It was there that I grasped the authentic spirit of astronomy. I had no teachers, and Shain was the only astronomer who influenced me—not so much by exhortation as by personal example. Sometimes we had long talks, usually on a bench under the old chestnut tree by the observatory building, and they were always a treat for me. Like nobody else (except, perhaps, Solomon Pikelner, who also worked at Simeiz Observatory in those years), Shain had a deep sense of the indissoluble link between astronomical observation and theory.

At the end of 1952, with a helpful boot from Andrey Severny, I left the Crimean Observatory.* Over the next two years I saw Shain only on infrequent visits to Moscow, but he spent most of the third year, the last of his life, in the capital seeking treatment

---

*[Severny (1913–1987) succeeded Shain as director of the Crimean Astronomical Observatory. Far from being the "triangular fool" of Moyseev's definition (see Chapter 10), Severny was a shrewd man and a good scientist who carried out pioneering work on solar magnetic fields and flares. As the director of the observatory until his death, Severny built it into a large and active organization, but his dictatorial style inhibited his corps of scientists. Shklovsky considered Severny, who was influential in the party and academy establishment, part of the "enemy camp." Severny reciprocated, disliking Shklovsky's attraction for students and aggressive development of new theories.]

for his ailing wife. I remember distinctly a conversation we had at the Hotel Moskva in late December 1955. The capital was celebrating the fiftieth anniversary of the Presnya uprising.* Shain said, "Can it really have been half a century ago? And I remember Odessa in 1905 as if it were today, the arrival of the *Potemkin* in the roads, the pilgrimage to the dead Vakulinchuk. . . ."†

After a short pause Shain began reminiscing about an episode from his early childhood. "The Turkish consul lived on our street. Such an elegant man, with a dyed mustache. . . . Every morning he left the house and, before getting into the waiting cab, he always gave a five-kopek coin to one of the little boys who gathered beforehand to await the consular departure. And one day I had the simple idea of getting up very early and occupying the best spot at his front door. The consul came out at the appointed hour, patted my head, and gave me the five kopeks." Shain paused again and then went on: "And now, if the appropriate organs were to interrogate me and ask whether I had connections with diplomatic representatives of foreign countries, as an honorable man I would have to answer that I had. 'And did you receive compensation from them?' 'Yes, indeed!' " Grigory Abramovich smiled with a slight tinge of sadness.

In his last years he agonized over a decent way of freeing himself from the large sum of money he had accumulated. The Shains lived modestly and hardly spent anything on themselves. Meanwhile money streamed in: the Stalin Prize first-class, the salary of the director of an Academy of Sciences observatory, and nearly as much from the Academy. Over a million old rubles piled up.** They had no children; there was only their adoptive

---

*[The end of the revolutionary ferment of 1905 came with repression of a Moscow general strike climaxed by an armed revolt in the Presnya district.]

†[Shain is recalling the mutiny of the sailors on the battleship *Potemkin* depicted in Eisenstein's famous film. The ship took refuge in Odessa harbor, and the body of the sailor who started the uprising was displayed on the docks.]

**[100,000 rubles of the Soviet nonconvertible currency, which was devalued in January 1961].

daughter, Inna, who was Pelageya Fyodorovna's niece and a cousin of Vera Ambartsumyan, the wife of the astronomer.*

Looking for a way out of this far from simple situation, Shain decided to spend some of his money on an eight-room house on the grounds of the new Crimean Astrophysical Observatory, which he intended to leave as a home for elderly astronomers. The builders cheated Shain shamelessly, and the whole affair upset him dreadfully. He also wanted to build an astronomical dome, a noble contribution to the construction of the Crimean Observatory. The local authorities, however, rebuffed the academician, and it is said that Severny egged them on: "Why this private philanthropy? Can't our government take care of the development of science?"

So after all that unpleasantness Shain still had the damned money, which went on growing as the needs of the two sick and elderly people decreased over the years. Fate dogged them. For many years Pelageya Fyodorovna sent 300 rubles a month to her father. That uneducated collective farm watchman in a small godforsaken village near Perm ended up having two close relatives by marriage, Shain and Ambartsumyan, in the Academy of Sciences. A man of classic peasant mentality, he went on living in miserly poverty and stashing away the remittances from his "successful" daughter in a savings account. When he died, two years before Pelageya Fyodorovna's own death, to her horror she inherited more than 20,000 rubles from him.

In 1954 Shain's wife was diagnosed as having a myeloma. In Moscow I did what I could to arrange medical help for her. Never before or since have I seen a more selfless relationship to

*[Viktor Ambartsumyan (b. 1908), longtime president of the Armenian Academy of Science and director of the Byurakan Observatory, is a competent astronomer, well known and respected abroad. As will become apparent, Shklovsky resented him greatly for various reasons, including his tireless self-promotion, and could never resist trying to puncture his ego. Shklovsky once compared Ambartsumyan to Ursa Major (the Big Dipper), explaining that "there's no logical reason why some constellations are more famous than others."]

a loved one than the care Shain took of his mortally ill wife. He rushed from one doctor to another and made endless trips to the Moscow clinic from the large, depressing Academy dacha in Abramtsevo where Pelageya Fyodorovna lay confined to bed. During one of those trips Shain felt ill himself. He was at the Academy clinic, and they took an electrocardiogram but didn't bother to develop it before he set out on the return trip over the bad road to Abramtsevo. The cardiogram showed that he had suffered a massive heart attack. Five days later Shain was dying before his wife, who lay in the next room. He was sixty-four years old and desperately wanted to live.

Zhenya and I got to Abramtsevo in the afternoon. Vera Ambartsumyan, Pelageya Fyodorovna's energetic niece from Byurakan, had already taken over the household. She received us more than frigidly and categorically refused to allow me to go upstairs to say goodby to Shain, but she did let us in to see Pelageya Fyodorovna. Drugged with painkiller and dreadfully emaciated, Shain's wife lay propped up on pillows, clearly oblivious to events around her. We went downstairs, and the Ambartsumyan woman gave us tea as we listened to occasional bursts of painful wheezing from Shain's room. I observed the proprieties by exchanging a few phrases with Vera Fyodorovna. "What are your favorite activities?" she asked Zhenya.

"Sports," answered my son, who at that time was the best sprinter among Moscow schoolboys.

"That's good," answered Ambartsumyan's wife. "You can play goalie for the Israeli soccer team."

On our return trip Zhenya asked me, "Why did she say that?"

"Because she's a nasty, vile woman," I replied, without bothering to elaborate.

Shain died the next day. I think he was laid out in state in the Presidium of the Academy of Sciences—I don't remember those days very well. For some reason I recall that young Kolya Kardashev (see Chapter 24) was among the last who stood in the honor guard. An official committee, of which both Severny and

Ambartsumyan were members, decided on a burial site near Simeiz Observatory. The committee flatly rejected my proposal to name the Crimean Astrophysical Observatory for Shain and limited itself to a resolution conferring his name on the large telescope then under construction at the Crimean Observatory.*

Several other astronomers and I accompanied Shain's body to Simeiz. From his gravesite you can see the windows of the apartment in the main observatory building where he lived for some thirty years. As we walked away from the burial, a terrible storm broke out. I felt sick at heart. Leaden, painful days dragged by. Pelageya Fyodorovna survived Shain by two weeks and died in the Simeiz apartment. Ambartsumyan's wife was displaying a frenzied peasant greed, taking over the Shains' property and sending off to Byurakan containers of the really fine old furniture of which Shain had been so fond. I would have liked to have had as a memento a book of Einstein's articles on public affairs which Shain had once lent me to read. The greedy woman wouldn't give me the book, but I picked the jacket with the great scientist's portrait out of the rubbish. Now the cover adorns my office—my only material souvenir of Grigory Abramovich Shain. She did give a couple of small books from his library to Pikelner, Shain's co-worker for many years and the person closest to him.

Pelageya Fyodorovna's will was read. The old merchant-class principle operated: money went to money. With the exception of insignificant sums (20,000–50,000 old rubles) left to their adoptive daughter Inna and two of Shain's cousins, the million-ruble estate was left entirely to Vera Ambartsumyan. Then something unexpected happened. Inna protested the will and sued. The girl had just turned eighteen and was engaged to the son of an Armenian from Yalta, an associate at the Magarach Institute, and it

---

*[In 1961 a 2.6-meter (102-inch) instrument, at the time the largest ever built in the USSR, was completed and named the Shain Reflecting Telescope.]

was her enterprising prospective father-in-law who egged her into contesting the will.

Later that fall I heard the outcome of the trial. By English law the suit should have been called *Shain* v. *Ambartsumyan,* but Inna had not been legally adopted by the Shains and her last name was Sannikova. Witnesses at the trial, however, proved that she had been adopted *to all intents and purposes.* The court decided that the entire million rubles plus the Academy dacha should go to the only legal heir, Inna Sannikova. She brushed off her Armenian suitor, and I heard rumors that she was sowing her wild oats. You can imagine how angry Vera Ambartsumyan was. Ambartsumyan himself pharisaically pretended not to care one way or the other. For some reason his wife decided that Inna had been put up to contesting the will by Solomon Pikelner, that most innocent of men. I am convinced that Ambartsumyan's spite, inspired by that vile slander, kept Pikelner from ever being elected to the Academy of Sciences.

I couldn't bear being a witness to the vile events going on over Shain's grave. Thoroughly depressed, I left Simeiz and took the steamer across the Black Sea to Sukhumi, where my old friend Mates Agrest was living. Over the next days I was restless and unsettled. Shain's image haunted me. I remembered that remarkable man's quiet voice and characteristic light cough and the hours we'd spent in conversation, mostly on topics only remotely connected with astronomy. I recalled how, just a few months before his death, he'd rejoiced at reading the paper by Oort and Wahlraven that so triumphantly confirmed my theory of the synchrotron origin of optical emission from the Crab Nebula. It was Shain who submitted my original work on the subject to the *Transactions* of the Academy of Sciences in the spring of 1953 (see Chapter 8). Throughout those days a troubled sense that I ought to do something for my dead teacher was brewing within me. The decision came quite unexpectedly. Mates' father-in-law performed some sort of unpaid duty (perhaps sexton?) in the Sukhumi synagogue. One Friday evening, after watching him recite the traditional prayers, arrayed in tallis and yarmulka with the tefilin wound around his naked arm, I asked him, "Can I order kaddish in the Sukhumi synagogue for one very good Jew?"

"Of course! What's his name?"

"Grigory Abramovich."

"Hirsch ben Avraham, that is. I'll find someone to recite kaddish for him in the synagogue and make sure it's all done properly!"

For the uninitiated, including modern Jews, I should explain that kaddish is a memorial prayer. As a child I recited kaddish for my father (in the language of our ancestors, of course) in the small synagogue of my native Glukhov. By tradition, kaddish is recited by a son who has reached "bar mitzvah"—the age at which he becomes a man. (For orphans, the age is twelve, and for boys with living fathers, thirteen.) All I remembered about the occasion was that it took a long time, at least half a day; a friend of my late father prepared me for it. I was rather surprised when Mates' father-in-law told me the next day that he had found a man who would recite kaddish according to the full canon of Jewish law every day for a year, for which I was to pay him 2,000 rubles. I was not prepared for that twist to the affair and didn't have that much money with me. It turned out that my childhood kaddish for my father had been a shortened variant, and a real kaddish is serious business. There was no turning back: I gave the man 1,000 rubles and sent the rest a month later.

My heart was light; I felt that I had kept a vow. I knew that Shain was deeply religious—he had confided as much to me. Of course, he wasn't a traditional believer; his faith had a pantheistic tinge reminiscent of his great fellow Jew Albert Einstein. For the next year the Sukhumi synagogue resounded with the ancient words of the memorial prayers for Hirsch ben Avraham, a good astronomer and a remarkable man.

Ilya Chavchavadze and the "Boy"

THE summer of 1956 was a good time for the Soviet Union. The cult of personality had been laid to rest. Peals of thunder were still reverberating from Nikita Khrushchev's secret speech in February, which stunned the whole world by demonstrating incontrovertibly that a criminal and butcher had headed our great socialist state for almost thirty years. The speech let a genie of monstrously destructive force out of the bottle, and it had to be corked up again. Twenty-five years later it seems that they still haven't succeeded.

The overwhelming majority of the Soviet population was in an excited, exultant state, especially the perpetually dissatisfied intellectuals. Thrilling things were expected. An era of "belated rehabilitation" began, tongues were loosened, and there was a lot of spicy chatter.

Against the background of general rejoicing, most if not all Georgians were going through a period tantamount to national mourning. This might seem surprising, since the Georgians had suffered heavily through the long years of Stalin's tyranny. Exceptional zeal was used in the extermination of old Georgian Bolsheviks, not to mention the Mensheviks who had been so numerous and active in the first years of Soviet power. Stalin dealt savagely with the Georgian intelligentsia as well. His beautiful little motherland was obviously not big enough to hold the Great Son of the Georgian People. He was never a Georgian nationalist, but a Russian one, a phenomenon "often observed among foreigners" (Lenin's words about Stalin).

The Georgian masses idolized the Leader anyway. Of course, there were material reasons—through the efforts of Stalin's stooges (but certainly not Stalin), the Georgians ended up in a privileged position.* It's not surprising that Khrushchev's famous speech aroused a wave of popular indignation. The "finer" feelings of the Georgians were offended. Young people in particular went on a rampage and got as far as open demonstrations, which were, of course, dispersed without excessive delicacy. In Tbilisi I was shown indentations from bullets, the result of one such demonstration on the anniversary of the Great Leader's death in March of that same 1956.

By late summer, when a regular plenary session of the Commission on Solar Research took place in Tbilisi, the storm had subsided, and the "timid Georgians," at least to appearances, had calmed down. Today such plenums are, God knows, minor events, but that one was organized with uncommon pomp. For the first time I had a chance to try the famous Georgian hospitality. The scientific and quasi-scientific sessions in essence occupied pauses between banquets. We were treated to delicious foods and the famous Georgian wines. The banquet element reached its apogee at Abastumani Observatory, to which the commission was transported in full.† Here, as in Tbilisi, the

---

*To a ridiculous degree. The line from Mikhail Lermontov's poem "The Demon" which read: "The timid Georgians fled" for a quarter of a century was printed and declaimed as: "The Georgians now defeated."

†[Abastumani is a mountain resort in western Georgia where the observatory of the Georgian Academy of Sciences is located.]

entire parade was commanded by the leading Georgian astronomer—Evgeny Kharadze, an intelligent and refined person who
is now president of the Georgian Academy of Sciences. It's hard
to imagine a more charming and yet restrained and strict host.

In addition to food for the body, our hospitable hosts treated
us to spiritual delicacies. We were shown the cultural monuments of Tbilisi and its surroundings. There were more distant
excursions, too. One of them is etched in my memory, a visit to
the memorial museum at the Kakhetian estate of the great Georgian educator, Ilya Chavchavadze. At every step we had heard
about him, his life, and his importance in the formation of modern Georgian culture.

Besides Kharadze and the members of the local organizing
committee, we were accompanied by a guide, a young, rather
short fellow who for some reason didn't sport the traditional
Georgian mustache. There was nothing special about the modest Chavchavadze estate. Since I preferred the real life throng-
ing the streets of Tbilisi to any museum, instead of listening to
our guide's explanations I detached myself from the group and
went on alone through the next rooms. In one of them I stopped
in astonishment. A huge, tasteless oil painting covered one large
wall. The scene was the editorial office of the progressive newspaper Chavchavadze headed, and a large desk with all its acces-
sories had been painted in the lower left corner. The rotund,
bearded Ilya Chavchavadze was portrayed rising from his editor's armchair, his eyes fixed in rapturous servility on a youth
standing in front of the desk in a proud and arrogant pose. The
youth was Soso Dzhugashvili.*

"It'll be curious to hear what the guide has to say about that
work of art," I thought maliciously. He couldn't ignore a canvas
that large, but at the time pronouncing Stalin's name out loud in
public was inadmissible.

Our group appeared. Unexpectedly the guide stopped in front
of the picture and made a sign to my tourist colleagues to stop

*[Soso was Stalin's childhood nickname.]

also. Then he said slowly and with heartfelt conviction, "Ilya Chavchavadze never printed the verse of young poets in his newspaper. He always said the youths should grow up and get to know life—and then he'd see. But when that boy came to see him, he printed his verse." I was put to shame.

On the way back I rode in the director's sedan beside Kharadze. "So what did Stalin write verse about?" I asked him.

Kharadze gave it some thought and answered slowly and quietly, "The sun, the rocks, the sea." I had no further questions.

Many years afterward I learned that one of Chavchavadze's unpublished letters contains another version of the meeting so effectively depicted by the local artist. The great Georgian educator found the young man's verse lacking in talent and without equivocation so informed the future Best Friend of All Poets.

"But what shall I do then? What should I take up?" Soso asked in dismay.

"Something else—for instance, politics."

It's interesting to speculate what might have happened if the young man hadn't heeded that imprudent advice.

My Contribution to Criticism of the Cult of Personality

THIS tragicomic history took place all of twenty years ago, and yet every time I reflect on it I come up against concepts like destiny, fate, and even the will of God—concepts that in daily life are totally foreign to me, a worker in the physical and mathematical sciences.

On June 15, 1961, I went to an All-Union Conference on Cosmic Rays, the first half of which was to be in Borzhomi, and the second in Erevan.* (Scientific conferences were certainly organized on a grand scale in those days.) I had to go—in the first place, purely as a tourist I never miss a chance to visit the Caucasus; and in the second, I had a paper to give on some astronomical aspects of the problem of the origin of cosmic rays.

I was more than ready to get away from Moscow, but, as so often happens, the last day before my flight was spent attending to niggling matters that couldn't be put off. The plane for Tbilisi left at two, and I spent all morn-

*[Borzhomi, "the pearl of the Caucasus," is a popular resort and mineral spring in Georgia; Erevan is the capital of Armenia.]

ing finishing off the dregs and didn't take time for a proper lunch. I managed to grab some dubious pirozhki on the street and barely made my flight, breathing a sigh of relief as I fastened the seatbelt. As events were to show, my relief was premature.

Since two eminent figures in our field, Bruno Pontecorvo and Sergey Vernov, were on the same plane, members of the local organizing committee met the flight with great ceremony.* The Georgian physicists put the future academicians into a waiting Volga and took me along, too. We drove rapidly from the airport through the capital of the sunny republic to a spot near the university building where several buses stood with a throng of conference participants beside them.

Although I didn't know our hospitable hosts, they offered me a seat in the Volga which had delivered us from the airport and was setting out immediately for Borzhomi. Since I can't stand extended contacts with bosses of any kind, I declined the flattering invitation as politely as possible. I preferred going to Borzhomi "on common terms" by bus in the company of cheerful young physicists. (When we arrived, I found out that my democratic gesture had been rewarded: on the road to the conference site the Volga overturned and Pontecorvo broke two ribs.)

Half an hour later I was seated in a good spot by the window right behind the bus driver. My seatmate was a man long known to me by reputation, Yakov Terletsky, a professor in the Moscow University physics department, a rather unpleasant character who was reputed to be a longtime secret collaborator of the Ministry of Love. Young physicists, mainly Leningraders and strangers to me, were noisily taking seats behind us. One of

*[Pontecorvo (b. 1913) is an Italian nuclear physicist who worked at Harwell in England and in the British-Canadian atomic research group in Montreal before defecting to the USSR in 1950 and continuing his research career there, first at the Institute for Physical Problems and afterward at the Joint Institute for Nuclear Research in Dubna. Vernov (1910–1987) was a well-known cosmic ray physicist and director of the Institute for Nuclear Research at Moscow University. He was active in the Soviet space program.]

them immediately brought out a guitar, and the group began singing popular songs.

I had already begun feeling queasy. Nausea nagged at me (which rarely happens), and in general I was out of sorts. I dearly love cheerful trips in faraway spots, but that day I found the young people's pointless merriment irritating. I couldn't figure out why I felt so lousy until a few dozen kilometers outside Tbilisi, when a sharp stab in the belly made the reason for my loathsome condition crystal clear: those damned pirozhki! Soon the Borzhomi road became my path to Golgotha. My turn had come to experience one of those repulsive (or rather, nightmarish) situations that I am convinced falls to everyone at least once in a lifetime. I base this conviction on my generally sound stomach, which, as we say in our field, eliminates the possibility of "observational selection."

Offhand I don't know of any depiction in world literature of the sufferings of a person in this unenviable position, and I will now apply my feeble pen to filling this substantive gap. Unbearable belly cramps came in periodic waves and, to keep from disgracing myself in front of the passengers on the bus and subsequently the scientific and nonscientific world in general, I managed to suppress them at the outer limit only by application of superhuman pressure to the affected internal organs. I fought off one monstrous attack and, covered in cold sweat, was looking dully at the rather wretched and, chiefly, treeless landscape of that part of Georgia flashing by my window in sunshine mixed with intermittent patches of rain. The absence of vegetation even in the form of bushes made it impossible for me to stop the bus, so to speak, on demand. And, of course, to do so would attract unwelcome notice from the male passengers, not to mention the female ones. I can't estimate the intervals between successive attacks, any one of which could have ended in catastrophe. I think there were five or six of them altogether, but for me time stood still. The amplitude of each attack was stronger than the last. My strength was fading. It seemed that my life was ending—and in a most embarrassing way. My God, why such punishment? But there was undoubtedly a reason, for, yea, I am a sinful man.

After the fifth or sixth paroxysm, I was watching the retreating landscape with a blank mind and tear-filled eyes, when a white stone road sign suddenly flashed by, bearing the inscription: "Gori 10 km." My tormented brain started working feverishly in an instantaneous series of disjointed thoughts, the sort of thing that happens to people in mortal danger: Gori, Stalin's birthplace. A memorial museum. There must be one. There has to be. I'll pretend I want to visit the museum and stop the bus, stop it at all costs! The museum was sure to have the ardently desired edifice which we students at the old Moscow University called the "annex to lecture hall 71."

I mustered the pitiful remnants of my strength and said with feigned casualness, "Kids, shouldn't we pay tribute to the cult? Gori's coming up—I suggest we stop and visit the memorial museum to Stalin."

"To hell with the cult of that old bandit! Let's keep going," came young voices from the back of the bus.

That was the last straw! Was I really to perish because of Comrade Khrushchev's 1956 speech to the Twentieth Party Congress? A pitiful witticism flashed through my mind: "One last victim of the cult of personality!"

Terletsky came to my rescue. Afraid of setting an example in what were still troubled times when nobody could predict the future course of events, he supported me energetically. Since Terletsky and I were by way of being "senior comrades," our combined wish had the character of a command. The driver turned off in Gori and started asking passersby for directions to the memorial museum. (Every Georgian knows where it is, but—oh, damnation!—our driver was an Armenian and hated Stalin.) My strength was gone, ardent hope for the memorial toilet was all that sustained me, and our bus's slow drift through the narrow streets of our Leader's birthplace sliced through me like a knife. Now I realize that it couldn't have taken us more than five minutes to reach the museum, but they seemed an eternity. I was all too aware that I couldn't withstand another assault from the lower organs of my tormented body.

The bus stopped before the waist-high stone enclosure of the memorial museum, and the passengers poured out onto the pavement. Thanks to my felicitous seating, I was first out of the bus. I covered the extensive grounds in a matter of seconds, running along the perimeter of the stone wall. A crowd of idle loafers strolled animatedly through the streets surrounding the shrine of the Georgian people. In the middle of the grounds, under a stone enclosure, stood a tiny hovel with two entrances. One led into the wretched room of Stalin's father, the shoe-maker Dzhugashvili, and the second into the similar apartment of the hovel's owner, from whom the parents of the Coryphaeus of All the Sciences rented their cubicle. The tasteless three-story stone building of the museum itself loomed at a distance.

My quick trip around the memorial convinced me, to my hor-ror, that the edifice for which I had organized the idiotic visit to that accursed spot was *nowhere to be found!* I had to admit that all was lost. The light grew dim before my eyes, and it took me a second to grasp the fact that the illumination had in fact dimin-ished greatly. My ancient Jewish God, the God of Abraham, Isaac, and Jacob, had seen the unbearable torments of a son of his long-suffering chosen people and performed a miracle. Unex-pectedly blackening stormclouds covered half the sky, and the heavens opened—all in substantially less time than the famous three minutes He had taken to create the Universe.* Mere mo-ments earlier the evening sun had been shining above the hori-zon and a festive throng sauntering around us. Now the sun was eclipsed, and the strolling Georgians and my scientific compan-ions were literally blown off by the wind and washed away by the

---

*See Steven Weinberg's fine book, *The First Three Minutes: A Modern View of the Origin of the Universe* (Basic Books, 1977).

rain. In short, the miracle followed the traditional Biblical scenario.

At that very instant a final belly spasm, the fiercest yet, seized
me. My strength was completely exhausted—I barely managed
to run to the shelter of the stone pavilion, where I performed an
unprecedented act of blasphemy at the door to the room where
little Soso had first seen the light of day eighty-two years before.

In blissful relief, soaked to the skin, I walked slowly back to
the bus through the pelting rain. My behavior must have looked
peculiar, because Terletsky, leaning out the bus window,
shouted maliciously to me, "Iosif Samuilovich, why that lei-
surely professorial pace?"

"I'm in no hurry to get anywhere now, Yakov Petrovich," I
replied, smiling broadly.

Wet and happy, I passed the rest of the trip in a state of
nirvana. Gradually, the transcendental and somewhat phantasmagoric nature of my action became etched, as they say, "in the
mind's eye." With epic composure I imagined the enraged
throng of aboriginal inhabitants of Gori applying lynch law to
me—and I'm convinced that if any of the local inhabitants had
seen that outrage I really would have been lynched. I also vividly
pictured the local Pinkertons finding an airplane hygiene packet
at the site of the vile crime and quickly applying Sherlock
Holmes' classic inductive methods to establish the loathsome
criminal's identity. But nobody saw me and there was no sign of
any guard at the shrine: to my good fortune, the cult of personality had ceased being universal, but had not yet become the local,
Georgian phenomenon of the last ten to fifteen years.*

I slowly became conscious of a growing feeling of pride in my
unique and audacious act. My attitude toward one of the greatest
monsters in human history had been formed in childhood. I vividly recalled the keen hatred of Stalin which my unforgettable
mother, a simple, uneducated woman, had always harbored. I

*[The Stalin Museum in Gori was closed in 1989.]

remember trying to moderate her overly loud imprecations against the Leader of the Peoples (after all, there were neighbors around, and they could denounce her).

By the time we got to Borzhomi late that evening I was bursting with pride, and I related my experience to Ginzburg and that congenial soul Evgeny Feinberg.* My colleagues burst out laughing and then with grave anxiety advised me not to prattle to anybody else. Of course, they were right: as I mentioned before, the future wasn't at all clear. I followed their advice.

A week later the Borzhomi part of the conference ended, and the participants went on to Erevan. On the way I couldn't resist stopping at Gori to visit the memorial museum—everybody knows that a criminal is always drawn back to the scene of the crime. I looked around tranquilly, without haste and with mixed emotions. First of all, I discovered that the facility I had sought in such torment was not in the courtyard, as my fevered imagination had somehow conceived it, but inside the museum. In the interests of justice, I should mention that it shone with a cleanliness and comfort which were a great rarity in sunny Georgia. The traces of my sacrilege had disappeared. After that, I devoted myself to a detailed visit to the museum. I was struck by a photograph of Soso's father, Visarion Dzhugashvili, fastened to the door of their wretched dwelling. I had often seen the photograph of his mother, Ekaterina, that hung beside it, but his father's picture was new to me. Where on earth had I seen that face before? Scrutinizing it closely (after all, I had once wanted to be a portrait painter), I realized why the man seemed so familiar: it was a little-known, clumsily retouched picture of Stalin himself in youth. The forgers had fixed a beard on him and forced him into a peaked cap obviously too small for his head.

The exposition itself was rather wretched and consisted primarily of various copies and huge, crudely made, tasteless pic-

*[Feinberg (b. 1912) is a theoretical physicist whose work has been primarily on cosmic rays.]

tures and cheap photoreproductions of oil paintings. Among the extremely limited genuine exhibits, I was struck by the correspondence between Stalin and his daughter Svetlana; there is no doubt he loved her. Stalin called her "dear little boss" and signed himself "your little secretary." I think "little general secretary" would have been more apt. Through the years the letters became less frequent, and their contents colder. The last note was in response to the birth of Svetlana's son (by Moroz). I recall the following lines from it: ". . . don't be distressed that you gave birth at seven months. The state needs new citizens, even premature ones." I'm surprised that the phrase didn't end up adorning the facade of every maternity clinic in our vast fatherland.

Last year, in 1980, I visited the memorial museum in Gori for the third time. The exposition had become even sparser, since the correspondence with Svetlana, naturally, had disappeared.*

A few months after the events described above, immediately after the Twenty-second Party Congress drove an aspen stake into the heart of the Stalin cult and decreed the expulsion of his remains from the mausoleum in Moscow, where he had lain beside Lenin, I ran into Feinberg on the street. He shook my hand heartily and congratulated me on my political perspicacity. Alas, he was mistaken—in that spontaneous affair I was merely the tool of God's will.

—September 1981, the Rest Home of the Georgian Ministerial Council (Stalin's former dacha), Sinop (Sukhumi).

---

*[Svetlana Allilueva's spectacular defection to the West had made her a nonperson in the Soviet Union.]

Complex Percentages

I MET a lot of curious people at the apartment of my friend Vladimir Turok (see Chapter 4). One frequent visitor was an elderly Jew named Lyovka, a man with little education but great intelligence and a rich past— for example, during the NEP he ran parimutuel betting at the races. This irrepressible old fellow was the inventor of an everlasting electric fuse, which he always carried in his pocket. He would ask everybody who came into Turok's hospitable apartment: "Let's assume you have a burned out fuse. What do you do with it?"

"I throw it away," came the invariable answer.

"But that's a waste. It was only the filament which burned out, and I calculate that the filament costs only 3 kopecks. To throw away the entire fuse, a device worth 46 kopecks, is a totally inadmissible extravagance."

"So what should we do?" Turok's guest would ask, with no sign of interest.

"I've invented an everlasting fuse. Look, here it is!" And he would thrust his creation under the other's nose.

The principle of the fuse was extraordinarily simple

and graphic. It had eight channels drilled into its butt end, and the filaments inserted in them were used one at a time. When one filament burned out, all you had to do was rotate the fuse by one-eighth to the next. The cost of this modernized fuse came to 72 kopecks, and its working life was eight times that of the standard fuse—for all intents and purposes it was everlasting.

Notwithstanding the obvious advantages of this apparently artless invention, putting it into production ran up against monstrous obstacles. For many years the mettlesome Lyovka waged a grueling lawsuit against the Ministry of Electrical Industry. All he ever managed to squeeze out of them was 3,000 rubles (old money). The ministry threw a cohort of lawyers into the titanic battle. Their trump card was that there was no way of knowing how much Lyovka should be paid: there were no data on the number of fuses which burned out in the country annually, and by law the inventor was entitled to a certain percentage of the economic benefits produced by the invention.

Every time we met, Lyovka buttonholed me and related in great technical detail his latest account of scandalous economic mismanagement, militant asininity, embezzlement, and monstrous waste of material resources. "You're a learned man, Iosif Samuilovich. Explain to me, please, why everything hasn't gone to pieces and collapsed altogether?"

I would reply to the effect that it must be proof of the scientifically valid basis on which our society is constructed. Lyovka found this explanation unconvincing, and he died in excruciating ignorance. Speaking frankly, I don't understand it either, so Lyovka's question has yet to find an answer.*

---

*[Perhaps Shklovsky should have shared with him one of his important, but unpublishable, scientific discoveries:] As we know, great Aristotle considered that motion (uniform and rectilinear, of course) could take place only because some force was acting *constantly* on the moving body. When that force ceases, sooner or later the body will stop. Great Galileo, and after him no less great Newton, came to the radical conclusion that the uniform and rectilinear motion of a given body *does not require* any force at all to maintain. This is the famous law of inertia, which many millions of schoolchildren on all

At Turok's apartment I have vivid memories of meeting an elderly woman who still bore the traces of majestic beauty. I was struck by the dainty, old-fashioned way she held her teacup. From the conversation I realized that she was a lonely ex-actress living on a miserable pension in the Home for Aged Actors, an institution which in the old days would have been called an alms-house.

After she left, Turok told me an amazing story, one connected in a roundabout way with his old friend the actress.

Around 1700 Peter the Great made one of his periodic voyages to West Europe. In Holland he undertook his usual important state business of recruiting craftsmen accomplished in various trades. (Today we associate that kind of activity with the "brain drain.") A boatswain known by the nickname Nachtigal or "nightingale" [in Russian *solovei*] was among the foreign specialists Peter enlisted. He was a respectable man, well off for the time, with 240 guldens on deposit in an Amsterdam bank.

In the newly built Petersburg, Nachtigal was appointed to a naval school to teach young aristocrats the art of navigation and sailing. As could be expected, the patrician minors showed no particular zeal for those sciences. The strict and demanding ex-boatswain gave his lazy students Ds and Fs for indolence and lack of effort and made the grades stick. Naturally, the blockheads' papas were far from pleased; through the ages the parents of D-students have maintained a certain family resemblance. The customs of the times were harsh, and to get rid of the intractable teacher, the lackadaisical schoolboys' parents denounced him to Peter. I don't know the exact nature of the calumny, but the tsar was so outraged that he ordered the unfortunate Nachtigal's arms and legs hacked off. Almost immediately after the excruciating punishment had been carried out, the

---

continents learn by rote without ever really grasping it. The crux of my discovery is that our great country lives by the *laws of Aristotelian mechanics,* and Newton's laws apply only to the decadent West.

emperor received incontrovertible proof that the denunciation was false. He went to the unfortunate exboatswain's apartment, collapsed to his knees before the human stump, and begged for forgiveness. What could Nachtigal do but forgive him? Peter awarded noble rank to the boatswain and all his farflung descendants, and that was the beginning of old Russia's aristocratic family of "nightingales," the Solovyovs.

About 1910, a certain Captain Solovyov, who had gambled away his estate at cards, was rummaging through the drawers of an old desk searching for a mortgage receipt. He stumbled across a packet of family papers and among them an ancient manuscript, which upon closer inspection turned out to be the equivalent of our savings-bank passbook. It was the long-forgotten Dutch deposit made by the unfortunate boatswain, the bankrupt captain's fully legitimate ancestor. Solovyov began making inquiries—in his lamentable situation, he couldn't afford to overlook 240 guldens. Astonishingly enough, the bank in which the boatswain had deposited the money was still doing business at the same premises.

The old boatswain's deposit was valid legally and subject to withdrawal on demand by his heir, but it proved impossible for the captain to get it. Complex percentages had been accumulating for two centuries, and the sum needed to pay off Solovyov was greater than the national income of Holland.* The Dutch bankers offered the Petersburg depositor compensation of some 15 million guldens. Before he could accept, the tsarist government, desperate for hard currency, intervened. The Russian Imperial Bank demanded the entire monstrous sum. Naturally, the Dutch refused to pay—would you expect them to be overjoyed at the prospect? There were rumors that the affair, which created an uproar in the press of the time, would be

---

*You have to take into account that eighteenth-century banks paid considerably higher percentages than they do today. Even at a base rate of 10 percent annually, in 210 years 10 billion (10^9) guldens would accrue.

turned over to the Hague Court. Only World War I saved the Amsterdam bank from inevitable failure.

The whirlwind of world war and the ensuing civil war swept over the land of boatswain Nachtigal's descendants. During Solovyov's numberless evacuations and moves, the priceless old paper, the bank deposit that had sparked a firestorm, was apparently lost. I'm not convinced, however: when the Russian Imperial Bank took over negotiations with Amsterdam, Solovyov might have given it the ancient passbook, which would have been lost when the revolution burst open the safes of tsarist institutions. One way or another the deposit vanished, and Captain Solovyov dragged out his existence in emigration.

Sitting in his armchair and drawing on a cigarette, Turok ended his story by saying, "The name of the old actress who lives in a special sort of almshouse is Solovyova. She's Captain Solovyov's only daughter. A rich heiress, isn't she?" I remained silent and despondent, but a thought stirred: What if the document were to appear again? Old papers end up in the damnedest places.

Five Billion Vodka Bottles to the Moon

ABOUT ten years ago, sometime in the early 1970s, I spent a pleasant afternoon in one of the small, cozy lounges in the writers' retreat at Maleevka chatting with the journalist Olga Chaikovskaya, whose specialty is crime and the judicial system. The late March sun flooded the room and cast a golden light. It was warm and cozy, and Chaikovskaya is a keen-minded woman of great charm. You can tell that she was once very pretty; like all former beauties, she is oblivious to the destructive work of time—that's the female nature. Buried in a newspaper in the far corner was the only other person in the lounge, Evgeny Bogat, a writer widely known for huge articles in *Literary Gazette* praising the high moral and ethical level of Soviet man. He was buried in a newspaper in the far corner.

"Olga Georgievna," I said, "you're a great authority on what is perhaps the bleakest sphere of Soviet life. I have a natural question for you: How many people are there in our prisons and camps serving time on criminal sentences?

She became embarrassed and even flustered. "To my shame, I've never given it a moment's thought."

I shrugged my shoulders in an eloquent way: women are amazing creatures, whose thought processes are quite different from ours. Details and trifles always excite their highly developed emotions, but they make no attempt to grasp a phenomenon as a whole. Instinctively sensing the trend of my thoughts, Chaikovskaya was clearly uncomfortable. "Of course, it's bad that I've spent my whole life studying the problem of crime and never even thought about the scope of it. I really don't know how many people are serving time. All I have to offer is my personal observation in Rostov, where I was head of the Izvestia bureau for some years. The city courts there sentence 10,000 people annually."

"Excellent!" I exclaimed. "I'm now going to demonstrate to you the power of scientific statistics. Back at the dawn of stellar astronomy, in the late eighteenth century, Sir William Herschel obtained the first reasonable picture of the population of the Galaxy by directing his telescope at representative regions of the Milky Way and counting the number of stars in the field of view. Over the centuries since, the use of statistics has developed tremendously in our sciences, and similar "sampling" methods are no less important in the humanities—for example, in the modern opinion poll. And so, 10,000 people are sentenced year in and year out in the Rostov courts? That's excellent—that is, it's lousy for the country, but excellent for our estimates. We will, quite arbitrarily, assume that the judges sentence defendants to an average of three years apiece."

"The average is five years," remarked Bogat from behind his newspaper. "The most widespread crime is malicious hooliganism, often due to alcohol and accompanied by serious bodily injury."

"Thanks for the information. And so, Olga Georgievna, we can assert that at any one time there are about 50,000 people in Soviet prisons and camps who were sentenced *only* by judges in

Rostov. Now we have to estimate the ratio of Rostov's contribution to the balance of the Soviet crime rate. The simplest way would be to fix it as equal to the ratio of the population of Rostov to that of the country overall, or 1:300. This estimate won't work—it gives us an implausibly large number of prisoners. Rostov is the classic city of bandits and the subject of famous thieves' songs, but nevertheless it undoubtedly yields in absolute numbers of criminals sentenced to the giant cities of Moscow and Leningrad. On the one hand, ascribing 10 percent of Soviet criminality to Rostov is too high, and, on the other, 1 percent is obviously too low. We can minimize error in the estimate by taking the logarithmic mean between these extremes, or 3 percent. This gives us the conclusion that at any one time approximately 1.5 million people are confined to the camps and prisons of the Soviet Union. I think that the probable error of this estimate is a few tens of percent, which isn't all that bad."

At that moment Bogat dropped his newspaper and said, "Where did you get that figure? It's a state secret!"

"One that isn't worth much. It's a pretty shallow secret, if such primitive means can dig it out."

Bogat's reaction gave me reason to assume that my estimate wasn't far off. A few years later I heard the same figure on the "voice of the enemy" from a former Soviet lawyer in emigration. Once again Herschel's old sampling method proved its validity.

Therefore, roughly 1.5 million people are serving sentences for crime. Today it might even be as many as 2 million—after all, crime is on the rise. Is that a lot or a few? It's a lot indeed! In West Germany, for example, there are 55,000 people in prison. When you consider that the population of the Federal Republic is one-fourth ours, you obtain a "proportional criminality" seven times less. In the United States the proportional criminality is somewhere in the middle (the logarithmic mean?) between the Soviet and German figures.*

*On May 24, 1984, *Izvestia* published an article by L. Koryavin, "Gunfire in Nighttime Washington," in which he writes: "One American in every 600 is in prison." From this it

The natural question arises of the number of political prisoners. And here we reach the surprising conclusion that, by comparison with criminals, there are strikingly few. Even Sakharov
never gave a figure of more than 3,000 people, and the majority
are the so-called religiousniks. The foreign "voices" and "liber-
ties" are always carrying on about the subject, but if you pay
close attention, the names they mention are always the same. I
can give some sense of the insignificance of 2,000–3,000 people
in an enormous country like ours by citing tiny Greece: not so
long ago that country had about 10,000 political prisoners in a
population of less than 10 million. In old Russia from 1907 to
1910 there were more than 100,000 political prisoners, not to
mention the millions of "enemies of the people" who served
time under Stalin. The current number of political prisoners in
our country is at a low point—at least, for the last hundred years
or so—and is convincing evidence that the overwhelming majority of our people are satisfied with the Soviet regime and only
grumble about "individual deficiencies" (primarily shortages).

I used statistical sampling several times after that to get
rough answers to other problems. For instance, five years ago I
asked myself a simple question: How much vodka do the Soviet
people drink annually? I don't have to demonstrate that alcoholism is a serious problem in our society. Everybody knows
there's a lot of drinking. But what does "a lot" mean? Alas, as on
so many other things, the official data on drinking are also a
"state secret." Somehow there have gotten to be a lot of state
secrets.

Just as in the previous case, there has to be some empirical
fact on which an estimate can be based and then generalized in a
rational way. For a start, let's try estimating the fraction of income the average Soviet family spends on drink. Clearly, it's
less than half or, let's say, one-third, but on the other hand daily

follows that 370,000 Americans are serving time. That would make the proportional
criminality 3.3 times lower than ours. According to Leo Tolstoy's article, "Nikolay the
Stick," 100 years ago there were 300,000 people serving time in Russian jails and penal
battalions.

observations show that the value is significantly higher than 1 or 2 percent. The sum of 20 or 30 rubles a year derived from that ridiculously low estimate wouldn't finance one good binge. Therefore, we can assume that the average Soviet family drinks something on the order of one month's wages annually. In some families, of course, that "item of expenditure" is considerably lower or even close to zero, but the badly off families who drink up to half their wages more than compensate for the sober ones. Finally, there are entire vast and at the same time prosperous regions (for instance, the North) where, as we well know, drunkenness reaches fabulous proportions. Therefore, my estimate of the expenditure on drink (a month's wages per year, or roughly 10 percent) is probably a rational one. This makes it all quite simple. The size of the annual wage fund for 1975 isn't a state secret: it was about 150 billion (150×10^9) rubles. From that figure it follows that our Soviet people drink about 15 billion rubles' worth of vodka and rotgut wine annually.*

As an astronomer, I have what you might call a professional sense for large numbers. In order for nonastronomical readers to grasp the magnitude of our alcohol budget, I'll give an example. Fifteen billion rubles in round numbers is 5 billion half-liter bottles. According to All-Union Standards, the standard half-liter is 8 centimeters in diameter. If you were to stand all those bottles in a line with each touching its neighbor, you would have an array $5 \times 10^9 \times 8 = 4 \times 10^{10}$ cm., or 400,000 km. long, which is exactly the distance from the Earth to the Moon. Of all

*This doesn't even touch the grave problem of moonshine, which is endemic to certain regions of our country. On the right bank of the Dnepr, for instance, hooch is widely distilled from sugar beets. With their irrepressible humor, the Ukrainians mark the bottles with indications of the quality of the contents, but where the French designate cognac in stars, "beets" are used in the Ukraine. "One beet" is a synonym for the lowest kind of turbid, raw poison. With further refining come "two beets, "three beets," and so forth. Finally, you get the highest quality hooch, "pure as baby's tears," which is called "five-beet" or "Maria Demchenko"—in honor of the famous "500ist." [The agronomist Maria Demchenko spearheaded a drive in the 1930s to increase the yield of sugar beets to 500 centners per hectare.]

our country's considerable achievements in space, that is surely among the most impressive.

Of course, I realize that my estimate of the scale of our drunkenness is crude and somewhat arbitrary. But what can we do when the Ministry of Trade and our liquor industry don't publish the data on fulfillment of its plan for the sale of vodka and other liquor? The Ministry of Finance might have some interesting things to say about the way in which the sale of vodka ensures almost normal functioning of the grass-roots financial organs, and they in turn ensure the population's wages.

I'm afraid my estimate is far from accurate—I say afraid because our alcoholism has reached threatening dimensions over the last decades. Everybody realizes it, but the press and other mass media feed our worried public on "individual facts" and general discussions which don't begin to suggest the scope of the calamity and the colossal increase of drunkenness in comparison with prerevolutionary times.* Eighty percent of the population of Russia before the revolution consisted of peasants, who, as a rule, confined their drinking to rare church holidays. On weekdays they had heavy work to do, and religion had a restraining influence as well. Artisans and factory workers drank heavily; the expression "drunk as a cobbler" was no accident. Statistical data reveal that workers drank four times more vodka per person than peasants. Since the revolution there has been a colossal process of urbanization which effectively liquidated the backwardness of the village; the entire country has pulled itself up to the level of prerevolutionary cobblers. It's all very sad, comrades, but we can't fight this national calamity without knowing its dimensions. The cover of state secrecy shrouding the problem of alcoholism obviously inhibits the important business, if not of eradicating drunkenness, at least of substantially reducing it.

---

*Not long ago I learned that 350 million rubles are spent annually on vodka in Latvia. This corresponds to 25 billion rubles for the whole country, which is not too far off the estimate adduced above.

The Question of Fyodor Kuzmich

"I HAVE a great favor to ask of you," said Lyudmila Romanovna, head of the therapeutic section of the Academy of Sciences Hospital, after she had finished a cursory examination of my person. "The hospital is overcrowded. Would you permit us to place a congenial doctor of science in your room temporarily?"

In early February 1968 I was recuperating from my first heart attack in the famous Academy of Sciences Hospital, familiarly called the "Akademichka." In that establishment rank was meticulously observed: as a corresponding member I was entitled to a semi-luxe private room, while "four-star generals"—full academicians, that is—languished and died in deluxe accommodations.

The crisis, when death was a serious possibility, had passed, and I had spent three weeks flat on my back, a position I don't wish on anyone. (They say this method is now obsolete, and a good thing, too.) I wasn't allowed up yet, but, thank God, my body was permitted any position in bed. I read a lot and received numerous visits from family and colleagues. Everyone showered me with love and pampered me. In short, I was doing fine.

Petty hospital happenings kept me amused. One funny episode sticks in my mind. A woman doctor I hadn't seen before
was making the Sunday rounds. I recall that she was dressed in
provocatively smart clothes for that vale of tears, but that was
hardly surprising. "She's probably the daughter or daughter-in-
law of some high priest in the Academy," I thought. Doctors,
male and female, with that sort of pull weren't rare in the facility.

I was feeling fairly chipper and took my own pulse. "Seventy-
three," I told the dear lady.

"That can't be," she observed didactically. "The pulse is always an *even* number."

I was too stunned by this remarkable revelation to burst out
laughing. It turned out that the ninny had reached that conclusion because she measured the number of beats for half or a
quarter of a minute and then multiplied by two or four.

I was used to life in the freedom of my private room, and I
wasn't enthusiastic about Lyudmila Romanovna's request. On
the other hand, you can't be an egotistical swine, so I consented
to take in a roommate.

The new tenant turned out to be an extremely interesting
man, the famous sculptor-anthropologist Mikhail Gerasimov.*
Unlike me, he was ambulatory and uncommonly active and vigorous for a man over sixty. For hours on end he told me stories
of his remarkable craft, which was on the frontier between science and art and completely unthinkable without both intuition
and a goodly dose of charlatanism. He suffered from the widespread "nobody-appreciates-me" complex. And indeed, my
brother, a sculptor by profession, emphatically asserted that
Gerasimov was not a sculptor at all, but at best a "modeler" (a
word sculptors find insulting). Since there are no anthropolo-

---

*[At age twenty, Gerasimov (1907–1970) began his career with an attempt to model
complete heads of Pithecanthropus and Neanderthal man from skulls in the Irkutsk
Museum. He spent his life refining the technique and created a wide range of sculpted
cranial reconstructions. Among the skulls he was given to work from were those of
Timur the Great (Tamerlane), Ivan the Terrible, and Fyodor Dostoevsky's mother.]

gists among my acquaintances, I don't know what people in that field think of Gerasimov's work, but I am almost certain that their opinion wouldn't be any more favorable. Gerasimov's fate was similar to that of many other talented people whose activities are in some way off the beaten path. Working "cross-field" is not always a happy lot in life, although it has its great successes.

After living with Gerasimov for almost two weeks, I ended up believing in his method. In particular, the historical personalities whom this remarkable man's unique talent and perspicacious intuition had resurrected from their remains looked exactly the way I imagined them. For instance, I find the face of an old Kazakh with prominent cheekbones—Great Prince Yaroslav the Wise as restored by Gerasimov—absolutely convincing.*

I was also impressed by Gerasimov's work in criminal investigation and contributions to the triumph of justice such as restoring the features of a murder victim from a skull that had lain buried in snow all winter. I couldn't tear myself away from his reconstructions of the frighteningly authentic physiognomies of Neanderthals and our other cave-dwelling ancestors.

After two weeks my unusual roommate had worn me out—I was still weak and our talks went on too long. Nevertheless one day I decided to take the initiative and said to him, "There's one problem, Mikhail Mikhailovich, that only you can solve: whether the Elder Fyodor Kuzmich, about whom Tolstoy wrote so superbly, was real or legend is not at all clear. The circumstances of Emperor Alexander I's death are shrouded in secrecy. Why did that healthy young man of forty-seven, who behaved so strangely during the last years of his reign, die unexpectedly in Godforsaken Taganrog? There may well be something fishy about it.† Who else but you can open the tsar's tomb in the

*[Yaroslav ruled the Kievan state from 1019 to 1054. His ancestry was undoubtedly a mixture of Norse "Varangian" and Slavic, but an admixture of Turkic can't be excluded.]
†[Alexander I's sudden death on December 1, 1825, gave rise to persistent rumors that he had faked his own demise and then reappeared in Siberia in the late 1830s as a

church of the Petropavlovsk Fortress, restore the face of the deceased from his skull, and compare it to the extremely rich iconography of Alexander I? That would settle the question once and for all!"

Gerasimov laughed in an uncommonly malicious way. "Oh, what a clever fellow! I've dreamed of that all my life. Three times I've appealed to the authorities for permission to open Alexander's tomb. The last time was only two years ago. They always turn me down, and they don't give any reason. It's as if I'd run into a brick wall!"

Gerasimov's answer intrigued me. My brain, well honed on the formulation of hypotheses about the nature of cosmic objects, went through one wild conjecture after another about the reason for the governmental organs' negative reply to the famous scientist's request. Could the odd position taken by the authorities be confirmation of the truth of the legend about Fyodor Kuzmich? After all, they showed no scruples about opening Tamerlane's tomb the day before the start of World War II, even though the action considerably complicated the mobilization of troops in Soviet Central Asia. Perhaps they saw in Alexander's renunciation a hint at the obscenity of clinging with all their might to worldly power.

A month and a half later I was released from the hospital. A new life began, new concerns arose, and the memory of both Gerasimov and the problem of Fyodor Kuzmich gradually faded. Not long afterward I heard that Gerasimov, so vigorous and bubbling with plans, was dead.

Ten more years went by. As usual I spent the end of February and early March at Maleevka. The days passed in pleasant monotony: breakfast, skiing, dinner, a nap, and a movie—most often a lousy one. In the evening I strolled around the circle outside the building in the company of familiar, half-familiar, and

wandering monk calling himself Fyodor Kuzmich. Leo Tolstoy left an unfinished story based on the legend, "Posthumous Notes of the Elder Fyodor Kuzmich" (1905).]

unfamiliar people. Now and then I took a turn with a man I had just met, a sturdy old fellow called Stepan Vladimirovich whose childlike eyes sparkled blue under thick gray brows. An ex-sailor, he was a veteran of the civil war and afterward a Red professor who had recently retired from teaching political economy. He knew Russian literature amazingly well, and in general I found him entertaining company.

As we were making the usual round one frosty evening, Stepan Vladimirovich suddenly asked me, "And what would you say, Iosif Samuilovich, if I were to tell you that I once saw Count Orlov-Chesmensky in court dress just as clearly as I see you?" (We were passing under a lamp.)

I made a lazy calculation: Count Aleksey Orlov was the brother of Catherine the Great's favorite. She died in 1796. He was probably younger than the empress, but even so he must have been dead by 1810. "I would say you were mistaken," I replied politely.

Stepan Vladimirovich laughed and went on to tell me an amazing story. We all know about Lenin's celebrated decree during the 1921 famine calling for the confiscation of church valuables. The decree also included a considerably less famous secret article directing that the graves of imperial aristocrats and patricians be opened and valuables removed to aid the starving. As a young sailor in the Baltic fleet, my companion took part in one such "grave-robbing" detachment to unseal the family crypt on the Orlov ancestral estate in the Pskov region. When the coffin was opened, Count Orlov-Chesmensky himself, totally untouched by decay and arrayed in court costume, appeared before the eyes of the astounded crew employed in that sacrilegious business. No particular treasures were found, and the count was thrown into a ditch. "By evening he rapidly started turning black," Stepan Vladimirovich recalled.

I had stopped listening to him. "So that's it!" I thought. "That's why they wouldn't let Gerasimov open the imperial coffin in the church of the Petropavlovsk Fortress! It's simply that there's nothing left—it's just like the vault of Count Orlov!"

By association, my mind jumped to my visit to the Parisian Abbey of St. Denis, where the rulers of France from the Carolingians to the Bourbons are buried. The noses of the marble kings and queens have been broken off all the memorial sculptures, traces of the "work" of the sans-culottes who broke into the abbey in August 1792.

I spent a long time walking among the mutilated marble rulers of France. When I came out of the gloom of the abbey into the bright sunlight, the first thing I saw was a sign bearing the name of one of the streets leading into the square: "Rue Vladimir Illitch."* The ancient Parisian suburb of St. Denis has long been a part of the so-called Red Belt of Paris.

*[Lenin.]

Paris Is Worth
a Dinner

THE happiest period of my life may well have been the years from 1966 to 1968. On my fiftieth birthday, July 1, 1966, I was elected to the Academy of Sciences—on the fifth try. After eighteen years I was at last permitted to travel abroad to meet my peers at international conferences. In 1967 alone I was in America in January and February, in Paris in May for my first trip to the greatest city in the world, and in Prague in August for the International Astronomical Union meeting. After a long period of suspended animation, it seemed that life was unrolling its red carpet before me.

Suddenly in the home stretch of that most felicitous year I ended up in the Academy hospital with my first heart attack, thanks to my old schoolmate and colleague Vitaly Ginzburg.* But the lucky streak trailed behind me and I was in good spirits and—I'm not afraid to say

---

*[For an account of the scientific quarrel that kept Ginzburg and Shklovsky on frigid terms for the rest of Shklovsky's life, see Ginzburg's article, "Notes of an Amateur Astrophysicist," *Annual Review of Astronomy and Astrophysics* 28 (1990).]

it—cheerful. Weak and helpless as I was, I felt keenly that good people loved me. Many friends visited me, perhaps too many, especially when I was on the mend and learning to walk all over again. A number of them unexpectedly turned out to have had heart attacks too, and they all competed to give me advice and recommendations about my post-infarct existence. Alas, their advice was distinguished for monotony and began with the word *Don't.* This plethora of prohibitions drove me to despair that my life was over. Happily I was wrong.

One day my friend the mathematician Sergey Fomin came to see me. Sergey was a year my junior and had already suffered two heart attacks; he died from the third not long afterward. Looking strong and vigorous, he began to trade experiences with me, droning away like all my previous visitors. Sergey, however, was clever enough to notice that I was getting depressed and abruptly cut short his tiresome litany by saying, "And, on the whole, you can live. While we're on the subject, I have a story for you about the career of a public figure I had a chance to observe when I was working in the KGB system. This character had one simple stratagem that advanced him from major to major-general in an unprecedentedly short time. At every meeting and every session this hidebound functionary would utter only one of two phrases: 'There's no need to complicate!' or 'There's no need to simplify!' Those two sentences gained him a solid reputation as a reliable, positive person and a profound thinker and led to his phenomenal rise. So," concluded Sergey, "that's what I have to say to you. On the one hand, there's no need to complicate, and on the other, there's no need to simplify." Those words of wisdom became fixed in my mind, and I still try to live by them.

In late March 1968 I was discharged from the hospital, and in early summer a stranger called me from the Soviet UNESCO Committee. "In August there's a roundtable conference at headquarters in Paris on the topic of 'Cultural Diversity in the Face of Common Technological Progress.' Professor Polikarpov, the organizer of the conference, would like you to referee some of the participants' papers."

"Send the papers, I'll look at them," I said.

A few days later I received a thick package with typescripts which had obviously been soaked in muddy water and were mostly in French, a language I don't know. The sight of them gave me a happy thought: "Why shouldn't I go to the crazy thing myself? I haven't been to Paris for a long time now." (It had been a year.) I dialed the Soviet UNESCO Committee and said offhandedly to the now familiar functionary, "I received the conference materials. Alas, the topic of space is not discussed anywhere."

"That's bad, oh, that's bad! What should we do?"

"I might be willing to give a paper myself."

"Okay, I'll arrange it right away."

The conference was less than two months off, and I expressed doubt that he could manage an exit visa for me in that short time.

"This isn't your Academy of Sciences, you know! Have you been to capitalist countries before?" inquired the UNESCO functionary. "You have. Then there's no problem; don't worry."

And having faith in my lucky star, I really, quite cheekily, didn't worry.

The Moscow summer passed. I didn't bother to read the materials which the unknown Polikarpov had sent me. For my paper I planned to read the manuscript of an article in press for *Problems of Philosophy*; I didn't make any changes or bother to get it translated. My total ignorance of French and my too modest knowledge of English were a worry, of course. "No problem, I'll muddle through," I thought.

One day at my brother's dacha, I caught a glimpse of the tall figure of the neighbor's daughter crossing our plot. "That's Lena," I thought. "She teaches French somewhere." An idea flashed through my mind: "Lena, what would 'There's no need to complicate' be in French?"

"Il ne faut pas compliquer," she answered in surprise.

"And 'There's no need to simplify'?"

"Il ne faut pas simplifier. Why do you want to know?"

"I need it," I answered, without bothering to elaborate, and copied down in Russian letters the French version of the phrases that had guaranteed the KGB general's meteoric career.

The day of my departure came, and there was the same trite foul-up as in our own dear Academy of Sciences. No travel authorization. For three days like an idiot I sat by the telephone with my neck washed and my bags packed. The UNESCO functionary was surprised at the silence from the directive organs and said he couldn't remember another instance like it.* By evening of the third day of my stupid vigil, I lost hope and called my functionary for the nth time.

"Unfortunately, there's no word. Forgive us. I have to leave here in half an hour to meet my wife, and tomorrow there'll no longer be any point in waiting."

No Paris for you, you imbecile! You were asking too much.

Ten minutes later the phone rang, and my functionary said calmly, "The authorization just arrived. The plane for Paris leaves tomorrow at 8 A.M. You should grab a taxi right away and pick up your ticket from the Aeroflot office in the Hotel Metropol. It closes in forty minutes. You'll be lucky to make it. The policeman on duty at the UNESCO building will have your foreign passport. Everybody will be gone, working hours are over."

I managed to yell into the phone, "What about money? Money—francs?"

"Alas, I couldn't manage to get the authorization signed. You'll get hard currency at UNESCO in Paris. I'll phone them this evening."

I dashed headlong out of the apartment. I was lucky—a free

---

*Afterward I realized that the government had other problems to worry about: it was early August 1968, and events were breaking in Czechoslovakia.

taxi stood right by the building. I had some difficulty locating the ticket office in the lobby of the Metropol, since it looked just like one of the bins where they sell the meager output of the Soviet press. The cashier was about to close. I found it absurd saying to her, "I want a ticket to Paris." She didn't seem surprised but, to preserve the conventions, she grumbled a bit. So there I was with the ticket in my pocket. I almost never get into the center of Moscow, and that summer evening seemed particularly beautiful. In no hurry, full of the joy of life, I walked over to Kalinin Avenue, where the Soviet Committee for UNESCO, one of many Moscow establishments of the harmless "don't kick a man when he's down" variety, has a small building opposite the Military Procurement Offices. I found it odd to ask the policeman on duty for my foreign passport. With no sign of surprise he handed me the desired document, and in exchange I poked my internal passport at him.

He wouldn't take it: "I have no instructions about that."*

I walked away from that pleasant building with two passports, and the next morning there I was at Le Bourget Airport. The joy that invariably sweeps over the normal Soviet citizen who is temporarily escaping his free country was overcast by the obscurity of my immediate future and the total absence from my pockets of even the smallest French coin.

I still can't understand how the man picked me out in the crowd of arriving passengers, but he came over to me and said with conviction, "You'll be Comrade Shklovsky." My benefactor, the chauffeur to the Soviet delegation, delivered me to UNESCO headquarters. In the Soviet offices—two small rooms in the two-story wing (every power has an equally wretched space)—I was met by Comrade Kolbasov, the permanent representative of the Belorussian Republic. I asked him to find me a room in a cheap hotel and arrange for me to be paid. I had never

---

*[Soviet citizens turn in their domestic identification papers in exchange for the temporary foreign passport.]

seen a room like the one they reserved for me in a suitable hotel nearby: a trapezoid eight meters across, 60 percent of it occupied by a monumental bed. The "facilities," of course, were down the hall.

I washed up, left my skinny suitcase in the room, and went back to the gigantic UNESCO building. It was not easy for a newcomer to penetrate its labyrinths and find the premises where the roundtable conference was already in its fourth day. I literally clutched the secretary to the Bulgarian delegation in a death grip and forced her to lead me to it. Not daring to enter, I asked her to call out Dr. Polikarpov, who turned out to be a gracious, round man who spoke excellent Russian, a graduate of the Moscow University philosophy department, and, beyond my most optimistic expectations, a Bulgarian Jew. Polikarpov greeted me heartily and took me into the conference room. There I got a shock. I had expected it to be the usual conference with hundreds of motley participants among whom I could easily get lost. To my horror, I stepped into a small room containing an actual large round table with only eight people sitting at it. There was no hiding place; everybody was in full view. An armchair with my name printed on the back stood empty waiting for me. I sat down and started making feverish plans for escaping with minimal damage from that idiotic situation. A huge black man sitting in the chairman's place had the floor. "Nigeria" was written on the back of his chair.

I heard the Nigerian mentioning my name more and more frequently, obviously inviting me to address the assembly.

Of course, there was no question of my making a speech. What was I to do? My roving eye lit on a small Japanese who looked to me as if he had been effaced by the professional windbags gathered around the table: "This year marks the hundredth anniversary of the Meiji revolution. It would be interesting if our colleague could cast light on the question of the interactions of traditional Japanese culture and the rapid technological development his country has undergone during that period."

The Japanese started to twitter happily—it was clear that the dear man had been bursting to speak—and I gained a respite.

I used it to open contact with my neighbor, an American. I said to him that the representative from the Federal Republic of Germany looked a little odd to me.

"And how," whispered the American. "He's a Jew. By the way, I'm Jewish, too, just like you." Further analysis led us to the conclusion that the Belgian representative was also a Jew. It was just like the good old days in Kiev or Lokhvitsa before the war.*

An hour passed in easy chat, and then it was time for lunch. I borrowed 25 francs from Polikarpov, who told me the UNESCO cashier would pay me the next day. For reasons that will become clear below, I was never again to eat as well in Paris as I did in the UNESCO lunchroom.

The next morning UNESCO settled accounts with me and gave me money . . . only for the day and a half I was actually at the conference. There it was, the dog-eat-dog law of capitalism. You came late—go fly a kite! At home, of course, we would have paid in full. But we have to be grateful for small favors.

I sat through another day of torment. I remember those professional windbags, for whom I had already developed a fierce hatred, avidly discussing the vital question of the need to set up a central book depository in Tanzania. Suddenly they flung themselves in chorus on the majestically silent representative of the Soviet superpower: What was the aforesaid power's opinion? The situation had reached a critical (or rather Ostap-Benderish) point, and I was forced to lead with my ace of trumps.

*Once in Erevan in the mid-1960s I happened by chance on a lecture that the American Nobel-winning physicist Murray Gell-Mann gave to a scientific gathering. The first rows of the auditorium were occupied by theoreticians from Moscow (for some reason, mostly Jewish) who tried as hard as they could to trap Gell-Mann with tricky questions. The American defended himself with wit and spirit and won the sympathies of the large audience of Armenians, who observed the scientific fray in silence. Afterward in the lobby, against the background of a steady rumble of incomprehensible Armenian, I suddenly heard one Armenian graduate student saying seriously to another in Russian, "You've got to admit that our yids are real lightweights compared to theirs."

Putting on the gloomy expression he's so good at, the Soviet representative said through pursed lips, "Il ne faut pas simplifier." My God, the effect that had! They began jabbering away in three languages, interrupting each other, while I held my majestically gloomy pose. The salvo got me through until lunch, which the other delegates devoted to staring at me in polite admiration. At last I understood the KGB general's spectacular rise.

One way or another I got through that difficult day, which ended up in full decorum. The problems of the diversification of cultures in the face of common technological progress received a powerful stimulus for further discussion. I was faced with a problem that was not as grandiose, but much more specific: What was I going to do next? I had a visa good for fourteen days, and there were still twelve left. Twelve days on my own in Paris, the rosy dream of many millions of people the world over! When I calculated my finances, my rapture faded. After paying for my hotel and putting 50 francs aside for a rainy day, I would have 7 francs a day left to live on. The cheapest meal in a cafeteria cost 11 francs, and a one-way metro fare, 1 franc. The season played an important role: in August the French are all away on vacation, and I couldn't count on the hospitality of my astronomer colleagues. I certainly couldn't expect any help from our famous embassy on rue Grenelle; they would simply ship me back to Moscow since, in the minds of our diplomatic scum, I had no business staying on in Paris at all.

It will be clear to everybody that there was only one decision I could take: to stay and fast for the remaining days. What the hell, I wouldn't die of hunger, and I would never again have a chance like that. I'll never forget those twelve days. At first I decided to economize on the metro—a round trip cost 2 francs—but by the second day I realized I couldn't do it, since the necessity of returning to my hotel each night would have confined me to practically one and the same route on foot around Paris.

After the metro fare, I had 5 francs a day. I allocated them as follows: every day I bought a kilo of really good apples for 2.5 francs from a Normandy peasant women at a tiny market near the hotel. I spent the other 2.5 francs on a delicious hot frankfurter smeared with mustard and stuck in a fresh roll, which I bought from an old woman who had a stand at the intersection of two famous Parisian boulevards—Saint Michel and Saint Germain. I chose the old woman's stand because, no matter what route I threaded through Paris, I found it easy to turn up at that intersection promptly at six in the evening, hungry to the point of cramps. She soon came to know me and would shout from a distance, "Monsieur Joseph!"

Later, on the trip back to Moscow, I calculated that I had walked over 300 kilometers down hundreds of different avenues and rues, a distance I haven't matched on all my trips to Leningrad. I can boldly state that I have walked farther in Paris than any other city in the world except Moscow. I was still recovering from my heart attack that winter and learning to walk again. My legs hurt badly. I kept wanting to sit down, but in Paris finding a place to rest is far from simple. You might expect to be able to sit in a sidewalk café in the fresh air long enough to catch your breath and stretch your aching legs. Even in quarters comparatively far from the center of the city, like the districts around our Garden Ring in Moscow, there are cafés every 50 meters or so, and in midafternoon they're usually deserted. I would choose the most remote table and begin the melancholy game of timing. Less than 20 seconds later a silent garçon would loom up (where on earth did he come from?) with his pad and pencil and set a glass of cold water down on the table. What does monsieur wish? Monsieur would be remembering those wretched Moscow restaurants and drinking establishments where—oh, joy!—he would wait for his native, frowzy, somewhat dirty waitress for at least half an hour. Dunce that I am, I had often seethed at the delay. How glorious it would be now to wait 10 minutes for that fellow already staring down impassively. Monsieur is counting every franc and can't permit himself even a small cup of coffee. Overcoming the pain in his legs, he gets up and trudges on. There's nobody to register a complaint with—that's capitalism for you!

When the endless walking wore me out, I would go under one of the famous Paris bridges, right to the edge of the dirty Seine, lie down, and stretch my legs out blissfully on the stones of the embankment. Genially cheerful, harmless *clochards,* Parisian vagrants, were usually clustered nearby. Under the Seine bridges all the *clochards* eat from baskets packed with food and wine. They didn't mean to disturb me with the smell of their meals, but I was much poorer than they and couldn't permit myself luxuries like wine and sandwiches. Parisians went about their business, and tourists loitered; the usual August population of Paris had no time to waste on me. That was both good and bad. Sometimes I felt painfully lonely and desolate, but more often I just lay there without thinking and looked at the high, cloudless sky. The weather was ideal for the entire twelve days.

Chance meetings satisfied my need for human contact. One day I decided to sit for a while in the Luxembourg Garden. I was attracted to the little metal chairs with curved legs scattered through the green grassy areas. It was more pleasant sitting by yourself than sharing a municipal bench. In my stupidity I didn't realize that you had to pay a franc for the pleasure of solitude. The old woman who collected the tribute covered the entire garden and was nowhere in sight—and that fooled me into thinking the chairs were free. I had no sooner sat down and gone blissfully limp when I heard someone behind me speaking impeccably correct, somewhat archaic Russian. Three old women, two of them really ancient, were walking by. Without turning, I remarked calmly, "How nice to meet fellow Russians in Paris!"

They courteously agreed with me that it was, indeed, nice.

In ignorance of the tribute collector, I gallantly asked them to take chairs next to me. Luckily the old Parisiennes said that they preferred to stand. If they had accepted I'd have been in a fine mess.

"Where are you from?" the oldest asked.

"Moscow."

"A long time ago?"

"It's been a week already."

They looked at me in an incredulous way. I realized in surprise that these women had taken me for an emigré, most likely from the so-called second wave after the war. "No, no, I'm a real Soviet. I came here from Moscow on business a week ago."

They didn't believe me. One of them began testing me. "And where is Paustovsky buried?" (The popular Soviet writer Konstantin Paustovsky had died recently, and ladies of that age naturally take funerary matters to heart.)

"At Novodevichy, I think," I replied uncertainly.

"Wrong. He's buried at Tarusa."

I was exposed as an impostor and, hoping to escape from that idiotic position, rummaged feverishly through my pockets until I found two crumpled tickets for the suburban Moscow electric train. This rehabilitated me.

"And where are you from?"

"We're from Tiflis!" my old ladies said with dignity.

"From Tbilisi, that is?"

"Please, just don't use that awful word. We're from *Tiflis.*"*

"In two weeks I'll be in your Tiflis!" It was the truth: I had a conference coming up in sunny Georgia.

"We have a great favor to ask of you: go to our old house and take a close look at it. We'll give you the address."

Touched by that rare form of nostalgia I promised, and a couple of weeks later I kept my word.

Another Parisian meeting with Russian emigrés has stuck in my memory. An old man joined me one day as I sat on a bench opposite the Ecole Militaire. It didn't take him long to recognize that I was Soviet, nor I to find out that he was a Russian emigré fallen on hard times. I told him that I wanted very much to

*[The prerevolutionary name of the capital of Georgia.]

visit the Russian cemetery at Sainte Geneviève near Paris.

The old man shed a few tears. "I've never heard a Soviet say that. Usually they are drawn to Père Lachaise.* The metro doesn't run out as far as Saint Geneviève; you have to drive. I don't have a car, but I have a friend, also Russian, with an old Peugeot. Meet me here tomorrow at eight."

So there I was, accompanied by emigrés, wandering around the small, clean cemetery which, notwithstanding the onion domes of the small church, didn't look at all Russian. My God, they were all there: the White Guards were buried in formation, and apart from them lay Kornilovites, Markovites, Drozdovites—a roll call of antirevolutionary factions. Only Denikin was missing; he's buried in Nice. Here was the grave of the ballerina Kshesinskaia, Nikolai II's mistress; not far off were Lvov, Guchkov, and other members of the Provisional Government.† Farther off lay the writers Dmitri Merezhkovsky and Zinaida Gippius and the touchingly simple grave of the Bunins.

And here was Zinovy Sverdlov, a man with a fantastic fate. In the early 1900s Maxim Gorky adopted the young Zinovy (it was the only way a Jew could live in Moscow), and thereafter he was always known by Gorky's real name, Peshkov. He went to Capri as Gorky's secretary, and they were trapped there by the war. Suddenly young Peshkov was seized by zeal for the cause; he quarreled with his adoptive father, joined the famous French Foreign Legion, saw action, and was gravely wounded, ending up minus an arm and with the rank of major. In return for shedding his blood for France, Pechkov (the French spelling he used) was granted French citizenship and had a dizzying career in the French army. A close friend of de Gaulle, he reached star rank and in World War II became one of the organizers of the Resist-

*[Père Lachaise is the cemetery in Paris famous for the world celebrities from Chopin to Oscar Wilde buried there; Saint Genevieve, south of Paris, is the pantheon of the postrevolutionary generation of Russian emigrés.]

†[The shifting factions which held power between the February and October revolutions in 1917.]

ance. Pechkov died in his bed in 1970. I stood by the gravestone of the old legionnaire and thought about the diverse fates of Zinovy and his younger brother, the equally famous Bolshevik Yakov Sverdlov, the first president of Soviet Russia, who died of typhus in 1919.

It goes without saying that penury precluded my indulging in typically Parisian diversions, but fate took an unexpected hand even in that apparently unambiguous situation. One evening I combed the area around boulevard Clichy famous for its cheap dens of vice. While I was observing the quarter's singular public, a sharp hunger pang told me that it was time to visit my old frankfurter seller at her stand on the opposite, left bank of the Seine. And then I had a simple thought: "Why the devil should I, hungry as I am, go that far? In Paris you can grab a bite to eat anywhere. The world doesn't revolve around that one congenial old woman!"

As events were to prove, it was undoubtedly the devil himself prompting me. I began studying the foodstands lined up at every step. Knowing I must avoid a mistake, I quite reasonably decided on the stand surrounded by the largest number of local people of modest means—a compact group of Algerians, negroes, and dark-haired men of indeterminate nationality. I was struck by the automaton-like rapidity of the work of the seller of hot cutlets in a roll. The cutlets cost the 2.5 francs I had to spend and so, hungry and under the spell of his precision, I pushed my way up to the stand and gave him a 5-franc note. I received my sandwich with lightning speed, and the seller immediately turned to serve one of the blacks. It took me a minute to realize that the brute had audaciously short-changed me. A lump rose in my throat, and the cutlet lost its first delicious taste. I stood there for a while, looking at the impudent fellow with sad Jewish eyes, but he didn't react. Thank God I didn't start clarifying relations with him the way a normal Soviet man would have done—I had enough sense to realize that a sound thrashing was the least I could expect. The police would report the affair to the

Soviet embassy, and they in turn would make haste to ship my precious person back to Moscow.

As I walked away from that dangerous spot, my glance fell on a fiery sign, "Permanent Striptease." I went over to the door and read, "2 1/2 francs"—the beggarly sum of which the sandwich seller had just robbed me. In my foul mood and with no pause for reflection, I approached the ticket booth in the dark lobby, cautiously inquired the price from a respectable-looking lady cashier, gave her exact change for a ticket, and entered the semi-dark, foul-smelling (garlic?) auditorium. The show was just starting. All the aisle seats were taken. I walked down the steep stairs of the amphitheater and took an empty armchair in the front row, very close to the sumptuous blonde disrobing up on the stage to the accompaniment of a nervous, ragged tune. I couldn't help noticing the large drops of sweat all over her broad rosy back, and that killed the effect the spectacle was meant to produce. I was left only with an impression of hard work in stuffy, stinking premises. Imagine what it was like for her, poor kid, slaving away for six-hour stints.

A uniformed boy came up to me and, insofar as I understood him, asked: "And what will monsieur drink?"

Monsieur answered to the effect that he had no intention of drinking anything. Only then did I grasp the simple working mechanism of the establishment: 2.5 francs was the entrance price, but after that you were supposed to drink something alcoholic at an enormous mark-up. Just as the sweaty blonde was reaching the culmination of her act, a wildly hairy, robust thug bent over me and asked earnestly, "But all the same, what will monsieur drink?"

I whispered, "Beer!"

"No beer," came a reply that Muscovites will find all too familiar.

"Then I won't have anything. My health doesn't permit it."

"In that case, monsieur will be good enough to quit the premises!"

I raised my eyes to the stage—just in time! With dignity, but without lingering, I left.

Out among the bright lights of the boulevard, a hot wave of joy poured over me. That was more like it! The scoundrel at the foodstand had stolen 2.5 francs from me and, with a stroke of genius, I had just cheated the owner of that den of iniquity out of at least 10. My light, happy mood was slow to fade as I floated along, barely touching the sidewalk.

For the rest of my time in Paris I bought my daily frankfurter from my dear old woman. Last year I went back for the first time in thirteen years. She, of course, was long gone, but that painfully familiar intersection of Boulmich and boulevard St. Germain was just the same. As I approached the memorable spot from the direction of Notre Dame, I started salivating just like one of Pavlov's dogs.

Rabbi Loewe and Lyosha Gvamichava

THERE was a large Soviet delegation—about a hundred people, including tourists*—at the Congress of the International Astronautical Federation (IAF) held in Prague in late September 1977. We were put up at the big International Hotel on the remote outskirts of the city. While we were waiting to register, I was pounced on by a group of space scientists led by Boris Petrov, head of our delegation and chairman of Intercosmos (who was finished off last year by the medical establishment of our Kremlin hospital, which has a sad reputation for that sort of thing). They were aflame with righteous wrath over my article, "Twenty Years of the Space Age," which had just appeared in the Soviet science magazine *Nature.* In the essay I defended the somewhat paradoxical thesis that the greatest achievement of the age was that no new principles had come from space

*[At international meetings only a small number of official Soviet delegates had their way paid; the majority had to buy a tourist excursion at their own expense.]

research. This fact, I maintained, brilliantly confirmed the *correctness* of the conception of the universe laboriously constructed by several generations of astronomers. Of course, I could understand the wrath of our leading figures in the space program, but they managed to ruin my mood anyway.

Seeking diversion, I proposed to a small group from our delegation who were in Prague for the first time that, since we were free until the congress opened the next day, we should take a ride into the center of that handsome, but now badly rundown city. After a long wait at the end of the line opposite our hotel, we caught the tramway, the only transport which came out that far.

I had been to Prague twice previously—in 1965 and in 1967. The first visit was an especially memorable one, because after an eighteen-year hiatus I "attained the first cosmic velocity."* Between 1947, when I went abroad for the first time in my life (to Brazil!), and 1965, I had applied dozens of times for permission to go to scientific conferences and congresses. During those years I had done more than a little internationally recognized work, and therefore I was always invited under the most advantageous conditions, but I was always refused. It was evident that somewhere in the secret chancelleries of the Ministry of Love there was a hitch in my dossier—I can't for the life of me figure out what—that made my pitiful but persistent attempts to take part in international scientific life totally unavailing. Lord, what can be compared to the humiliating position of a person who has filled out those exit applications so offensive to human dignity dozens of times and always in vain? With difficulty I would overcome my natural feeling of nausea and revulsion and stubbornly write that abomination over and over again—and every time without result. There's a limit to everything, and by 1965 I was ready to give up the odd conceit of wanting to associ-

*The expression is Zeldovich's. The second cosmic velocity is communicated to a body (human) on a trip to a capitalist country.

ate with colleagues abroad. Then one day a man I barely knew began talking to me in the university dining hall and asked me politely what I was working on. Since I had just finished writing an application, I muttered gloomily, "My hobby keeps me busy—hopelessly filling out the usual travel forms."

"Come and see me tomorrow—I work in the foreign section of the university." I went, and three days later I was on the train to Prague. My benefactor attached me to an ongoing exchange, called somebody—and that was it. Czech colleagues had repeatedly invited me to give lectures at Ondřejov Observatory, and at last I had the chance to do so.

Thanks in part to my election to the Academy of Sciences in 1966, I went abroad often over the next six years. But that first trip to Prague in 1965 will always stand out in my memory as one of the most exciting adventures in a life which has not been that rich in joys.

The train made an unexpected four-hour stopover in Warsaw. All the passengers poured out of the cars, and I went, too. What was there to interest me in the Polish capital? I didn't have a single złoty in my pocket, but there was one spot I had an obligation to see. I had no idea how I was going to find it, until a miracle occurred. The train had stopped at Gdansk station, close to the center of Warsaw. I crossed under a viaduct and in the vista at the end of the street saw a ridiculously large building which I immediately identified as the creation of Comrade Rudnev.* "That means this is Marszalkowska Avenue," I thought. I didn't ask any of the Poles scurrying back and forth for information. I simply couldn't—it was as if I had lost the power of speech. Without any idea where the goal of my excursion might lie, I walked in silence down the right side of the avenue.

No more than five minutes later I suddenly saw a sign on a

---

*[After the war the Soviets built a huge "Palace of Culture and Science" in Stalin wedding-cake style in the center of Warsaw; Poles sometimes refer to it as the "House of Genghis Khan." Lev Rudnev was the architect.]

narrow side street that bore the name of Mordechai Anielew-icz—which to my shame I didn't know. But the first name left no room for doubt that I was on the right track.* I took the sharp turn into the street and soon came out into a small square. In the middle of it stood a dark structure which from a distance looked like a cube. Amazingly, I had gone straight to my goal. As I came closer, I saw that all four sides of the marble cube bore sculptural reliefs depicting fellow Jews who had been destroyed on that spot. It had an inscription in two languages. I could make out the Polish: "From the Jewish people—to its heroes and martyrs." The inscription evidently sounded more dramatic in Hebrew, but alas! I couldn't read it. I liked the Polish inscription, however; it went to the heart of the matter with maximum terseness.

I sat down on a stone bench and remained there for three and a half hours. Where else was there for me to go in this foreign city which had suffered such a terrible fate? I was struck by the absence of people in the square. Every once in a while a flock of kids came running into it to play a game something like hopscotch, but the bustling life of Warsaw went on outside the spot where twenty-two years earlier the ruins of the ghetto had been cleared away. The square used to be called Nalewki; I've never figured out what the word means. Fifteen minutes before my train's scheduled departure, I finally left the cube and the deserted square where there wasn't even a whiff left of the smoke from the uprising in the Warsaw ghetto, terrible in its futility, that broke out at Passover in 1943. During those four hours, and for some hours afterward, I never uttered a single word.

In that spring of 1965 Prague was enchanting. I wandered around the city for a long time, soaking up its ineffable aura of antiquity. I was totally unprepared for the old Jewish monuments in the heart of the Czech capital, five minutes' walk from Old Town Square. In the Jewish cemetery, gravestones from

---

*[Mordechai Anielewicz was a leader of the uprising of the Warsaw ghetto against the Nazis on April 19, 1943; against all odds the besieged community managed to hold out for three weeks.]

the fourteenth to the sixteenth centuries stand in incredibly crowded conditions, totally without orientation—the ancient stones stick up every which way, and it looks as if the dead people lying there are arguing bluntly and fanatically about something important. You can see that they didn't get the argument settled during their lifetime. . . . I go back to the cemetery every time I come to Prague. I don't know why, but I find it symbolic of my people and their grim fate.

Near the cemetery is a Jewish museum, in which extremely rare artifacts of the old synagogues—not just Czech ones, from all over Europe—have been collected. I couldn't imagine why the Germans hadn't destroyed all those things, when they had been so ruthless in destroying everything else related to the Jews, starting with the people themselves. Synagogues in Kiev and Minsk and throughout occupied Europe were razed. Jewish cemeteries were dug over. But here, in the center of Europe, if you can imagine it, those artifacts have been preserved! The answer was at once simple and terrible. The minutes of the notorious secret Wannsee conference in early 1942 laid out with German scrupulosity all the technical details of the "final solution *(Endlosung)*" of the Jewish question—the layout of the extermination camps, production of the gas Zyklon-B, training of cadres of executioners, transport problems connected with deportation, and much, much more. It also included a paragraph directing the establishment, after the *Endlosung,* of a Jewish Museum in Prague, where the treasures of the Jewish people would be assembled from all over Europe, so that future generations of ethnographers would remember with gratitude the German high command's foresight. A special department run by Alfred Rosenberg painstakingly looted Jewish synagogues. You can't deny that the Germans are a cultured nation.

Stunned by learning why the Jewish antiquities in Prague had been preserved and feeling a bit like a museum artifact myself, I spent a long time looking at gold menorahs and gold-embroidered altar covers. The only other person there was an elderly, withered German woman who gave me appropriate explanations. I asked her about the origin of the word *golem* used for the gigantic robot which, as legend has it, the great sage Rabbi Loewe manufactured in the sixteenth century. The German woman started muttering something to the effect that there were several versions of the word's origin, but nobody really knew. And at that moment I realized where the enigmatic word must have come from. A picture from far-off childhood swam up from the depths of my memory. Whenever I committed some minor mischief out of clumsiness—breaking a cup, for instance—Mama used to clasp her hands in vexation and call me a *leimener geilom. Geilom*—that's it exactly! *Geilom* is the mysterious *Golem.* In old Yiddish the word meant *idol. Leimener golem,* literally "clay idol," was often used in Jewish families as a caustic definition of bunglers and clumsy people who wrecked and broke things. The medieval Jews saw Rabbi Loewe's creation as an idol. I didn't share my philological research with the German woman.

Those were the thoughts running through my mind as the tramway carried me and my companions across Prague twelve years later. "Well, it's gotten noticeably worse," I thought. The city looked like an abandoned construction site. The urban landscape was marred by the Prague version of our construction scaffolding—rusty, thin pipes twined around or used to repair buildings. The sites were deserted and somehow eerie. My beloved Old Town Square was also entangled in the carcasses of rusty pipes.

As an old Praguer, I showed my companions the famous clock on the Town Hall with figures of the apostles coming out of a small window and death with his scythe following them sedately. In the cathedral we spent a long time standing beside the gravestone under which lies Rabbi Loewe's great contemporary Tycho Brahe.* For some reason we couldn't spot the famous

*[The Danish astronomer Tycho Brahe (1546–1601), his pension withdrawn because of disagreements with the new king of Denmark, moved to Prague under the patronage of the Emperor Rudolph II.]

epitaph he wrote for himself: "He lived like a sage and died like a fool." I explained the origin of this melancholy saying: Brahe fell mortally ill at a court ball because he was too ashamed to go to the toilet—he wasn't sure that court etiquette permitted it.

Afterward we went to the old Jewish cemetery, and there I noticed that one of our group, the young and congenial Lyosha Gvamichava, wore an expression of indescribable suffering. I asked him what was wrong.

"Tooth," the poor boy barely managed to whisper. What a shame! His first trip abroad—and to have a stroke of bad luck like that! What could we do? Was there really no hope?

Then I got an idea that I can in all confidence call magnificent. We were just approaching the central section of the cemetery and the site of Rabbi Loewe's large vault. I explained to my compatriots what this servant of the ancient monotheistic cult was famous for: "There's a legend connected with Rabbi Loewe's grave. If you write out a petition and slip the note into this crack, they say it will be granted. So perhaps, Lyosha, you should appeal to the rabbi about your tooth."

The group broke out laughing, but Lyosha just asked, "Which language would be better, Russian or Georgian?"

"Write in Georgian. I think it will be the only note in a language rarely seen in Central Europe, and therefore it will instantly attract the attention of the great kabbalist's shade."

Lyosha tore a sheet from a notepad, wrote something on it, and added his jottings to the hundreds of pieces of paper welling up out of the crack in the vault. The group and I went on to another synagogue, one with walls covered with the names in calligraphy of 147,000 Czech Jews destroyed by the German fascists. An artist who had been driven mad by the loss of his entire family in the gas chambers at Teresienstadt created this titanic work. Alas, bad weather and natural damage have wiped out a considerable number of the inscriptions, particularly on the lower section of the walls. The authorities in Prague, of course, are doing nothing to preserve this unique monument.

All at once I sensed a change in my sympathetic audience. I

didn't realize what had happened until I saw Lyosha's beaming gaze. "So, Lyosha, your toothache's gone?" I asked confidently.

"Like magic. It happened all at once, five minutes ago."

What a miracle you worked, most revered rabbi! The congress lasted ten days, and together Lyosha and I gave a paper on the KRT-10 telescope and took part in numerous discussions. He was in fine fettle the entire time. After the conference, when we were all at Prague airport waiting to board our Il-62, Lyosha came over to me—and he was so pitiful that I couldn't bear to look at him. "Tooth," the poor devil groaned.

"There's nothing you can do now, Lyosha. Rabbi Loewe's spells don't extend to the territory of the international airport. The best advice I can give you is to go straight from Sheremetevo Airport to the clinic." And that's what he did.

This true story took place in Prague on September 28, 1977, in the presence of a dozen witnesses. I think it can be explained within the framework of contemporary medical science (autosuggestion and the like). But on the other hand, God only knows. . . .

Elections to the
Academy of Science

LAST week I was voted down at elections to the Academy of Sciences. I calculate that I've been on the ballot ten times over the past twenty-five years, and I was elected only once.* That gives me a good basis for making a few remarks about academic elections "from a professional viewpoint." I shouldn't have stood for election at all, since I had no doubt that I was already a *chansonette.*† There was another circumstance that precluded my election: word was getting around about the literary memoirs I had impetuously begun writing. In them I incautiously bruised Landau's untouchable posthumous prestige and permitted myself to express negative feelings about a base act Zeldovich once committed (see Chapters 11 and 5). This wrecked my rela-

---

*[Shklovsky became a corresponding member in 1966; he explains the distinction between that rank and academician proper below.]

†An election term, designating a candidate who has no chance of being elected (from Russianized French, *shansov net* [no chance]). Candidates who will make it are called rogues [*prokhodimtsy;* literally, those who "make it through"].

tions with the so-called "progressive left" flank of our academic elite and, since my relations with the right flank (Ambartsumyan, Severny) have long been close to saturation, ended any chance I might have had for election. I agreed to be a candidate this last time while I was on vacation (a debilitating state) and in the sober calculation that failure would untie my hands once and for all.

I assessed the situation from purely tactical considerations. In principle, it is possible for me (or any other candidate) to be elected—the party and government never interfere. I was turned down in the best parliamentary tradition on an honest secret ballot. Can you name another institution in our country where important business is conducted in that democratic manner? Can you imagine another group of a few dozen men, no longer young, picking up ballots bearing the names of dozens of candidates (for two or three spots), dispersing to the corners of the conference hall of the Institute of Physical Problems (where elections to our physics and astronomy section are usually held) and, after an interval of reflection, marking either "agree" or "disagree" beside each name? The choice isn't usually guided by the elector's feelings about the candidates—he may not even know most of them—but by tactical considerations and combinations as complex as anything in chess. In short, this is not your election to the Supreme Soviet of the Russian Republic.*

Factors besides the laws of probability theory and statistics influence the elections. There are several substantive stages before that important final ballot. The initial, or what might be called the zero, stage takes place in deep secret from the scientific community: the Presidium of the Academy of Sciences wrests vacancies from our "directive organs" (more simply, the

*To be elected you have to receive more than two-thirds of the votes against fantastically high competition. For example, at the last elections in our section thirty-six candidates were originally advanced for two vacancies as corresponding members. More vacancies were announced later, but one of those remained unfilled, since after three rounds of balloting no candidate had the requisite percentage of votes.

party and the government). Distributing those vacancies by section and within sections by specialty is also a clever combinational and positional game concealed from outside scrutiny. When the vacancies are finally announced in *Izvestia,* the experienced eye can often tell that one or another is meant for a specific candidate. (For instance, there was a series of electoral campaigns in which there were openings for candidates in "physics and astronomy" as a unit. The fact that no separate vacancy was announced in astronomy indicated that a physicist was almost sure to be elected.) The publication of the list of vacancies in *Izvestia* is the official beginning of the campaign.*

Before analyzing our academy elections further, I should address the important question of why learned (and not so learned) people are eager to occupy Academy armchairs. I will start with an anecdote from life. A delegation from the English Royal Society headed by the vice-chancellor, a professor of chemistry named Martin, came to Moscow—I think it was in the summer of 1960.† Most Academy members were away on vacation, and the Presidium sent out an appeal to Academy of Science institutes to fill the Presidium Conference Hall with as many of their co-workers as they could find (in the way that burning theaters call out the fire brigade). I was among the nonacademicians present. Since the president and the chief scientific secretary were out of town, one of our Lysenkoites, a rather crude type named Sisakyan, served as chairman.** Martin's speech was rich in humor and facts and cast a favorable light on the activities of the Royal Society, especially in contrast to our academy's moss-covered and sluggish bureaucracy.

In an attempt to dispel the impression Martin had made, the

---

*In recent years the announcements have been printed in the *Bulletin* of the Academy of Sciences.

†[David Christie Martin (b. 1914) has been the executive secretary of the Royal Society of London since 1947.]

**[Norair Sisakyan (1907–1966), a biochemist, who in 1963 became the chief scientific secretary of the Presidium of the Academy of Sciences.]

chairman asked him through the translator to explain one thing not quite clear to him, Sisakyan: What were the rights and obligations of a member of the Royal Society? The subtext of the wily Armenian's question was to the effect that Soviet academicians are servants of the people, and the British, lackeys of imperialism.

Martin's reply was a fine example of the famous English humor: "I understand you, Professor Sisakyan. I will begin with the duties: every member of the Royal Society is obliged each year to pay £5 to the Society's treasury. Now we can speak of his rights: every member of the aforesaid society has the right to receive completely free the periodical publications of his division. On average, that amounts to £ 7.50. So to be a member of the Royal Society is profitable, gentlemen!" the Briton ended, to thunderous laughter from the assembled company.

The story has a sequel. Two years afterward I was elected to the Royal Astronomical Society and began receiving the leading English astronomical journals, *Monthly Notices of the Royal Astronomical Society* and *The Observatory*. My joy at receiving the journals, which are hard to get in our country, was somewhat clouded by the impossibility of paying my yearly £ 5. When the British physicist Professor Bates came to visit us in Moscow and congratulated me on my election, I confided my embarrassment over the £ 5.

"Oh," said Bates, "I see that Martin didn't tell you everything. Foreign members of the Royal Society are relieved of the disagreeable obligation of paying £ 5. So it is particularly profitable to be a foreign member of the Royal Society!"*

Membership in the Soviet academy is profitable indeed, comrades. "For his epaulets," so to speak, the academician receives 500 rubles a month, and the corresponding member, 250. These are sums equivalent to a decent salary.† Insofar as I know, for-

*[In fact, the Royal Society and the Royal Astronomical Society are separate institutions.]

†[In the 1980s, the average monthly wage in the Soviet Union was about 250 rubles.]

eign academies do not pay their members. The only exceptions are those in socialist countries and, I think, the "closed" Académie Richelieu in France, whose members (the "immortals") receive for each session a louis-d'or apiece minted for the purpose. Before the war, in Mussolini's time, the Italian academy was also paid.*

Full academicians and corresponding members also receive many other benefits. There are the excellent conditions in the Academy of Sciences Hospital, where aging men of learning unhappily sometimes end up—I've been there three times myself. The greatest privilege is that members can't be forced to retire. How many tragedies have we seen when a strong, healthy sixty-year-old doctor of science becomes first a consultant, and then a pensioner drawing a beggarly 100 rubles a month? Access to the Academy restaurant in Moscow would seem to be a trivial matter, but in our chronically famished country the convenience and delicious food are also important privileges.

The sharp rise in a Soviet scientist's social status after his election to the Academy is equally important. He isn't actually any smarter or higher in rank, but it certainly seems that way. His own and others' bosses and Academy and ministerial bureaucracies treat him quite differently. The result is that things go perceptibly better in his laboratory. A special atmosphere is created around the "chosen one"—a propitious microclimate, if you like.† Academicians can talk as much nonsense as they please (as the example of Ambartsumyan shows). So you see, there are many considerations of a strictly material kind for standing for election to the Academy of Sciences. Compared to

*[Members of the American academy pay $50 a year in dues, and the chief privilege is the right to publish articles without peer review in the *Proceedings of the National Academy of Sciences.*]

†That our powers behave totally differently to academicians can be seen in the example of Andrey Sakharov and the fate of Trofim Lysenko after he fell from favor. [Both Sakharov and Lysenko retained their Academy membership and privileges through all vicissitudes.]

the West European and American academies, election as recognition of achievement and scientific prestige plays a subordinate role.

Another curious circumstance about our academy is that it's the only one in the world (excluding, or course, the socialist countries, which copy our structure down to the last detail) that has a two-level membership: full academician and corresponding member. The division made sense in tsarist times, when the Academy was located in Petersburg and high-ranking academic officials were supposed to be on the spot. Scientists who didn't live in the capital of the empire naturally enough became *corresponding* members. The original meaning has long since been lost, and the two ranks have acquired a different significance: there are *real* academicians and *semi*-academicians, who must grow into that rank and then go through the purgatory of new elections to full membership. The presumption is that the corresponding member will contribute something new and valuable to science, but any competent person realizes that this is utter nonsense—certainly in the physical and mathematical sciences, which I know best, and I'm convinced in other fields as well. As a rule, the people elected to corresponding membership are about fifty years old. Scientifically they have accomplished everything they are going to. There are rare exceptions, of course, but those exceptional specimens never get elected to the Academy at all. By the time a scientist becomes a corresponding member he has usually long been a "figure"—the director of an institute, the head of a major department or engineering center, and so forth. When the candidate's outstanding achievements are described in glowing terms during the campaign for full membership, you can be sure that those same achievements were cited at his election as corresponding member. Everybody realizes this, but nobody mentions it—after all, the electors were once in the same position.

What lies at the heart of this archaic two-level system? There is actually a vital reason for it: the two levels of Academy membership make scientists easy to manage. Immediately after his election as corresponding member, the candidate starts thinking about the higher rung of the academic hierarchy. He can't help realizing that he has to stay on good terms with the academicians in his section who will vote for him for full membership, and he spends years building cordial relations with them. I don't need to stress that this leads to an atmosphere of stagnation, the absence of real criticism without respect to person, and the decay of genuine science. The corresponding member resembles a hare running in harness after a carrot swinging on a pole in front of him. There's no need to simplify, however. Independent characters exist even among corresponding members, and there's always that strange secret vote. Surprises are one of the charms of our Academy.

The weighty, crude, and highly visible privileges of academicians have naturally made membership an attraction for people with only a tangential relation to science. The change in the nature of scientific creativity since the war has been one factor leading to the appearance of bosses of every sort in the Academy. The experimental sciences have become a collective process, in which the role of the creative individual has steadily diminished. So-called scientific administrators have moved into the most prominent posts; they are often untalented people who know their way around in other areas and, above all, in human relations. Attracted to the Academy by stability, material benefits, and prestige, this contingent supplies the largest number of candidates for academic chairs. On the eve of the 1953 elections, for instance, the all-powerful directress of the Moscow Energy Institute, Madame Golubtsova (the wife of Malenkov, then the head of state), decided that her institute should have its own academician and corresponding member. No sooner said than done. Two quite ordinary professors, Vladimir Kotelnikov and Vladimir Kirillin, were immediately elected. And now? The Malenkovs are probably living on their pension (120 rubles?), but Kotelnikov is still in the Academy. Kirillin tripped himself up a couple of years back, but that was pure coincidence and doesn't change the essence of the matter.*

Over the last dozen years I have observed a change in the nature of my physics and astronomy section. The military-industrial complex, which in our country as in America has become powerful and independent, has swept the Academy at all levels, starting with President Aleksandrov, whose only role at meetings is promoting Academy chairs for the complex's routine set of candidates.† From the point of view of the heads of the Academy and the section, we long ago became the technical physics section: science is whatever shoots, explodes, regulates, or guides itself. Not satisfied with having powerful branch institutes and "mailboxes" [secret establishments] which take up the lion's share of the country's funds and personnel, they would like to turn the entire Academy into the annex to a super-gigantic mailbox. The fools—they know not what they do!

Among the "scientific administrators" who make their way into the Academy, sons and sons-in-law—relatives of Politburo members—occupy a special place. At the most recent elections in our section, the son of Defense Minister Dmitry Ustinov got in; it was a close squeak, however, and Aleksandrov had to work hard for him. The sons-in-law of Andrey Kirilenko and Mikhail Suslov were roundly rebuffed in voting in the sections for mechanics and control processes, respectively. (In the latter case, the section failed to live up to its name.) Never fear, things will be back to normal at the next election. The director of the Institute of African Countries, Comrade Gromyko junior, recently became a corresponding member, and sociologist Dzhermen Gvishiani was very lucky to be elected to the Academy in 1979,

*[Kirillin lost his post as chairman of the State Committee of Science and Technology about the time that Andrey Sakharov was banished to Gorky in January 1980.]
†[In 1986 eighty-three-year-old Anatoly Aleksandrov, who had been the director of the Kurchatov Institute for Atomic Energy before becoming president of the Academy, was succeeded by the head of the Academy's Siberian division, mathematical physicist Gury Marchuk (b. 1925).]

just before his father-in-law, Prime Minister Aleksey Kosygin, quit the arenas of politics and life. Gvishiani makes a superb toastmaster, but I can't say anything definite about his sociology.*

It's easy to grasp the attraction the Academy has for broad strata of the scientific and managerial communities, but as we have seen, crossing its threshold is not easy even for highly placed sons and sons-in-law. There are numerous pitfalls. The first hurdle is the sectional commissions, whose task is to guide the voters by recommending one or two candidates per vacancy out of the great number of those up for election. In practice, however, in addition to previous vacancies, the directive organs sometimes announce one or two supplementary ones, which, in clear contradiction to the Academy charter, are obviously designed for their own candidates, as in the case of Ustinov's son at the last elections. These maneuvers take place under a useful veil of secrecy, and the members of the selection commission also vote in secret. Its decisions (essentially those of the party group) are very important; over the years I have observed that over 50 percent of those recommended by the commission get elected. This substantially narrows the freedom to maneuver during elections, but some possibilities still remain.

The next round of the pre-election carousel is the "president's tea." By tradition the president invites the members of the section to hear the selection commission's recommendations, after which there is a first exchange of opinions about the slate of candidates. Waiters pass watery tea with lemon and cookies. The slate of corresponding members is discussed in the presence of the entire section, and then the corresponding members are driven from the hall in shame, like schoolboys from a teachers' meeting—and these are important middle-aged

---

*[The word *nauka* in Akademiia nauk [Academy of Sciences], which is usually translated as "science," in fact refers to scholarship in general, and the Academy's sixteen sections include history, philosophy, economics, and literature and linguistics.]

people, many of them directors! The remaining academicians then proceed to discuss the candidates for full membership, for whom only they vote.

At the president's tea, the first advance-guard clashes among hostile groupings break out, and there are times when decisive electoral maneuvers take place. For instance, in 1946 Grigory Neuymin, the director of Pulkovo Observatory, was up for election as corresponding member. He should have been elected: restoration of Pulkovo, which had been razed during the war, was impending, and the director traditionally has a seat in the Academy. Neuymin was a sound astronomer of the old school, known for his research into comets and asteroids.*

The people speaking in Neuymin's favor at President Vavilov's tea were physicists who didn't know his work, but they all tried to support him by running on about comets until everybody was sick of the subject. Ambartsumyan was the only astronomer present, and he didn't say a word.

At last Vavilov became impatient and turned to him. "Why are you silent? After all, Neuymin is a worthy candidate—he discovered comets."

Ambartsumyan said in all apparent seriousness, "Yes, but my wife's aunt also discovered three comets."

Titters were heard: they were proposing to elect a man whose field was something an aunt could do! A few days later Neuymin was voted down at the elections. Ambartsumyan was perfectly correct, but he didn't bother to mention that his wife's aunt, Pelageya Shain, was a well-known astronomer.

During the 1976 elections I was fighting for the candidacy of my most talented student, Kolya Kardashev. The commission hadn't included him on its slate, and very few people knew him. In that situation my only possible strategy at the tea was to attract attention to his candidacy—and I did so by scandalous

*[Neuymin (1886–1946) was an astrophotographer who discovered sixty-three new asteroids and seven comets.]

heckling. It turned the trick: everybody remembered Karda-shev's name and he was elected.

At last the final (and principal) part of the election drama is played out, and we encounter the basic motive forces directing the flow of this seemingly elemental process. On the sectional level the elections are marked by conflict and deals among vari-ous "mafias." Riccardo Giacconi, the famous Italian-American x-ray astronomer, once remarked, "You Russians have a com-pletely erroneous idea of the mafia. You naively imagine a mafi-oso as an evil-looking guy in a mask with a knife in his teeth and a machine-gun. That's the wildest nonsense! The best transla-tion of the word *mafia* into Russian is the word *blat* [pull]. Favor for favor! You for me, and I for you. And all of it tinted in the optimistic hues of good family relations!" In speaking of mafias, I have in mind Giacconi's subtle and reliable definition.

There are two basic mafias in our physics and astronomy section. The mafia grouped around the Landau Institute, the Solid Body Institute, and, to some extent, the Institute of Physi-cal Problems is the most powerful. It has to be admitted that those boys do a clean piece of work; they're a very tenacious company and work together with discipline to get almost all their leading figures into the Academy. Their style is the use of high-flown, terribly progressive turns of phrase. The mafia of the Kurchatov Institute of Atomic Energy, where our late Acad-emy secretary Lev Artsimovich shone for so many years, had to yield first place to them. Artsimovich was a master at making deals. It will be many years before there are any real discoveries in thermonuclear fusion, but we already have three young acade-micians from the field. That mafia draws its strength from the president's participation and has a powerful ally in the neighbor-ing atomic section of the Academy.

Small groups, like the circle of classical astronomers sur-rounding Ambartsumyan, function between these basic mafias, and there is also a rather extensive area of quicksand with unsta-ble and shifting banks. In order to be elected, every candidate realizes that he must either be a member of a mafia or secure its support by appropriate behavior. I was always voted down because I never belonged to a mafia or sucked up to any of the various mafiosi. I was elected corresponding member by accident in 1966. In violation of the charter that year, a rather harsh age qualification was introduced. (It was repealed at the next election.) Also, for some unknown reason Artsimovich was well disposed to my candidacy.

It's amusing to listen to the discussion of candidates which precedes the voting. It follows the Jesuitic tradition of avoiding abuse of those under discussion—that's considered bad manners. There is, however, a rich arsenal of ways to downgrade an undesirable candidate and extol one's own protégé. Opponents speak briefly of the candidate's scientific contributions and then often take advantage of the ignorance of the basic mass of electors to talk demagogic nonsense. The candidate's membership in foreign scientific societies and academies usually works against him: "Look at that sharp fellow! He's in, and we aren't; let's make him wait a while."

Much depends on the situation in the particular section. The mathematics section is known for its anti-Semitism. They repeatedly turned down our most eminent mathematician, Izrail Gelfand, a member of the world's greatest academies.* My membership in those same foreign academies worked against me also. Stout fellow that he is, in the latest elections Gelfand refused even to be a candidate. Our best astronomer, Solomon Pikelner, was voted down five times and never became even a corresponding member of our section.†

I could cite many other such examples. Does that mean, however, that the Academy never elects real scholars? Not at all! That's the paradox. Over the past two centuries the overwhelming majority of important Russian scientists have been members

---

*[Like Shklovsky, Gelfand got as far as being elected corresponding member (in 1953).]

†[In 1971 Pikelner was elected to the British Royal Astronomical Society.]

of the Academy of Sciences. The Academy must elect genuine scientists to maintain its prestige. Being part of an institution founded by Peter the Great in which Lomonosov, Pavlov, Chebyshev, Krylov, Landau, Kapitsa, and Sakharov lived and worked is very flattering.

There aren't many genuine scientists. There are particularly few of them in our country, where the administrative-bureaucratic flood long ago overwhelmed us. This makes it both possible and necessary to permit the occasional election of such harmless eccentrics to the Academy. Quiet, talented young scientists who have not made enemies have a comparatively good chance of being chosen. Each one of them serves to justify the comfortable existence within the Academy walls of at least a dozen personalities who can only be called ballast.

Despite its deficiencies and absurdities, of which I have given only a pale sketch, the Academy of Sciences is a fine institution, one in which things get done, and for that we have to be grateful.

Antimatter

IN 1962—I think it was December; the days were short—I received orders to appear at a certain hour at the Presidium of the Academy of Sciences to attend a meeting. Not a word was said about the character of the gathering, which meant that the business to be discussed was top secret. At that time I was enthusiastically involved in the space program and quite often attended meetings of the Interdisciplinary Council called by Mstislav Keldysh, president of the Academy and chief theoretician of the space program, but those sessions took place in his office at the Institute of Applied Mathematics on Miussy Square. I was puzzled by the fact that this meeting was being held in the president's office at the Presidium instead.

Intrigued, I arrived ten minutes before the meeting began. The first thing that struck me was the number of people I'd never seen before. Of course, familiar faces turned up, too—I remember Ambartsumyan sitting in absolute silence in a corner. I think Pyotr Kapitsa was present. Among those I didn't know, I noticed a corpulent man, getting on in years, who was totally bald and looked remarkably like Fantomas: it was Aleksandrov, the future president of the Academy. The central spot in this small, elite gathering was occupied by an energetic middle-aged man, also completely bald, who was busy giving orders to his assistants. It was instantly clear that this stranger was used to power and on close terms with high authorities. The man's colleagues were hanging large sheets of drawing paper all over the walls of Keldysh's office, but I couldn't figure out the graphs inked on them.

Keldysh opened the meeting, and I began to feel ill at ease. I was clearly the only one present who had no idea what was going on. Boris Pavlovich—that was what they called the important stranger—took the floor. But he was a stranger only to me, the interloper in the room. Everyone else knew him so well that *not once* did anyone utter his last name.

The stranger began talking about a topic the essence of which I had trouble understanding. He reminded those present that two years earlier a government decree had been passed authorizing and funding the Leningrad Institute of Physics and Technology (or Phystech for short) to carry out top secret work of great importance to the state. Since then much had been done and highly promising results obtained. Therefore he was asking this distinguished gathering to approve the work to date, extend the period of the decree, and, accordingly, allot a few million more rubles for the project. Briefly presenting the results obtained, the speaker gave some rather nebulous explanations of the graphs on the walls, and gradually I got a general idea of the Phystech's activities. I almost fell off my chair. My first impulse was to burst out laughing. I repressed the instinct with great difficulty, but as I looked around the room at the consequential faces of men well on in age and weighted with high rank, I got angry instead. Ambartsumyan, the only other astronomer in the room, rhythmically nodded his head like a Chinese idol. For a moment I thought it was all a bad dream or I had gone mad.

And, in fact, the whole thing was enough to drive an astronomer mad. Boris Pavlovich asserted, as if it were a proven fact, that astronomers had long since made a definitive mess of the question of the origin of comets and meteors. They (the astronomers), being ignorant of contemporary nuclear physics, had failed to realize that comets and the products of their disintegration (i.e. meteor showers) are actually made up of *antimatter*—atoms with negatively charged nuclei and positively charged electrons.* If antimatter particles were to impact on the Earth's atmosphere, they would be annihilated and their mass converted into powerful gamma rays. By government decree, a scientific team from Boris Pavlovich's institute was observing (in complete secrecy!) atmospheric gamma-ray flashes which supposedly coincided with individual meteors impacting on the atmosphere. There was no doubt that the work was organized on a grand scale. Among other things, they had set up their own radar service for meteor observations and flown specially equipped airplane-laboratories, while as many as a hundred people simultaneously worked out the theoretical aspects. You can understand the roots of my outrage: the resources our country spent on actual research in meteor astronomy were hundreds of times less than those devoted to this peculiar venture. Then there was the tone in which that functionary, that dense ignoramus, permitted himself to speak of astronomers. And that goose Ambartsumyan knew the whole thing was gibberish and said nothing. He didn't want to damage his relations with those important people, you see, and so he said nothing. Good Lord, what had I gotten myself into?

The meeting was over in less than thirty minutes. The Phystech's activities were approved, the money allocated, and the

---

*[It is a great mystery of cosmology why all naturally occurring atomic nuclei consist of positive or neutral particles (protons or neutrons), while the light particles that circle around them, electrons, are negative. In principle, antimatter—nuclei of negatively charged antiprotons with positrons spiraling around them—could exist undetected from Earth, but antiprotons and positrons have been found only in products of collisions involving cosmic rays or in accelerators.]

speaker highly praised. Against that background it would have
been simply unthinkable for me to make a row. When the group
broke up, I asked a friend of mine on the Presidium staff, "Who
is he, strictly speaking, this Boris Pavlovich?"

"What do you mean, who? That's Academician Konstantinov,
director of the Leningrad Institute of Physics and Technology!"

The name was empty noise to me—I'd never heard of any
physicist named Konstantinov. Right there on the spot I relieved my long restrained emotions by using my command of
railroad-laborer's profanity to explain to the fellow from the
Presidium what I thought about that "vitally important" subject,
Comrade Konstantinov, and the idiots taking part in the farce. I
made these explanations quite loudly in the anteroom outside
Keldysh's office, and there can be no doubt that my friend wasn't
the only one to hear them. A few days later I got a phone call
from Keldysh.

An unfamiliar female voice said, "Mstislav Vsevolodovich
wants to speak to you." The president of the Academy and chief
theoretician of cosmonautics had never before honored me with
his attentions; our relations were strictly one-way. The occasion
had to be extraordinary.

"Now, Iosif Samuilovich," sounded the quiet, peevish voice I
knew so well, "instead of making nasty remarks in the corridor
about Konstantinov, you ought to go see him in Leningrad and
investigate his work on the spot—that is, at the Phystech. You'll
leave on the Arrow *today*.* I've already arranged it with Konstantinov. You'll be met. And please, be polite—pretend you're
chatting with a foreign colleague. Is that clear?"†

Stunned, my only reply was the idiotic question: "But who's
going to pay for the trip?" (At the time I wasn't working in the
Academy of Sciences system.)

---

*[The Red Arrow is the overnight express train between Moscow and Leningrad.]
†That bit about the "foreign colleague" was a good jab—he caught me right between the
"horns-ashvili," as a friend from student days used to put it. [In Russian, *rog-ashvili*
(*rog*—horn), a play on Stalin's real name, Dzhugashvili.]

"What?" uttered the president in mixed revulsion and astonishment.

"Excuse me, that was foolish. I'll go today." Short beeps sounded from the telephone.

Keldysh's order brought home the fact that I had gotten involved in an unsavory business. Naturally I had no desire to go to a hostile Leningrad institute—and not least because I had never in my life worked on meteors and comets. "Konstantinov's place is the best physics institute in the country, and there must be people who know more about the meteor business than I, a total amateur," I thought. "But in the last analysis, truth is on my side. What's going on there is nothing but delirious ravings, and what good am I if I can't expose it? Forward into battle!" I spent the few hours before my departure for Leningrad studying a popular pamphlet about meteors by Millman, a Canadian specialist in the field. It was thirty-five pages, just long enough to get across the essentials.*

It was still dark the next morning in Leningrad when two men from the staff of the institute met me at the Moscow station, put me into a car, and drove me to the Phystech. Konstantinov was waiting for me in his office, which was covered with the graphs I had seen a few days earlier in the Presidium of the Academy. A dozen people I didn't know were sitting on chairs along the walls—Konstantinov's closest co-workers in the search for antimatter in the Earth's atmosphere. They greeted me with cold civility.

I rushed straight into a decisive attack, seized the initiative, and never again relinquished it. Even now, over twenty years later, I marvel as I remember that battle. I fought like the cruiser *Varangian* and, I must say, with greater success. At any rate, I

---

*[Canadian astronomer Peter M. Millman never produced a popular pamphlet on meteors. He suggests that Shklovsky had access to an article he wrote with D.W.R. McKinley, "Meteors," which was published in *The Moon, Meteorites and Comets,* edited by Barbara M. Middlehurst and G. P. Kuiper (University of Chicago, 1963). Millman sent a bound preprint of the article to a colleague in Moscow.]

didn't follow the sad tradition of the Russian fleet and valiantly scuttle the ship.* The engagement developed roughly by the following scenario:

First, I made clear to them that astronomers are by no means the dunces that Konstantinov thought them and that they understand something about meteors and comets. At this point, by the way, it became clear that worrying about their erudition in the subject had been a waste of time: their knowledge of astronomy, like that of most physicists, was quite primitive. Millman's summary was a revelation to them. (It goes without saying that for tactical reasons I didn't reveal the source of my erudition.)

After the introduction, I struck a blow that seemed to me crushing. I named the amount of meteor matter, deduced from the brightness of their streaks, which impacts on the Earth daily (about 500 tons), multiplied it by the square of the velocity of light, and demonstrated precisely that, if it were antimatter, the output of irradiation of our poor little globe by annihilation gamma rays would be equivalent to daily explosions of millions of hundred-megaton hydrogen bombs.† "I don't have to explain to you what that means—after all, that's your field, isn't it?" I finished impudently.

I thought that would do it. But Konstantinov mounted a counterattack: "Your estimate of mass is based on the optical effect produced by meteors and under the assumption that they consist of *matter*. But I believe them to be *antimatter*, and in that case immeasurably less material would be needed to produce the same number of flashes."

"Their boss is quick-witted," I thought and felt an instant relief. I had wavered in my assessment of the Phystech director—was he obsessed or a swindler? I have always preferred the obsessed, and now it was clear that this was the category to

---

*[In 1904, during the Russo-Japanese War, the *Varangian*'s captain, trapped in the harbor at Chemul'po (Inchon), sank the ship rather than surrender it to the enemy.]
†[The mass would be converted into energy by Einstein's famous equation $E = mc^2$.]

which Konstantinov belonged. Realizing this, I hit him a second time: "But, Boris Pavlovich, there are many thousands of meteor *spectra,* from which you can analyze the light produced by incoming meteors. You can use them literally to *count* the number of meteoric atoms falling to Earth (I was exaggerating, of course, but in principle I was absolutely correct). Those calculations give approximately the same amount of mass for the meteoric material falling to Earth as one obtains from the energy of their bright streaks. I don't have to prove to you, do I, that the spectrum of anti-atoms is absolutely identical to that of ordinary atoms?"

The blow was a strong one and brought confusion to the enemies' ranks. From the faces of Konstantinov's co-workers I saw that they had gotten the point—after all, they were first-class physicists. There wasn't another peep out of them, but Konstantinov was made of sterner stuff. Recovering somewhat from the knockdown, he tried an evasive tactic: "You see, I don't really believe that *all* meteors are antimatter. For instance, sporadic meteors may well be made of ordinary matter. I think that only meteors which are products of the disintegration of comets are antimatter. You can't tell from the spectra, can you, what kind of meteor it is—sporadic or cometary?

Millman came to my rescue. "I can, indeed!" I said, exulting in total victory. "I don't need to remind you that all meteor showers originate in comets, from which they may overtake the Earth or meet it head on! The meteor spectrum is determined by the relative velocity of the collision between the corresponding shower and the atmosphere. The spectra of overtaking meteor showers at low relative velocity has an incomparably lower excitation than that of head-on showers. A specialist can distinguish the spectrum of a meteor belonging to the Draconid shower from, let us say, Leonids.* But if the radiated energy

---

*[Meteor showers are named after the constellations from which they appear to come, in this case Draco and Leo. The head-on Leonids hit the Earth with three times the relative velocity of the overtaking Draconids and are consequently much brighter.]

was due to matter-antimatter annihilation, the velocity difference would be insignificant compared to the nuclear process."

The victory was complete. It was already late in the afternoon when Konstantinov dismissed his co-workers. I felt nauseated from hunger—I hadn't had a bite to eat or drink since the evening before, and I came right out and told my host so. "We'll get you something right away."

His secretary brought tea and some sugary pastry. Over tea Konstantinov went on raving almost incoherently about his obsession; he was indeed a fanatic. Dead tired, I dreamed of a good piece of meat and kept silent. We parted cordially, and the director's chauffeur drove me to the Moscow station, where I sat waiting for the train in a semidoze. In Moscow nobody asked me for an account of the trip. Of course, nobody reimbursed me for it either.

After this adventure I began thinking seriously about the fortunes of our science. I found it all very sad. Of course, rationally I realized that outrageous things often go on in our country. In the antimatter business, fate cast me into the thick of our "great projects," and in that instance, as in a number of others, the power of preposterously incompetent functionaries decided everything. Khrushchev himself, intrigued by the supposed military applications of that monstrous idea, authorized the antimatter project. They say that was what he meant when he stated, "The imperialists try to scare us with their neutron bomb. . . . But our scientists have something even better in their briefcases."

Every cloud has its silver lining, however. At the Leningrad Institute of Physics and Technology a strong astronomical section with some clever young people arose out of the ruins of the antimatter project.

Not long afterward Konstantinov became the first vice-president of our Academy of Sciences without resigning as director of the Phystech. A man of ebullient energy, he burned himself out with unproductive administrative work and died prematurely in 1969 at the age of fifty-nine. He was, God knows, a decent fellow and a fully qualified *acoustical* physicist, whose doctoral dissertation was on the theory of woodwind instruments. He made a major contribution to the creation of nuclear power in our country. Konstantinov loved science, insofar as he understood it. Perhaps his obsession with antimatter is most easily comprehended as a human flaw: he wanted to make a name for himself in science. He liked to say, "A real scientist is one you read about in the schoolbooks"—and he'd never done anything worth recording. Most of his colleagues were and are in roughly the same position, and it is not by chance that Konstantinov often advised them never to abandon a stipulated program of applied research, citing the famous story of Khodja Nasreddin.*

Inside the cozy courtyard of the Phystech building stand pedestals bearing three busts. One has the inscription: "Here from 1927 to 1969 worked the outstanding *Russian* physicist Boris Pavlovich Konstantinov." A second bust honors the atomic physicist Igor Kurchatov, and for many years the plaque on it told us that an outstanding *Soviet* physicist worked there. Last year—I suppose as a result of my sarcastic gibes about that strange hierarchy of epitaphs—the word *Soviet* was altered to *Russian.* The third bust, that of the institute's Jewish founder, Abram Ioffe, bears no memorial plaque at all.

---

*[What Khodja Nasreddin, the subject of endless popular anecdotes in the Near East, said when the shah ordered him to teach a donkey to read, has become proverbial in Russian: "It will all work out somehow—somebody, either the shah, the donkey, or me, is bound to kick the bucket, and meanwhile . . ."]

Cannibals

I WENT to the United States for the first time in January 1967, to attend the Second "Texas" Symposium on the rapidly developing field of relativistic astrophysics. The meeting was in New York. It's hard now to reproduce the atmosphere of animation and enthusiasm of those times. Quasars had been discovered four years earlier, and the boundaries of the observed metagalaxy* were expanding incredibly. The symposium was held just a year after the discovery of the fantastic relict radioemission of the universe, which gave us a glimpse far back into an epoch when neither the stars nor the galaxies had yet originated and the world was only a fiery hydrogen-helium plasma. At that time the expanding universe was thousands of times smaller and tens of thousands of times younger than it is now. I took pride in having originated the widely used term "relict radiation."†

*[The entire system of galaxies.]
†[In the West the term "three-degree radiation" is more commonly used.]

The weather in New York was fantastically warm and sunny for winter, and the city made an unexpected impression on me. Like everyone else who has not seen this amazing, gigantic place, I had unconsciously assumed that it was gray, probably as a result of reading American and Russian literature (Upton Sinclair's novels, Gorky's "City of the Yellow Devil," and so forth). In fact, New York impressed me by a multicolored diversity which I had always associated with southern cities. The resemblance to, say, a greatly expanded Naples (which I've never seen) was intensified by the staggering narrowness of its streets. I measured the width of Broadway and the famous, glittering Fifth Avenue with my own legs; the avenue is nineteen paces wide from curb to curb, and Broadway (despite its name) only seventeen.

New York is one of the few cities in America where pedestrians in colorful throngs rule the streets. The negro faces are fascinating in their unexpected diversity. I felt at home in the New York crowd—is it perhaps because three million of my fellow Jews live in that gigantic city?

I found the New York skyscrapers stunning, especially the comparatively new ones. Some of them were so colorful that you might think they were faced with the same tiles as the mosques of Samarkand. All the symposium participants lived and met in the forty-story Hotel New Yorker on the corner of Eighth Avenue and Thirty-fourth Street. Four short blocks from our hotel the icy beam of the Empire State Building soared skyward.

There was the customary reception in the hotel's huge conference hall on the evening of our arrival. In an incredible crush the flower of world astronomy, more than a thousand participants with whiskey glasses in their hands, diffused and sniffed each other out.

"Hello, Dr. Shklovsky, how are things going?" Before me stood the middle-aged, thick-set Jesse Greenstein, with his close-clipped mustache, the director of the largest and most famous observatory in the world, California's Mount Palomar.* "I know you're in our country for the first time; what would you like to see?"

All the Soviet delegates had been given exit visas good for a month, but the symposium (and with it our scanty supply of hard currency) would end in five days. Coolly and calmly I told Jesse that I would like, if possible, to visit his famous observatory, as well as the National Radio Astronomy Observatory at Greenbank and the California Institute of Technology in Berkeley.† In the heady atmosphere of the reception I wasn't even horrified at my own audacity.

"O.K.," said Greenstein, and he melted into the crowd.

Every few seconds another American colleague with an eminent name appeared out of the crush to greet me. Fifteen minutes later Greenstein surfaced again, this time all business. He handed me a large envelope and asked me to acquaint myself with its contents: a little book of airline tickets with the routes already indicated (New York–Los Angeles, Los Angeles–San Francisco, San Francisco–Washington, Washington–New York) and the schedule of my journey ("timetable") written on a magnificent typewriter with the date, route, who would accompany me, and who would meet me at every point of the itinerary clearly indicated. "You'll get expense money at each place. Is there anything else you'd like?"

Stunned, I could only mutter words of gratitude. My benefactor melted back into the crowd. Igor Novikov, a member of our delegation who had been watching the scene, came over to me, "Iosif Samuilovich, maybe I could go too?"

Shamelessly I located Greenstein in the crowd and asked the same favor for my young colleague. Unhindered by Igor's pres-

*[Greenstein headed the academic astronomy program at the California Institute of Technology. Palomar Observatory is the property of Caltech, but at that time it was controlled by a joint entity called the Mount Wilson and Palomar Observatories, the director of which was Horace W. Babcock.]

†[Caltech is in Pasadena.]

ence, Jesse asked, "And is he a *real* scientist?"* I assured him that he was, and soon Igor had an envelope like mine. Besides Novikov and me, the Americans did the same great favor for Ginzburg, who acted independently. Others in our delegation (for example, Terletsky [see Chapter 14]), who had only a distant relation to relativistic astrophysics, not to mention astronomy in general) were turned back at the gates, and a few days later they went home.

Worn out by the profuse impressions of my first day on American soil, I found a little sofa and sat down. Here Greenstein came over to me for the third time, accompanied by a heavy man getting on in years, who stretched out his meaty hand and introduced himself, "Edward Teller. I know your schedule. You'll be in San Francisco on February 6 [seventeen days later—I.S.]. I'll expect you at my house at 6 P.M. Pacific time." I grunted a reply, and Teller disappeared. Events were moving so fast that the unusual invitation didn't even startle me.

The intense five days of the symposium flashed by, leaving me with only scrappy memories. I recall meeting the guest of honor, the eminent physicist-defector George (Georgy Antonovich) Gamow, who was the first to predict relict radiation back in 1948.† Alas, although he was far from old, he had only months to live. Despite my imperfect knowledge of English, I was honored by being asked to chair the panel on relict radiation.

*[Igor Novikov is a leading Soviet cosmologist, coauthor with Zeldovich of a two-volume work on relativistic astrophysics. In later years he joined Shklovsky's group at IKI.]

†I consider Gamow one of the greatest Russian physicists of the twentieth century. Science is cruel: the only thing that counts are the concrete results of a researcher's work. To use a soccer analogy, it is not elegant feints and dribbling that count, but *goals scored.* Gamow immortalized his name with three outstanding "goals": 1. the theory of beta-decay or, in more general terms, "sub-barrier" processes (1928); 2. the theory of the "hot universe" and, consequently, prediction of the relict radiation (1948), the discovery of which in 1965 marked a new epoch in cosmology; and 3. the discovery of the phenomenon of the genetic code (1953), the foundation of modern biology. Of course, it's too bad that Gamow was a defector. But can you imagine the musical culture of twentieth-century Russia without the emigrés Chaliapin and Rachmaninov? Why is recognition possible in the arts but not in science?

During the discussion Gamow said something in rapid English from his seat. "Georgy Antonovich," I begged him, "speak Russian; it'll be more fun!" To the audience's loud laughter, Gamow immediately switched to his native language.

Afterward, figuratively speaking, I was set on the rails of the unsurpassed, businesslike American hospitality and sent rolling around the great transoceanic superpower. A profusion of impressions, meetings, discussions, and excursions overwhelmed me. Hollywood and Disneyland. A nighttime trip on a six-lane highway from San Diego to Pasadena with an unbroken ruby band from the rear lights of a stream of cars running backward along the neighboring lanes. The driver was Maarten Schmidt, the man who discovered quasars.

In San Francisco, the fairytale city of my childhood dreams, my guide was Harold Weaver, who, just a year earlier, with Nan Dieter discovered the cosmic masers "working" on the radio-line of interstellar hydroxyl (OH) at a wavelength of 18 centimeters, a phenomenon I had once calculated and predicted.* I reveled in the view of the bridges across the bay, especially the beautiful Golden Gate; I was astonished by the funny cable cars and enchanted by the fish market. But then Weaver said anxiously, "Please don't forget that you're due at Professor Teller's at six this evening."

Dear God, I had totally forgotten—too much had been happening. Weaver reassured me by saying that he would set me down promptly on Teller's doorstep.

"And you're coming with me, of course?" I asked, ill at ease.

"No way! Teller's too much of a big shot for me. I don't know him at all."

At five minutes past six I entered the brightly lit, luxurious bungalow of the famous physicist and "father of the hydrogen bomb." The elite of American science was at Teller's reception.

*[Harold F. Weaver is a professor at the University of California–Berkeley and director of its Hat Creek Radio Observatory. Shklovsky published an article explaining the emission as maser action in the OH molecule pumped by strong infrared emission from stars in formation.]

There were at least six Nobel laureates, two of whom, Charles Townes and the chemist Melvin Calvin, I knew personally. To my great embarrassment, Teller dashed up to me as soon as I crossed the threshold and started quizzing me about those incomprehensible quasars. This made me the center of attention at a time when all I wanted was to fade into the background. The owner of the house obviously had no use for the etiquette requiring him to pay more or less equal attention to all his guests, and the agony lasted for a good fifteen minutes before I decided to find a way to turn him off. I abruptly changed the subject by saying, "Do you know, Mr. Teller, that a few years ago your name was extremely popular in our country?" I had in mind a feature article in *Literary Gazette* with the screaming headline, "Teller the Cannibal." When I tried to tell my intrigued host about it, to my horror I couldn't think of the English for cannibal, even though it was probably the first English word I had learned as a child. With only seconds to reflect, recalling that Teller was a Hungarian Jew who must speak German like a native, I said, *"Menschenfresser."*

"Oh," Edward moaned in delight, "cannibal! But what is it in Russian?"

"Lyu-do-yed," I pronounced distinctly.

Teller pulled out his notebook and entered the easily pronounceable Russian word. "Tomorrow I'm giving a lecture for students at Berkeley, and I'll tell them I'm a—*liyu-do-led!*" The other guests, who hadn't caught much of our conversation, laughed politely. I castled to a corner of the veranda and took time out to think about Teller's reaction to the accusation of cannibalism.

The whole scene reminded me to a surprising degree of my first meeting with Soviet atomic physicists. Sometime in the late 1950s a friend of mine dragged me to a birthday party for some relative of hers who was prominent in the atomic establishment. The apartment was crowded with people I didn't know or knew only slightly, primarily physicists. They were rapidly getting drunk. In response to persistent requests, the host performed his famous trick of playing some unthinkable fugue on the family piano with his fat backside.

Singing started. The crowd harmonized melodiously, at first choosing the thieves' songs popular at the time among the intelligentsia. I don't know why, but I remember one heartrending song with the words, "but he who's free in spirit is free in prison, too," which goes on with a jaunty refrain picked up by a dozen voices, "And he who weeps is just a broad—why should we pity him?" Then somebody proposed, "Fellows, let's sing our atomic song."

All the drunken guests launched into a product of amateur nights at the secret mailboxes. The jocular song tells the story of a fellow named Gavrila who decided to make an atom bomb using, so to speak, domestic means. He filled his bathtub with heavy water, climbed in, and picked up hunks of uranium in both hands. ". . . And the next thing to tell you I've / Is that it was uranium two three five" are the devil-may-care words I still remember from that cheerful ditty. "It's not too late for edification / To read the Stockholm proclamation," the singers' intoxicated voices warned. Gavrila's irresponsible actions and disregard of safety precautions weren't long in taking effect: there was an atomic explosion, and the ill-fated hero of the song was vaporized. The final words, sung to general laughter, were: "All warmongers would sure do well / To remember what to Gavrila befell." Yakov Zeldovich was the honored guest among the roistering physicists, and that evening was the first time I had ever seen him up close.

I was struck by the shameless cynicism of the creators of the atomic bomb. No ethical problems weighed on their disciplined minds. In 1973, six years after my conversation with Teller, I asked Andrey Sakharov whether he suffered from the Eatherly complex.*

---

*Claude R. Eatherly, the American army colonel who dropped the first atomic bomb on Hiroshima from a B-29 bomber, was later tormented by remorse, became deeply depressed, and ended his days in a psychiatric hospital.

"Of course not," one of the greatest humanists of our planet calmly replied.

In my country I know of only one man who behaved worthily with the chief of the atomic (and not only atomic) cannibals, Lavrenty Beria. That man was Pyotr Kapitsa, the present patriarch of Soviet physics. I was never able to get the details first-hand, but the story has long since become legend. (One knowledgeable person told me the following version. At a crucial meeting chaired by super-cannibal Beria, whom the Politburo had named to direct the atomic program, the production of separated uranium isotopes was under discussion. The research had been successful, but the scientists reported that a few additional experiments requiring about six months remained before large-scale production could begin. The enraged Beria displayed his usual style of management by rudely interrupting the speakers and unleashing a stream of filthy abuse. Kapitsa got up and replied to the crazed super-butcher in exactly the same terms, concluding: "When you talk to physicists, mother and double your mother, you should stand at attention!" The apoplectic Beria couldn't say a word. The following day Stalin ordered Kapitsa relieved of all his posts, and for all intents and purposes he remained under house arrest until 1953.) Whatever the details, the fact remains that, during the gloomiest period of the Stalin terror, Academician Kapitsa displayed great courage and strength of character. He was transformed into a cottage industry academic, but his indomitable spirit was never broken. I think, however, that Kapitsa's behavior was largely determined by his being a product of Cambridge University's famous Cavendish Laboratory. He proved himself a worthy disciple of his great teacher Rutherford, who, as head of the committee to aid scientists fleeing from Hitler's Germany, refused to shake hands with Fritz Haber because of the latter's decisive contribution to the exploitation of chemical weapons. It should be emphasized, however, that Kapitsa's position was immeasurably more difficult than Sir Ernest's.

Just recently I came across echoes of that story in Khrushchev's curious reminiscences. At some point during the early
1960s Nikita asked Kapitsa directly why he wouldn't go into
defense work.

Kapitsa's answer was couched in terms that the primitive but
crafty Nikita could comprehend: " 'I'm a scientist, and scientists
are like artists. They want other people to talk about their work,
to make movies about it, to write articles about it in the newspapers. The trouble with military topics is that they're all
secret.' "* Stalin's times were over, and the repression that
followed the conversation was quite modest: for the nth time
Kapitsa was denied permission to accept an invitation from
abroad.

The ex-premier makes another curious comment later in the
same work. He reports that Sakharov petitioned him not to test
the hydrogen bomb (evidently in the early 1960s, after a series
of tests of multimegaton "toys"): "Obviously, [Sakharov] was of
two minds. On the one hand, he had wanted to help his country
defend itself against imperialist aggression. On the other hand,
once he'd made it possible for us to develop the bomb, he was
afraid of seeing it put to use. I think perhaps he was afraid of
having his name associated with the possible implementation of
the bomb" (p. 70). Sakharov's tragic mistake seems to have
been in thinking he could play games with the cannibals and even
try to deceive them, but he was young and didn't have Kapitsa's
lifetime of experience to draw on. Afterward he became wiser.

Two months ago chance brought me to the famous museum
at Los Alamos. I spent a long time looking at the steel column
singed by a hellish flame which had withstood the world's first
atomic explosion in the Alamogordo Desert nearby. There was a
puny-looking replica of the Hiroshima bomb standing beside it. I
was struck by photocopies of business correspondence between

*[*Khrushchev Remembers: The Last Testament,* trans. Strobe Talbott (Little, Brown,
1974): 65.]

the administrators of the laboratory and certain high authorities, possibly military, which were on display. The letters referred repeatedly to the necessity of giving orders to drive a nail into the wall of Mr. Oppenheimer's office so he could hang up his hat. Life at the Los Alamos Laboratory in its stellar period was completely normal.

I know personally one American scientist who displayed real heroism and civic courage in his relations with the cannibals. He is Phil Morrison, who is now one of America's leading theoretical astrophysicists. Seriously ill, to all intents and purposes a cripple, even back in the far-off 1940s he realized that a scientist's probity and honor are incompatible with the service of Beelzebub. Morrison left the Los Alamos Laboratory in disgrace and slammed the door behind him. He had serious difficulties, but he was never broken. Sitting with him at a table in a small Mexican restaurant in the old section of Albuquerque, some hundred miles from Los Alamos, I looked into his deep blue, childlike, clear eyes—the eyes of a man with a crystal-pure conscience—and my heart was uplifted.

—October 1981, Mountain Sanitarium of the Ministry of Medium Machine Industry.*

*[The Ministry of Medium Machine Industry was a cover name for the USSR atomic program. It has now become part of a ministry like our Department of Energy.]

"Harden and Guide Me"

ON November 5, 1973, my son Zhenya delivered me to the Academy Hospital on Lyapunov Street, an establishment with which I was already only too familiar. I had suffered my second heart attack, a massive one, and it might easily have been my last. Wearing a light overcoat, I lay in the cold premises of the hospital admitting room on a structure resembling a catafalque. The nurse on duty, busy registering a middle-aged patient with a face covered with bruises and abrasions, was in no hurry to admit me. For some reason I was calm. As I waited my turn, I asked the somber Zhenya for the newspaper, which I recalled seeing him pull out of the mailbox as we were getting into the ambulance. The first thing I spotted was an obituary: the Writers Union and other institutions and organizations announced with profound regret the demise of Vsevolod Kochetov. Totally unexpectedly I burst into a loud guffaw and, while everyone in the room stared at me in alarm, kept laughing. The thought that I might die almost simultaneously with that type seemed somehow inexpressibly funny.* During the next

*[Vsevolod Kochetov (1912–1973) was a Stalinist novelist and editor, the worst type of literary bureaucrat.]

hours my life hung by a thread, and the positive emotional jolt I got from that obituary may have tipped the scales toward my survival.

For the next three weeks I felt lousy. One peculiarity of a heart attack is that you lose the feeling that you can rely on the bodily systems whose functioning is a synonym of life. You're acutely aware that any second the machine might stop without warning. There is an indescribable tinge to the realization that the machine is you, your own self.

Lying in my private room, I gradually reestablished contact with the outside world through my little Sony radio. For several hours a day I listened to various "enemy" voices over the short-wave. At the time they were paying a good deal of attention to Andrey Sakharov and his wife, whom I've known for a long time as "Lyusya," even though the name on her passport is Elena. The public prosecutor, Comrade Malyarov, kept pulling her in for questioning. Every day the academic couple informed foreign journalists of the ups and downs of their complex relations with the authorities, and foreign radio kept me up to date on the affair.

One day after my regular portion of news I dozed off into semi-somnolence. I was awakened by noises and realized that I had passed over into the next world. Judge for yourself, what else could I think? Academician Sakharov and his wife in person were standing beside my bed. When it finally got through to me that I was not hallucinating, I was naturally overjoyed to see this pair of old friends. They had had the clever idea of escaping from Comrade Malyarov by checking into the Academy hospital, and a day earlier, on Friday evening, they had appeared like a bolt from the blue before the orderly on duty in admissions. You can't help feeling sorry for the fellow. The problem was far from simple. After consultation with hospital administrators, the Solomonian decision was reached to put the academician into a deluxe private room (rules are rules, and you can't get around them) and his wife into an open ward. The couple had somehow heard of my presence in the hospital and, indignant at this arbitrary act, come to see me as an "old timer" to get my advice on fighting the outrage.

"Whatever you do, don't hold a press conference," I said. "Over the weekend there's nobody in charge. Be patient for two days longer—and on Monday you'll be reunited." That's how it turned out.

That marked the start of a new and colorful phase in my hospital life. In the haste of their flight from Comrade Malyarov, the couple, like the ancient Judeans fleeing from Egyptian captivity, forgot to take along one important item. The Jews left leavening behind, and the academic couple forgot their transistor radio. Every evening after supper Sakharov, either alone or with his wife, came to my room to listen to my assortment of voices. I was touched to see them sitting by my bed, listening to the radio, and holding hands the entire time. Even newlyweds don't do that.

We were amused, of course, to hear the BBC reporting that Academician Sakharov was supposed to have been carried off to the hospital by force and that the progressive community in Moscow was gravely disturbed.*

The number of visitors to my room increased sharply. I hadn't seen many of them for years. They got wind of the time the renowned conjugal couple visited my room and came mainly in the evening. Often, as we listened to the radio, the door would open slightly and a completely unknown face poke through it. Visitors told me that ambulatory patients—the principal contingent of the Academy hospital—brought chairs and lined up along the corridor. Long before the academician and his spouse progressed in state through the corridor of my wing, this audience, who certainly had nothing better to do, would be waiting for the "happening." The result of this way of life, so rich in vivid im-

---

*[Dissidents were sometimes hospitalized for "mental illness" and treated with psychotropic drugs, and the rumors were that that was happening to Sakharov.]

pressions, was that by the evening rounds my blood pressure jumped twenty points.

Despite these complications, my talks each evening with one of the most remarkable men of our time gave me enormous pleasure. From them I gained a better understanding of my marvelous companion's character. We talked about science, scientists' ethics, and the climate of scientific research. I still remember his remarkable epigram: "You, astronomers, are happy people: the poetry of facts is still intact in your field!" How true that is, and how profoundly he must have grasped the spirit of a discipline in essence little related to his own interests to sum it up that neatly. By contrast, I am involuntarily reminded of the absurd definition of astronomy as a "pathological science" once given by the talented but limited Landau, a man short of his fair share of real imagination.*

I was struck by the punctilious objectivity and boundless benevolence of the opinions Sakharov expressed about his colleagues, prominent physicists. Sometimes I even found it irritating—for instance, when he rated Bogolyubov as highly as Landau, notwithstanding some of the loathsome traits of the present director of Dubna, including an inordinate love of power.†

Of course, we talked about other things as well. Once I asked Andrei, "Do you really believe your social activism can accomplish anything in our country?"

Without a moment's hesitation he answered, "No."

"Then why do you behave as if you do?"

"I can't do otherwise!" he snapped.

In general, a combination of inflexible firmness and a sort of childlike spontaneity, kindness, and even naiveté are the distinc-

*[Lev Landau (1908–1968) is considered the greatest physicist of the Soviet era and often compared to Richard Feynman. A pioneer in many fields and the teacher of a bright array of physicists, he received the Nobel prize in 1962 for his studies of condensed matter. His loyal students were offended by Shklovsky's description of him.]

†[Nikolay Bogolyubov (b. 1909), a mathematical physicist, is head of both the Steklov Institute of Mathematics and the Joint Institute for Nuclear Research in Dubna.]

tive traits of Sakharov's character. Once I asked him whether he had ever read the program of the Russian Constitutional Democratic party (which has long been stuck with the demeaning nickname "Cadets").* He replied that he hadn't. "In my opinion, their program was similar to yours, and in some things went even further, but under the conditions of Russian reality, the Cadets got nowhere. They promised all sorts of freedoms, and Lenin promised the peasants a bit of land—the outcome is well known."

"Times are different now," Andrey replied briefly.

Sometimes he would share with me reminiscences of people now deceased or affairs now over. The story that most impressed me is one which I had already heard at second hand from physicists of the older generation. In the summer of 1953, the first thermonuclear device was exploded at a test site far from Moscow, a few months before the similar American "experiment." You can imagine the delight, pride, and enthusiasm of the participants in that tremendous achievement. Even before the government commission had officially accepted the future hydrogen bomb, the traditional sumptuous banquet was promptly organized for the scientists and military men who directed the work.

At the large banquet table, everybody's attention was focused on the two heroes of the celebration: General Mitrofan Nedelin, the commander-in-chief of the installation, who had been chosen toastmaster; and the young physicist who had contributed decisively to the realization of the experiment, Andrey Sakharov.

The banquet began, and the toastmaster gave the first word to Sakharov as the guest of honor. He got up and said, "I raise my glass to the hope that the awesome phenomenon of nature we observed a few days ago will never be used to the detriment of mankind!"

Nedelin immediately exercised the toastmaster's rights by

*[The moderate party headed by Aleksandr Kerensky, prime minister of the Provisional Government between July 1917 and the October revolution.]

interrupting Andrey and in a farcical, rowdy way telling those around the table the old Russian soldier's joke about the Orthodox priest who was standing one night before the icon in a corner of his chamber. His wife, already in bed, was languishing under the covers in expectation of a moment of bliss. "Most Holy Mother of God, Queen of Heaven," the priest prayed, "harden and guide me—" Impatient, his wife interrupted the prayer, "Father dear, just ask to be hardened and I'll do the guiding!"

"What a clever fellow that Nedelin was! A simple, rough soldier, and he explained to me so precisely the relationship between science and the state! In my youth and stupidity I didn't even catch on right away," Sakharov said to me in the Academy Hospital almost twenty years to the day after that banquet. Field Marshal of Artillery and Commander-in-Chief of Strategic Rocket Forces Mitrofan Ivanovich Nedelin perished tragically in 1960 during the test of a new rocket system.*

Just before curtain time of a new life, when I had almost recovered, I contracted serum hepatitis in the hospital and was hastily evacuated to the Botkin Hospital isolation ward. Sakharov spent a long, frustrating time searching for me—nobody would tell him where I was.

*[The USSR has now officially revealed that Nedelin and fifty-three others were killed in 1960 in an ICBM explosion at the Baikonur launch pad.]

The Search for Extraterrestrial Civilizations

ON October 1, 1961, a score of us gathered in Keldysh's memorable office in the Institute of Applied Mathematics on Miussy Square for one of our regular discussion of space projects. The enthusiasm generated by the launch of the first Soviet Sputnik had yet to cool, and our ventures into space had gone from one success to the next. The world had just witnessed Gagarin's magical flight and shared the rapture of our glimpse of the reverse side of the Moon. Our first Venus rocket produced an indelible impression. I was filled with pride and delight and constantly aware that I was playing a role in historic events. Already over forty, I felt like a kid who'd fallen in love, and that state lasted more than five years.

At the start of the space age, together with my young colleagues and despite the bad will of my institute's sluggish administration, I plunged head first into that new and absorbing field of research. I was the one who proposed the simple, but effective, "artificial comet" method of observing interplanetary stations in flight by vaporizing on board a small quantity (2–3 kilograms) of sodium. The vapor produced intensive scattering of the yellow rays of the Sun, and the resultant bright cloud, known as "resonance fluorescence," was bright enough to be observed optically from the ground. In those years we didn't have the radio apparatus to track our *sputniks* accurately, and the administration of the space program, headed by Sergey Korolyov, resolutely supported my method.* I was so carried away by the artificial comet project that all too often I left my mortally ill mother alone in one pitiful little room with deaf-mute neighbors, and I will never forgive myself.

The decisive test of the "artificial comet" took place at the famous launching site of Kapustin Yar. On a summer night which was already as cold as autumn, a five-stage rocket was launched. My young colleagues and I were standing approximately a kilometer from the launching pad. Now we are all used to the sight of a rocket taking off—for some years they've been shown on Soviet television. But then we were all too aware of our responsibility for a launch made especially for our "comet" and found the spectacle unforgettable. Minutes went by after the launch. The hellish flame streaming from the rocket's nozzles faded, and the rocket itself became a barely visible weak point of light—absolutely nothing was happening in the agate-black sky. Time stood still. Did we have a catastrophic failure on our hands?

Suddenly, right at the zenith, a bright spark shone and, like paint on a tablecloth, a blindingly beautiful, vivid orange spot crawled across the sky, spreading slowly for half an hour until it extended over twenty degrees. Only then did it start fading.

My young colleague Vladimir Kurt used a series of photographs he took at that flight as the basis of his dissertation: he derived the density of the terrestrial atmosphere at an altitude of 500 kilometers from the velocity at which the sodium atoms diffused. I remember saying to Dima at the acme of that colorful

*[Korolyov (1907–1966), a pioneer in rocket work from the early 1930s and director of the Institute for Jet Research, was killed in a plane crash.]

and magical spectacle, "Admire it—that's your dissertation glowing up there!"

The method's effectiveness had been graphically demonstrated. Soon afterward another "comet" worked flawlessly on our lunar rocket, halfway between the Earth and the Moon. It's sad that the artificial comet wasn't further exploited. I proposed using lithium instead of sodium, which would have produced the same optical effect while vaporizing tens of times less matter. A lithium comet would be crimson and make spaceships look like tracer bullets. Nobody took the idea seriously. I proposed strontium and barium comets and stressed the method's rich possibilities for investigation of the Earth's magnetosphere. Many years later the West Germans successfully carried out those experiments.

At that October 1961 gathering of space scientists, Keldysh addressed us with uncharacteristic fervor. He reminded us that the fifth anniversary of the launch of the first Soviet *sputnik* was only a year away and should be properly celebrated. In particular, monographs should appear reflecting the universal significance of the event.

An idea popped into my head. I said that in the given time (the manuscripts would have to be handed in by July of the following year, 1962) I could finish a monograph I had already started (I hadn't!) on the unusual subject of the possible existence of intelligent life elsewhere in the Universe. Keldysh approved my initiative on the spot.

My calculation was an exacting one. I was convinced that the time was too limited for any of my colleagues to write a decent article, let alone a monograph. They just weren't that sort, and besides, the endless details of the space program kept them very busy. The months would fly by, the editor's briefcase would be empty, and mine would be the only manuscript handed in on time to meet the deadline of the fifth anniversary on October 4, 1962. In that situation I would have a better chance of escaping the embraces of the general censorship. Works on space topics had their own censor, a man named Kroshkin, whom I knew to be far from stupid. I had been greatly impressed by Cocconi and Morrison's 1959 article discussing the possibilities of radio communications over interstellar distances.* I intended to write a broad-ranging book going far beyond astronomical topics. In it I would demolish Oparin's notorious theory†—in 1961 Lysenko was still in favor, and Oparin was his close confederate—and indulge in a bit of futurological speculation. Under normal circumstances those aspects of the book would run considerable risk of suppression.

The chapters on molecular biology were especially difficult to write. Molecular biology was at best semi-licit in those Lysenkoist times, and there were no real textbooks in Russian on that far from simple topic. The futurological aspects of the book were much easier to deal with: I could use my natural bent for fantasy. Even my notorious "artificial satellites of Mars," which had kicked up such a fuss in 1959, would come into the picture. They weren't just a joke—even then I was giving serious thought to the fabulous possibilities of intelligent life in the universe. Overall, it was great fun and a badly needed distraction at a time when my mother's death had left me deeply depressed.

I began working feverishly. I still had all my other obligations and wrote the book in snatches, taking small "excursions" of three or four days at a time. I recall that in early July (my favorite time of the year) I retreated to my brother's dacha at

*[In 1959 Giuseppe Cocconi and Philip Morrison published an article in the British science journal *Nature* proposing that the spectrum line emitted by interstellar hydrogen at 1410 MHz could be used to communicate with distant civilizations. In our hydrogen-rich universe that frequency would be known and important to intelligent life forms. The article is considered the seminal work in the Search for Extraterrestrial Intelligence (SETI) movement.]

†[Aleksandr Oparin, director of the Academy of Sciences Biochemistry Institute, proposed that life should originate in protein molecules which swarm together in giant clumps called coacervates and then split up or replicate as they grow too large. However such forms, even if they grow, do not have the ability to transmit genetic code that is the mark of living organisms.]

Velyaminovo to write the difficult molecular biology chapter, but the weather played a dirty trick on me. The temperature fell nearly to freezing; there was occasional light snow and more often a wind-driven, icy rain. I retreated to the kitchen, the only room that could be heated, and shutting myself in, tried heroically to write with hands cramped with cold. I endured that torment for four days, got the chapter written somehow, and fled the dacha. The chapter had to be redone: if the book was to be more than a vain conceit, all of it had to be written with inspiration.

The manuscript was finished early in August, and my calculation proved correct. On a cold December day in 1962 my colleague Nadya Sleptsova and I received our twenty-five author's copies from the publisher. It brought me a rare feeling of joy. To all intents and purposes the book had escaped censorship. There was an uproar over it, but nothing terrible happened. Oparin squealed in indignation. I wrote him a polite letter, but he ripped it into little pieces and returned it in the same envelope. And they say that science nowadays lacks passion! The book sold out a printing of 50,000 copies in a few hours, went through five editions, and was translated into many foreign languages. I am especially proud of the edition in Braille for the blind: the four thick volumes in slick cardboard make a strange impression.

The American translation has a curious history. A young and little-known planetary astronomer from Cornell University named Carl Sagan undertook to see it into print. By education he is a biologist, and therefore I asked him to make any additions he wished to the American edition, since, as I said, biology is not my element.* Sagan interpreted my request broadly and, long afterward, in 1966 I received an elegantly produced, fat volume entitled *Intelligent Life in the Universe.* The size had doubled, and on the cover were crammed the names of two authors:

---

*[Sagan received a Ph.D. in astrophysics from the University of Chicago in 1960 and then got into the problems of the origin of life and various space investigations.]

Shklovsky and Sagan. I should say that Sagan showed a certain integrity; he left my text unchanged and set off his with little triangles. This frequently led to amusing misunderstandings. For instance, I wrote, "... in accordance with the philosophy of dialectical materialism, ..." and immediately after that paragraph came Sagan's text: "However, Kant's positivistic philosophy teaches. ..." It was just like E.T.A. Hofmann's diaries of Tomcat-Murr. I was quick to realize that my American "coauthor" had done me a priceless boon in distinguishing his text with triangles. Otherwise our vigilant official "readers" could have made things tough for me.

In America and the West in general that "book by two authors" was sensationally successful; there was even a mass paperback edition. When I came to New York for the first time in early 1967, like every normal Soviet abroad I was transformed into a skinflint forced by our beggerly stipends to watch every penny. I noticed that my American colleagues were perplexed at seeing me deny myself the necessities of life, down to a glass of beer. Finally one of them said frankly, "Forgive me, but we find your behavior surprising. After all, you're a rich man!"

"How's that—rich?" I wondered.

"Come on, your book with Sagan came out in paperback. That's worth tens of thousands of dollars!" Alas, the Soviet Union hadn't yet signed the international copyright agreement.

With his American business sense, Sagan effectively used the "Soviet-American book" as the springboard to a dynamic pop-science career, the apotheosis of which was his thirteen-part TV series *Cosmos.* Now he's a very progressive millionaire, an active fighter against the threat of nuclear conflagration, and a scientist out on the rosily optimistic flank of the spectrum on the question of extraterrestrial civilizations. I have no grievance against this businesslike, cheerful, and congenial American: at my request he did all he could to help my brother when he fell sick in Paris.

The appearance of my book had a stimulating effect on our

country's young astronomers. Nikolay Kardashev worked with the energy and creative independence which mark his characteristic style of unrestrained optimism combined with elements of fanaticism, a style I somewhat maliciously (and, I think, correctly) have dubbed "adolescent optimism." It is based on faith in human society's unbounded progress and places exaggerated emphasis on the radio-technological prospects for extraterrestrial communication, while ignoring both the humanities and biological aspects. To my mind, this is inadmissible. In brief, from the beginning I have been convinced that the problem of extraterrestrial civilizations is in essence and effect *complex.*

At about this time Kardashev published the famous work in which he classifies civilizations in space by a level of technological development characterized by the quantity of energy resources they exploit. The highest form of civilization, which uses the resources of the entire stellar system transformed by the force of intellect, is type III. A suitable candidate for such a super-civilization in the sky was soon located, the extragalactic source of radio emission CTA-102, in which my colleague Evgeny Sholomitsky had detected variability. There was a great uproar over it. I'll never forget the press conference that the Shternberg Institute gave to announce the great discovery. The entire courtyard of the institute was crammed with luxurious foreign cars belonging to some 150 of the leading accredited correspondents in Moscow. I led off with a few conservative and skeptical principles. Sholomitsky was extremely restrained. The director of the institute, Dmitry Martynov, basked in the limelight. Unfortunately, it soon became clear that CTA-102 was just an ordinary quasar with a large (but not record-breaking) redshift.

In early 1963 Kolya Kardashev decided to put together an all-union conference on the problem of extraterrestrial civilizations. Kolya was always full of big plans, and amazingly enough he almost always managed to realize them—for instance, the installation of our gigantic radiotelescope RATAN-600 and the

six-meter optical telescope, the realization and launch of the first
space radiotelescope, the launch of a telescope designed to
study the relict radiation of the universe, and much more besides. Under our conditions those projects took incredible effort
and persistence. In addition to Kolya's exceptional natural abili-
ties, high principles, and firm and independent character, he has
an element of natural luck to thank for his successes.

Kolya and I agreed completely and immediately on two
points: to keep the conference from becoming a circus, the press
would be excluded; and we wanted to hold it at Byurakan Observatory. Such a rare conference had to take place against the
background of the ancient stones of Armenia, witness to bygone
civilizations, and within view of the dazzling beauty of Mount
Ararat.

We put a lot of time and effort into the preparations. Our first
task was to reach an agreement with the master of Byurakan
Observatory, Viktor Ambartsumyan, and we were forced to
track that not easily trackable person to the most unexpected
places. I recall that Kolya and I went to see him at the Central
Committee's sanitarium in Lower Oreanda on the south shore of
the Crimea. The decisive talks took place at Byurakan, and we
flew in from Baku for the purpose.

I remember that trip with great clarity. Nobody met us at the
Erevan airport, and we had to get to Byurakan under our own
steam. We arrived late on Saturday evening, and the observatory was deserted. We went to sleep hungry and tired in the
guest quarters. I woke as usual at dawn and went to my favorite
spot by the south stone gates of the observatory, the best place
for seeing Ararat. No matter how often I've been to Byurakan, I
always revel in the indescribable beauty of the scene. The valley
of the Araxes River across the Turkish border was still sub-
merged in a deep blue predawn darkness. There was not a single
light; the area has been uninhabited since the 1915 Turkish mas-
sacre of the local Armenians. High in the sky was a band of
delicate pink, the snowy summit of Great Ararat. Daylight came

quickly, and the entire astounding beauty of the panorama was sketched like a delicate watercolor against the various shadings of blue sky. I don't perceive Ararat the way that Saryan has repeatedly painted it—too harsh, too much contrast.* To my mind, Ararat could best have been depicted by the old Japanese masters. Only they could have transmitted that incomparable airy perspective. From childhood on I wondered why Ararat, a good 1,500 kilometers away from the "scene of the action"—an inordinate distance for hoary antiquity—plays such an important role in the Bible. When I first stood lost in admiration of the mountain back in 1955, I understood immediately: the valley across the frontier is only 400 meters above sea level, and the massif of Ararat a few dozen kilometers farther south rises as if out of nowhere to 5,200 meters. Even the summit of the Himalayas is not that high above the surrounding crests, and the peak of Tenerife, which as late as the eighteenth century was considered the highest in the world, doesn't loom that far over the desolation of the Atlantic Ocean. Ararat was clearly the ancients' idea of a *mountain*.

After my morning view of Ararat, I went back to our room, which opened onto a covered terrace. At the door I discovered a packet of walnuts, a touching gift from Ambartsumyan himself. It couldn't have been more timely, since Kolya and I had missed supper the evening before. We filled up on walnuts and went for a walk through the picturesque village of Byurakan. For some reason I've never forgotten the sight of a homely donkey cropping grass beside the road. The appearance of a little girl from a neighboring cottage was all it took for this modest herbivore unexpectedly to produce monstrous signs of his adherence to the stronger sex. "And you doubt the possibility of establishing contact with civilizations on other planets," remarked Kolya reasonably.

---

*[Matiros Saryan (1880–1972) was an Armenian painter who worked in bright colors and simplified shapes.]

Not far away stood an antenna pointing in a completely incomprehensible direction. Later the local astronomers explained to us in all seriousness that it was observing Cassiopeia-A through its back lobe. We were more than a little surprised by that purely Armenian way of investigating objects in space.*

The first All-Union Byurakan Conference on Extraterrestrial Civilizations in October 1964 was a great success. Ambartsumyan, the absolute monarch of his observatory, supported it with enthusiasm, and everything took place as if by a wave of his magic wand. More than a few of our eminent scientists participated, and interest in the problem rose sharply.

After that conference, we got the idea of organizing an international conference on the same topic, and once again Kolya furnished the motive power. About that time we established contact, not with extraterrestrial civilizations, it is true, but with a Czech enthusiast in the field, Dr. Rudolph Pešek, who proposed holding the conference in a medieval Czech castle. We found this a splendid idea and began working out arrangements during our meeting with Pešek at the International Astonomical Union meeting in Prague in August 1967. Unfortunately, a year later the Czechs found that they weren't up to holding an international conference, and we decided to return to Byurakan. During a trip to the United States Kardashev came to a definitive agreement with Sagan on the subject.

The second Byurakan conference was essentially Soviet-American. Stressing the complex character of the topic, I felt that we shouldn't limit participation to astronomers and radio physicists (the only people Kolya took seriously; to him the rest were "philosophers"—i.e., windbags), but insisted that we invite people from a broad sector of the humanities as well. The

---

*[While radio dishes are designed to be most sensitive in the forward direction, they often (depending on type) have good sensitivity in the backward one, and that arrangement can sometimes minimize interfering signals. An ordinary TV antenna displays this pattern. Cassiopeia-A is one of the strongest radio sources in the sky and might lend itself to that kind of observation.]

Americans felt the same way. Our Soviet "humanitarians," however, made a wretched and decrepit impression.

The entire Byurakan staff put intense effort into organizing that unprecedented conference, at which some twenty-five Americans were received in comfort at a remote observatory. It couldn't have happened without Ambartsumyan.

The conference opened on September 4, 1971. Never, before or afterward, have I taken part in a more imposing scientific gathering. Among the Americans were two Nobel Prize winners, one of them the eminent physicist and astrophysicist Charles Townes, who shared the glory of the 1964 Nobel Prize for the invention of lasers and masers with our Nikolay Prokhorov and Aleksandr Basov. He arrived at Byurakan just after his striking discovery of the masers of water vapor (wavelength 1.35 cm.) that accompany the formation of stars from the interstellar medium.* Sagan, Philip Morrison, and Frank Drake, widely known for their pioneering works on the question of extraterrestrial civilizations, were there. Famous historians (W. H. McNeill, University of Chicago), cyberneticists (Marvin Minsky, Massachusetts Institute of Technology), and even an ethnographer, Richard Lee (University of Toronto), attended.

Lee, a frail-looking man whose grandfather (by the name of Liberman) had come from the Russian pale of settlement, was a pioneer of the new science of experimental anthropology. One of his exploits was spending half a year in the Kalahari Desert (Namibia) with a tribe of Bushmen, imitating their behavior, sharing their diet of lizards and other repulsive things, freezing on cold nights, and mastering the language and customs of those ancient African aborigines. Another and even more impressive feat was spending several months in a herd of ferocious ba-

---

*[A number of molecules in interstellar space have been found to exhibit maser action, intense emission in limited spectral bands pumped by strong infrared radiation from dense clouds in which stars are being formed.]

boons. "The main thing is not to look full-grown males in the eye," that fearless man told me.

Among the Americans, a strapping, bulky man named Bernard Oliver who seemed older than his fifty-five years attracted wide attention. He was a real millionaire, the vice-president of the famous computer firm Hewlett-Packard. He had a tragicomic adventure: on the way from America to Erevan—I think in London—his suitcase got lost. Without his baggage, in which he had packed everything necessary for life if not in interplanetary at least in socialist civilization, the poor millionaire didn't even have a change of underwear.

The foreigners were put up at the Armenia, the luxurious Intourist hotel in Erevan, forty-five kilometers away, while the Soviet participants in the conference stayed in great comfort at the observatory. Twice a day, morning and evening, the foreigners jolted their way up and down the mountain road in buses; those trips were not a source of great joy to them. One evening when our foreign guests, still deep in animated discussion, were reluctantly boarding their waiting buses, I saw Lee standing apart from the crowd and signaling to me. When I went over to him, he told me that he had secretly decided to spend the night at the observatory—he liked it there, and he would have a chance to revel in the morning view of Ararat. In dismay I began muttering something to the effect that there's no room, and so forth. He looked at me significantly, and I realized how ridiculous my excuses must sound: a night in the clumps of prickly grass beside the Byurakan dome was no big deal to a man who had slept with a herd of baboons. In the morning when I went to check on the highly rumpled Liberman, he assured me that he'd had a good night and asked for toothpaste.

In the Byurakan conference hall and the open galleries adjoining it, scientific passions seethed. One surprising paper followed another even more impressive. Hot discussions flared sporadically, and in the breaks and over lunch the scientific battles continued. The dapper young Sagan introduced the effective term *subjective probability* to describe estimates of the probable distribution of intelligent life in the Universe, based on Drake's famous formula.*

I remember the absorbing paper given by Professor Morrison, one of the founders of Communication with Extraterrestrial Intelligence, or CETI. His topic was the possibility of transmitting by radio all the wisdom of a civilization (in this case, Earth). He showed that it could be done, and in a rather short time. (I had made similar calculations in my book *Universe, Life, Intelligence.*) With a large margin of error, the estimate is that everything written by everybody who ever lived on Earth (including not only the contents of every book printed in all languages, but the vast bulk of vacuous papers-receipts and the like) could be expressed in binary code by 10^{15} bits. A radio transmitter with a bandwidth of 100 MHz, working without pause, could transmit this product of human "intelligence" in a few months. The effect of Morrison's impressive but simple result was somewhat dampened by the calm and phlegmatic Drake's innocent question: "How many bits of information do you think Einstein's formula $E = mc^2$ contains?" That flustered the usually resourceful Morrison, and the gathering burst out laughing.

I recall another discussion dedicated to the "topical" problem of the danger to Earthlings posed by contact with inhabitants of other planets. The most interesting answer came in writing from Sakharov, who didn't attend the conference: "To an intelligent and good person contact will be useful; to a stupid and bad one, harmful."

My particular contribution to the success of the well-organized conference was inviting Bob Belitsky, my comrade on the 1941 Moscow-Ashkhabad convoy, to serve as chief synchronous translator. Without Bob we would have had our own tower of Babel. None of us, neither Soviets nor Americans, had ever

---

*[Drake's formula, $N = R \times L$, stated that the number of communicating civilizations in the Universe is equal to the rate, R, at which they appear, multiplied by their lifetime, L.]

heard such translation: he was lightning swift at improving the text of questions and answers at both ends. Miss Evans, the American stenotypist, also struck the imagination of the participants, especially the Soviets. Watching her fantastically rapid and accurate work, we realized that there can be poetry in the secretarial field. The sum of her labor was greater than its parts: by the time the conference was over she had prepared a stenographic record, and this ensured the publication of a volume of collected articles with an alacrity beyond our wildest dreams.*

The end of the conference left us all sad. We weren't ready to leave Byurakan without reaching total agreement, settling our quarrels, and cementing our friendships. Our grief was lessened only by the prospect of the farewell banquet at Lake Sevan.

So there we were, sitting at huge banquet tables. Beyond the broad veranda the famous lake stretched in splendid panorama. An eighth-century monastery was visible on a nearby peninsula (once an island) in the heavily drawn-down lake. The American participants were excited by the fact that Oliver's suitcase had turned up. Oliver himself had skipped the banquet to go to Erevan and retrieve his belongings.

Ambartsumyan was unanimously elected *tamada,* or toastmaster, but everybody realized that he was too grand and stiff to fill the post in anything but ceremonial fashion. A vice-toastmaster was needed, and I was chosen. I think that was the highest office to which I have ever been elected. Those were my stellar hours—Ambartsumyan, sitting to my left, occasionally nodded his head slightly, and I did the rest. To my right sat Francis Crick, the Nobel Prize winner who discovered the structure of DNA.

I was truly inspired that day. Following local Caucasian customs, I called for a toast from Professor Lee, demanding that he respond in the Bushman language. The magnificent landscape

---

*[*Communication with Extraterrestrial Intelligence (CETI),* edited by Carl Sagan (MIT Press, 1973).]

around us resounded with weird clicks and sibilants. The anthropologist explained that he was chanting a primeval hymn which accompanied the ritual of sharing a collective delicacy, some rare bird or other. The toast made a strong impression.

At the end of the banquet I spoke to the assembled company: "Gentlemen and comrades! Throughout these unforgettable days we have talked a lot about subjective probability. But if yesterday I had asked you to estimate the subjective probability that Mr. Oliver's lost suitcase would be returned to its owner, you would have responded to me in chorus, 'Zero.' And what happened? Today the worthy vice-president of Hewlett-Packard received his suitcase, with it the shorts so necessary in this Eastern republic, and apparently his gloves as well! This joyful event serves to convince us that somewhere, far beyond the limits of the constellation Tau Ceti, so expressively sung by the remarkable Russian poet Vysotsky, a banquet like ours is taking place.* At any rate, the subjective probability of that joyous event is far from small. Let's drink to it. I recommend the local three-star product."

I would like to think that this speech appreciably increased the percentage of adherents to the "optimistic" approach to the question of communication with extraterrestrial intelligence.

---

*[In a song by that title, guitar-poet Vladimir Vysotsky recounts a crude Earthman's visit to the civilization on Tau Ceti. He is horrified to find it populated by female creatures who reproduce by asexual budding, or gemmation.]

Index